The Moral Epistemology
of Intuitionism

Also available from Bloomsbury:

A History and Philosophy of Expertise, by Jamie Carlin Watson
Knowledge, Number and Reality, edited by Nils Kürbis, Bahram Assadian and Jonathan Nassim
The Futility of Philosophical Ethics, by James Kirwan
The Value of Giving Reasons, by Felipe Oliveira de Sousa

The Moral Epistemology of Intuitionism

Neuroethics and Seeming States

Hossein Dabbagh

BLOOMSBURY ACADEMIC
LONDON • NEW YORK • OXFORD • NEW DELHI • SYDNEY

BLOOMSBURY ACADEMIC
Bloomsbury Publishing Plc
50 Bedford Square, London, WC1B 3DP, UK
1385 Broadway, New York, NY 10018, USA
29 Earlsfort Terrace, Dublin 2, Ireland

BLOOMSBURY, BLOOMSBURY ACADEMIC and the Diana logo are trademarks of
Bloomsbury Publishing Plc

First published in Great Britain 2023
This paperback edition published 2024

Copyright © Hossein Dabbagh, 2023

Hossein Dabbagh has asserted his right under the Copyright, Designs and
Patents Act, 1988, to be identified as Author of this work.

For legal purposes the Acknowledgements on p. ix constitute an extension
of this copyright page.

Cover image: Concrete wall (© zhihao / Getty Images)

All rights reserved. No part of this publication may be reproduced or transmitted
in any form or by any means, electronic or mechanical, including photocopying,
recording, or any information storage or retrieval system, without prior
permission in writing from the publishers.

Bloomsbury Publishing Plc does not have any control over, or responsibility for, any
third-party websites referred to or in this book. All internet addresses given in this
book were correct at the time of going to press. The author and publisher regret any
inconvenience caused if addresses have changed or sites have ceased to exist,
but can accept no responsibility for any such changes.

A catalogue record for this book is available from the British Library.

A catalog record for this book is available from the Library of Congress.

ISBN: HB: 978-1-3502-9757-9
PB: 978-1-3502-9761-6
ePDF: 978-1-3502-9758-6
eBook: 978-1-3502-9759-3

Typeset by Deanta Global Publishing Services, Chennai, India

To find out more about our authors and books visit www.bloomsbury.com and
sign up for our newsletters.

For Roshi

Contents

List of illustrations	viii
Acknowledgements	ix
Introduction	1

Part I Mind — 7

1. Philosophical intuition's mental ontology — 9
2. Moral intuition's mental ontology: Shifting from philosophical to moral intuition — 32
3. The use of intuition as evidence — 48

Part II Epistemology — 57

4. Shaping classic moral intuitionism: An examination of H. A. Prichard's and W. D. Ross's ideas — 59
5. Towards the new moderate intuitionism: Recent revivals of contemporary moral intuitionism — 104

Part III Neuroethics — 135

6. Scepticism about moral intuition: How my favoured account of intuition rebuts the neuroethicists' position — 137
7. Scepticism about moral intuitionism: How my favoured account of epistemological intuitionism rebuts Sinnott-Armstrong's position — 166

Afterword — 199

Notes	201
Bibliography	227
Index	247

Illustrations

Figures

1	A taxonomy of views about what philosophical intuitions are	13
2	Adelson's checker shadow illusion	25
3	Müller-Lyer illusion	35

Table

1	Views about intuition in philosophy and psychology	47

Acknowledgements

This book grew out of a dissertation I wrote between 2011 and 2015 at the University of Reading and Oxford. I am especially indebted to, and could not have finished this project without, my supervisors Philip Stratton-Lake and Brad Hooker, who kindly and tirelessly supported me throughout my doctoral study, reading multiple drafts of my work without complaint. I could not have wished for anyone better to supervise my work. I would like to express my deep gratitude to Regina Rini, my advisor at the Oxford Uehiro Centre for Practical Ethics in the final year of my doctoral study, whom I benefited and learnt much from. Together, they all made this project possible with their sharp, insightful and thorough critical comments, which were invaluable to this study as well as the structure and arguments. It goes without saying that their input was integral to this work, and their comments have made it considerably better than it would otherwise have been.

Some of the material in this book was presented at the Understanding Value Conference, University of Sheffield, 2014, the Moral Psychology Conference at Kyoto University, 2014, the Practical Ethics Seminars at the University of Oxford, 2013, the Aristotelian Society Conference at the University of Exeter, 2013, the iCog Conference at the University of Sheffield, 2013, the Experimental Philosophy Workshop at the University of Bristol, 2013, the Central European University's Summer Course, 2013, the Experimental Philosophy Workshop at the University of Nottingham, 2012, the thirty-fourth International Wittgenstein Symposium, Vienna, 2012 and the University of Reading's Graduate Research Seminars from 2011 to 2013. I have benefited from discussions with – and in some cases, written comments from – numerous people, including very helpful feedback from participants at these events.

To the following people, I extend my special thanks for helpful discussions on topics pertaining to this book: Robert Audi, John Broome, Sophie-Grace Chappell, Soroush Dabbagh, Jonathan Dancy, Alex Gregory, Guy Kahane, Chrysovalantis Margaritidis, George Mason, Nilou Mobasser, Charlotte Newey, Geraldine Ng, David Oderberg, Derek Parfit, Richard Rowland, Julian Savulescu, Tim Scanlon, Russ Shafer-Landau, Rob Shaver, Peter Singer, Anthony Skelton, Abdolkarim Soroush, Galen Strawson and Tim Williamson.

My family have always been an unfailing source of love and encouragement. I would like to thank my parents, Hossein and Zahra, for their love, faith and support. I am beyond indebted to them in more ways than I can imagine. My father's philosophy has always been a source of deep inspiration for me to pursue my career. My mother always encouraged me to finish my project even though she is not particularly fond of philosophy! Without their support, writing this book would not have been possible.

Last but not least, I would like to end by giving a special mention to my wife, Roshi, who was a source of hope in moments of frustration and whose emotional support was vital to the commencement and completion of this project. I will never forget her vibrant enthusiasm and encouragement, which inspired and drove me throughout these years. This book is wholeheartedly dedicated to her patience and sacrifice.

I have extensively borrowed from some of my published articles. I thank the editor and publishers of my following articles for giving me permission to reuse them in this book:

- 'Intuitions about Moral Relevance—Good News for Moral Intuitionism', 2021, *Philosophical Psychology*, 34 (7): 1047–72.
- 'Sinnott-Armstrong Meets Modest Epistemological Intuitionism', 2017, *Philosophical Forum*, 48 (2): 175–99.
- 'Feeling Good: Integrating the Psychology and Epistemology of Moral Intuition and Emotion', 2018, *Journal of Cognition and Neuroethics*, 5 (3): 23–52.
- 'Intuiting Intuition: The Seeming Account of *Moral* Intuition', 2018, *Croatian Journal of Philosophy*, XVIII (52): 117–32.
- 'The Seeming Account of Self-Evidence: An Alternative to Audian Account', 2018, *Logos & Episteme*, IX (3): 261–84.
- 'The Problem of Explanation and Reason-Giving Account of *pro tanto* Duties in the Rossian Ethical Framework', 2018, *Public Reason*, 10 (1): 69–80.

Introduction

This book will combine work in epistemological intuitionism with work in neuroethics. It will develop an account of the role that moral intuition and emotion play in moral judgement and utilize this account to argue that moral intuitionism will be in a better position if we construe moral intuition and emotion in terms of non-doxastic intellectual seemings and perceptual experiences. This book introduces and elucidates what seems to be the best understanding of moral intuitionism with reference to the seeming states. In this narrative, I reevaluate, in a coherent manner, all elements of moral intuitionism, including moral intuition, self-evidence, non-inferentiality, adequate understanding and moral emotion, with reference to the seeming states. I argue that the seeming-based account of moral intuitionism will equip us in a more tenable way to defend the epistemology of moral intuitionism and that it can resist the empirical challenges derived from empirical moral psychology (neuroethics).

Although there is a rich literature on the seeming account of moral intuition and intuitionism, the raison d'être for this book is that it reevaluates and redefines all elements of moral intuitionism in terms of seeming states with the aim of removing the lacuna in the tradition of moral intuitionism that deals with how moral intuitionism can embrace empirical findings derived from neuroethics without creating an epistemic threat.

Epistemological moral intuitionism is ordinarily thought of as an account of non-inferentially justified moral intuitions. Investigating the reliability of moral intuitions is one of the hot topics in moral psychology and of high importance for philosophical questions. In different studies (Sinnott-Armstrong, 2008a, 2011), the influence of framing on people's intuitions about the moral relevance of certain properties of moral scenarios was investigated to assess the validity of some crucial assumptions of moral intuitionism. While it was found that people's intuitions about moral relevance were not affected by framing effects, the findings were not fully satisfying news for moral intuitionism since a worrisome proportion of participants disagreed with the purportedly self-evident moral relevance statements (Andow, 2018).

However, the moral intuitionist epistemology claims that there are certain moral self-evident propositions that our moral intuitions can give us non-inferential justification for believing. (Audi, 2004 and Stratton-Lake, 2002). In this book, I focus on the *epistemology* of moral intuitionism without addressing metaphysical discussion and the defensibility of moral *realism* per se. I defend the epistemology of moral intuitionism against empirical challenges derived from moral psychology. I argue that the epistemology of moral intuitionism is compatible with admitting a role for emotion and that moral intuitions and emotions can be partners without creating an epistemic threat. I develop my work on these topics by focusing on three subjects in recent moral intuitionism, that is, *Mind*, *Epistemology* and *Neuroethics*.

Mind

Part I of this book, which consists of Chapters 1, 2 and 3, deals with intuitionists' mental ontology. In Chapter 1, following Bealer (1998) and Bengson (2010), I defend the non-doxastic account of *philosophical* intuition, which understands intuitions as *seemings*, against the doxastic account, which understands intuitions as *beliefs*. According to the non-doxastic account, to have an intuition that p is to have the intellectual seeming that p. Understanding intuition in terms of seemings implies that 'S has the intuition that p if it seems to S that p'. For example, as far as someone adequately understands the proposition 'John murdered his partner for fun', one can be 'intuitively' struck by the seeming wrongness. In Chapter 2, I introduce and elucidate what seems to me the best understanding of *moral* intuition with reference to the seeming account (Stratton-Lake, 2016a, 2016b and Huemer, 2005). In Chapter 3, based on the seeming account of intuition, I argue that intuitions, both moral and philosophical, can serve as evidence for beliefs.

Epistemology

Part II of the book, which consists of Chapters 4 and 5, deals with the central epistemological ideas of moral intuitionists. In Chapter 4, I highlight the tenable elements in the epistemology of classic moral intuitionists, for example, Prichard and Ross. In Chapter 5, I discuss the new moral intuitionist epistemology (e.g. Audi) and offer responses to the famous objections to the ideas of self-evidence, reflections and non-inferentiality. Meanwhile, I present my alternative account of self-evident propositions in terms of intellectual seeming.

Having equipped myself with a strong form of seeming-based epistemological intuitionism, I will proceed, in the rest of this book, to elucidate and defend the moral intuitionist epistemology against the data gleaned by experimental philosophers that seems to challenge the epistemology of moral intuitions.

Neuroethics

Part III of the book, consisting of chapters six and seven, deals with the empirical challenges moral psychologists raise in neuroethics. In Chapter 6, I argue that seemings are compatible with emotional experiences; so, my favoured account of moral intuition, i.e. the seeming account, helps rebut the neuroethicists' challenges derived from brain science's fMRI studies. In Chapter 7, I argue that my favoured account of epistemological intuitionism can rebut one of the most important grounds for scepticism about intuitionist epistemology.

Plan of the book

In Chapter 1, I defend the non-doxastic account of philosophical intuition, which understands intuitions as intellectual seemings, against the doxastic account, which understands intuitions in terms of beliefs. In the first part, I argue that the intellectual seeming account is superior to the *mere* belief account of intuition. Although I echo some parts of Bealer's argument against the doxastic account, I will add more fuel to his argument with new articulation and concrete moral examples to qualify his account and present it in its strongest form. In order to do that, I will respond to the criticisms raised by Nimtz against Bealer's account to save the intellectual seeming account. In Part II, I will explore whether the so defended intellectual seeming account of intuition in this chapter can stand against the inclination or disposition-to-believe account. I argue that although the inclination or disposition-to-believe account of intuition is superior to the mere belief account, the intellectual seeming account looks more fundamental.

In Chapter 2, I introduce and elucidate what seems to me the best understanding of *moral* intuition with reference to the intellectual seeming account. First, I will explain Bengson's quasi-perceptualist account of *philosophical* intuition in terms of intellectual seeming. I then shift from philosophical intuition to moral intuition and will delineate Audi's doxastic account of moral intuition to argue that the intellectual seeming account of intuition is superior to the doxastic account of intuition. Next, I argue that we can apply our understanding of the intellectual seeming account of philosophical intuition to moral intuition. To the extent that we can argue for the intellectual seeming account of philosophical intuition, we can have the intellectual seeming account of moral intuition.

In Chapter 3, I argue against those sceptical philosophers about using intuition as evidence. I introduce some special technical use of intuition in terms of phenomenological or non-comparative use of seemings, that is, intellectual seemings. This technical use of intuition, I believe, shows how intuitions can have an episteme role as evidence. However, to see whether intuitions can be used as evidence, I will start by explaining what evidence is. Next, I argue that intuitions can play an epistemic role as evidence and how intuitions should be treated as evidence. Based on my understanding of evidence, intuition as evidence can only be accepted if we assume that the intuition that p is not the belief that p.

Chapter 4 will delineate the history of moral intuitionism and its different classifications. I will focus on the epistemological ideas of two significant classic intuitionists, that is, Prichard and Ross. Following the Wittgensteinian idea of 'family resemblance', I argue that we have many moral intuitionisms with different properties. However, this does not entail that it is impossible to define moral intuitionism or refer to it meaningfully. Similar to Wittgenstein's usage of the concept of 'game', I will show that although there are many forms of moral intuitionism throughout the history of moral philosophy, there are different properties of moral intuitionism that we can use as markers. These markers, I believe, can be used as moral intuitionism's definition. Thus, we can meaningfully refer to moral intuitionism even though we have many moral intuitionisms.

In Chapter 5, I argue against Audi's doxastic formulation of self-evidence and those contemporary moral intuitionists who believe that the notion of self-evidence should be read in terms of the doxastic account of intuition. Quite the contrary, I argue that the notion of self-evidence should be read in terms of the non-doxastic account of intuition if intuitions are construed as intellectual seemings. First, I will start by elaborating on Robert Audi's account of self-evidence. Next, I criticize his account on the basis of the idea of 'adequate understanding'. I shall then present my alternative account of self-evidence based on the seeming account of intuition. Finally, I show how the seeming account of self-evidence can make the moral intuitionist epistemology more tenable.

Chapter 6 argues that moral intuitions and emotions can be partners without creating an epistemic threat. I start by offering some empirical findings to weaken Singer's (and Greene's and Haidt's) debunking argument against moral intuition, which treat emotions as a distorting factor. In the second part of the chapter, I argue that the standard contrast between intuition and emotion is a mistake. Moral intuitions and emotions are not contestants if we construe moral intuition as non-doxastic intellectual seeming and emotion as a non-doxastic perceptual-like state. This will show that emotions support, rather than distort, the epistemic standing of moral intuitions.

In Chapter 7, I will first introduce Sinnott-Armstrong's argument against the epistemology of moral intuitionism on the grounds that it is not justified to have some moral beliefs without needing them to be inferred from other beliefs. He believes that our moral judgements are inferentially justified because the 'framing effects', mostly discussed in empirical psychology, cast doubt on any non-inferential justification. I then argue that Sinnott-Armstrong's argument is question-begging against intuitionists and his description of epistemological intuitionism is a diluted version that most intuitionists do not believe; therefore, he is not attacking the epistemological intuitionism in its strongest form. I then propose my alternative modest account of epistemological intuitionism. I also reconsider the concept of 'non-inferentiality' as one of the key elements of intuitionist epistemology and propose a modest account of non-inferentiality.

The target audience for this book will be academics and graduate students in the field of philosophy and psychology, both in departments of philosophy and experimental psychology. Since the book covers issues both in moral philosophy and neuroethics, it can be particularly useful for master's and PhD students studying moral philosophy (moral epistemology) and experimental psychology (neuroethics). It is also beneficial for those scholars who follow contemporary revivals of moral intuitionism. This book might also be used as a text or supplementary text for a list of courses, such as moral philosophy, moral epistemology, contemporary moral psychology, moral intuitionism, moral intuitions and emotions, and neuroethics.

Part I

Mind

1

Philosophical intuition's mental ontology

1 Introduction

In his *Republic*, Plato considered four stages of the emergence of the idea of *perception*: (1) intelligence, (2) reason, (3) belief and (4) illusion. However, according to him, nóêsis (νόησις) is higher than the four aforementioned stages in the process of consciousness. Plato believed that we could see the very idea of 'truth' with the aid of nóêsis. Aristotle, following Plato, viewed nóêsis as an *intellectual virtue* and as the *ability* to know first principles non-inferentially.[1] For example, in one passage, Aristotle talks about a form of comprehension as 'an unmediated grasp of important foundational concepts' (*APost*. 99b20–211). In this phrase, as in Plato's works, translation of nóêsis normally corresponds to 'intuition' or 'intuitive knowledge'.[2]

The use of the concept of 'intuition' (from the Latin word for 'look into') in *modern* philosophy started with René Descartes, focusing on the epistemology of intuition.[3] According to him, as we cannot arrive at knowledge through experience, we have to make room for something that is both cognitive and *a priori*. The very idea of intuitive thinking has to be taken into account in this respect. Intuitive judgement, in the Cartesian sense, is something that can be achieved non-inferentially – that is, it is a direct apprehension of truth.[4] Descartes writes in his *Rules for the direction of the mind* that

> [W]e distinguish at this point between intuition and . . . deduction; because the latter, unlike the former, is conceived as involving a movement or succession . . . From this we may gather that when propositions are direct conclusions from first principles, they may be said to be known by intuition or by deduction, according to different ways of looking at them; but first principles themselves may be said to be known only by intuition; and remote conclusions, on the other hand, only by deduction. (1626–8, Rule III)

To make the point clearer, consider the following sentences: 'Nothing can be red all over and green all over at the same time' or 'Every event has a cause'. These sentences are not analytic in the sense that the predicate concept is not contained in the subject concept. For example, the concept of 'cause' is not contained in the concept of 'event'. They are nonetheless *a priori*; that is, the way in which we *see* that 'every event has a cause' or 'something is not green and red at the same time' is *a priori*. However, these propositions might be non-inferentially justified depending on how someone came to believe them. The way we are justified in believing them might be non-inferential because the justification of belief in the propositions might not be based on premises.[5]

Like Descartes, there are some other rationalists and empiricists who talked about such a non-inferential state which they call intuition, a state in which we can just *see* (or perceive) that something is thus-and-so. For example, Spinoza, as a rationalist, described such a state in his *Ethics* that

> Given the numbers 1, 2, and 3 . . . we arrive at the fourth number [6] from the ratio which, in one *intuition* [uno intuito], we *see* [videmus] the first number to have to the second. (2p40s2, italic added)

And Locke, as an empiricist, writes in the *Essay* that

> For should the soul of a prince, carrying with it the consciousness of the prince's past life, enter and inform the body of a cobbler, as soon as deserted by his own soul, everyone *sees* he would be the same person with the prince. (1969, II.27.15, italic added)

Henry Price also writes in his *Perception* that

> In discursive consciousness (as the name suggests) there is a passage of the mind from one item to another related item, for instance . . . from premise to conclusion. . . . In intuitive consciousness, on the other hand . . . there is no passage of the mind. (1932, 151–2)

According to Price, we can think of two notions of 'inference': one is the proposition that is a conclusion from some argument. The other is when we come to believe some proposition through a 'passage of the mind'.

However, it seems that two things must be distinguished in these philosophers' intuition-talk, although some of them might not mention the word intuition. Talking about intuition-as-perceiving is one thing, and thinking that intuitions are non-inferentially justified is another. Talking about intuition-as-perceiving is an ontological (or even psychological) claim about the nature of the mental state we call 'intuition', claiming that intuitions are like perceptual experiences.

Thinking that intuitions are non-inferentially justified is an epistemological claim stating how intuitions are justified. Although these two issues are somehow interrelated and one can learn something about epistemology by studying the ontology of intuition, for the purpose of clarity, I believe these two issues should be separated. So, in this book, I will first delineate philosophical and moral intuition's mental ontology in Part I. I investigate different theories about what philosophical and moral intuitions are like and argue in favour of the seeming account. I will discuss the epistemology of moral intuitionism in Part II. In order to do that, I focus on the epistemology of moral intuitionism's central idea according to which we have some non-inferentially justified moral intuitions.

2 The psychology of intuition

The nature of a given mental state, such as intuition, need not necessarily be regarded as an epistemological issue since it concerns the psychology or even ontology of the mind.[6] In fact, there is a mutual (reciprocal) relationship between the psychology and epistemology of intuition. By reflecting on the psychology of a given mental state, such as intuition, that is by explaining *what intuition is*, one can understand more about the epistemology of intuition.[7] This is because having a different ontological or psychological theory about the nature of intuition may impact epistemological claims about the justificatory status of intuitions.

The ambiguity around the concept of intuition even leads philosophers to ask *what is it like to have an intuition*. For example, Ludwig Wittgenstein writes,

> What do we know about intuition? What idea [have] we of it? It's presumably supposed to be a sort of seeing, recognition at a single glance; I wouldn't know what more to say. 'So you do after all know what an intuition is!' . . . but do I therefore know what it means? (1976, 419)[8]

However, since there are many distinct candidate definitions for the generic title 'intuition', I am encouraged to make a distinction between my definition of intuition and the definitions used in the majority of the literature on intuition.[9] This will help me to clarify my target in this book.

For my argument's sake, following Bengson (2010), by the word 'intuition' in this book, I signify the occurrent and conscious mental state of *intuiting that p*, or *having the intuition that p*, where p is some proposition.[10] So, put simply, 'intuition' denotes 'having the intuition that p', and p is just the content of the intuition, for example, that 'killing is wrong'. Such *occurrent, conscious* and *contentful* intuitions, which can be of intuiting properties and intuiting concepts, should be distinguished from the other phenomenon of having a 'special faculty' of intuition or phenomena discussed in mysticism or mathematics.[11] As a result, in this book, I will say *nothing* about the mathematical and logical intuitions. However, I do not rule out that something that can be labelled 'philosophical intuition' can explain and justify such mathematical intuitions (e.g. Gödel's view of mathematical truth). I assume in this book that mathematics and logic differ from philosophy and need further examination, which is outside the scope of this book.

However, as Bengson (2010) correctly argues, we should also make a distinction between our usage of 'intuition that p' and the phenomenon of being *intuitive* as a property of propositions, theories and methods. Although the English words 'intuition', 'intuitive' and 'intuitively' are often used interchangeably, there are important differences. For example, when we say 'X has the intuition that p, at T', this occurrent, conscious and contentful intuition only requires subject (X) and time (T) at which that p comes into the subject's mind. However, saying that p is *intuitive* has an entirely different connotation from saying that we *have an intuition that p*. For example, it may be intuitive to one that flipping the switch turns on the light, but it is another issue whether one has the intuition (intuits) that flipping the switch turns on the light. To the extent that the distinction between having the intuition that p and the potentially different state of finding a property of a proposition being intuitive that p sounds plausible, it is the occurrent mental state of having the intuition that p which is relevant here and that is my concern in this book.

Let us return to the questions that this chapter started with: What is 'intuition'? What are intuitions like, and what is it like to have an intuition that p? There are different expressions that have the connotation of 'x has the intuition that p'. For example, expressions such as 'it is *obvious* to x that p', 'x *sees* that p', 'It is *clear* to x that p', 'it is *self-evident* to x that p' and 'It *seems* to x that p' have the same role in our ordinary language.[12] Yet, Herman Cappelen talks about this ordinary intuition-talk with various labels. According to him, this intuition-talk sometimes denotes 'some kind of quick, spontaneous, and relatively unreflective judgment' (2012, 38) or 'an incomplete answer meant for easy consumption' (2012, 38).[13]

We find a range of accounts of 'what an intuition is' or 'what it is like to have an intuition that p' when we consider the philosophical literature in this area. For instance, here is a taxonomy of theories about what I call 'philosophical intuitions', which are discussed mostly by *philosophers* (Figure 1).

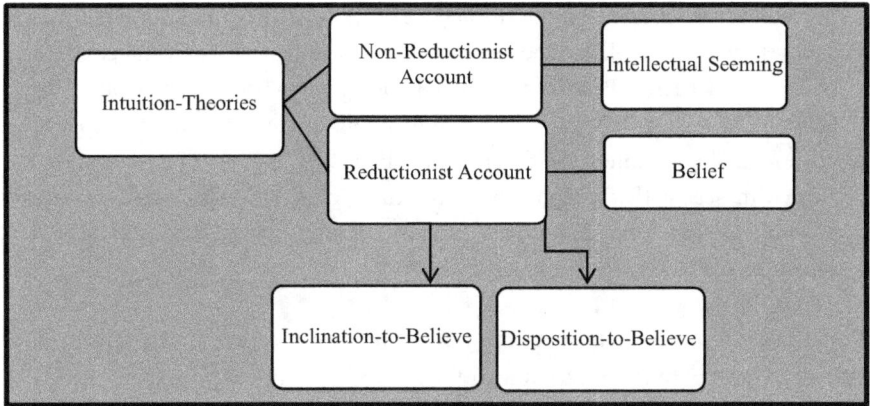

Figure 1 A taxonomy of views about what philosophical intuitions are.

But what is the basis of this categorization? Although many philosophers take intuition as a mental state, some of them think of intuition as a sui generis mental state, and others think of intuitions as a subset of other mental states like belief. Since these philosophers all think that there are intuitions and do not aim to eliminate them, I call these two groups of philosophers *non-reductionists* and *reductionists*, respectively. In other words, philosophers who reduce intuitions to a particular subset of beliefs, inclinations, or dispositions-to-believe are reductionists and philosophers who think that intuitions *do not* reduce to any other mental states are non-reductionists.[14]

Non-reductionists: George Bealer, a prominent intuition theorist, for example, thinks that intuition is a sui generis mental state that cannot be reduced to other mental states. He states two claims: one negative and one positive. On the negative side, he argues that one can have an intuition with certain content while one does not believe that content. Also, one can believe that p whereas one does not have the intuition that p. Bealer also differentiates between intuition and guess, hunch, judgement, and inclination-to-believe.[15] On the positive side, however, he introduces a new terminology instead of intuition, i.e. 'intellectual seeming'. Following Bealer (1998), John Bengson (2015) developed and defended a non-reductionist account, which he dubbed a 'quasi-perceptualist' view of intuition. By quasi-perceptualism, he means that intuition is basically similar to perceptual experiences, in a way that there are some shared phenomenological features between intuition and perceptual experiences.

Reductionists: Prominent philosophers like David Lewis and Timothy Williamson (based on one reading) think that intuition denotes *a certain* belief, inclination or disposition-to-believe.[16] There are also other reductionists who think about belief or inclination-to-believe differently. They think that intuition denotes a *particular* subset of beliefs or inclination-to-believe. For instance, some philosophers, such as Plantinga, think that intuition is a belief or inclination-to-believe that comes with a special phenomenology.[17] He states that this special phenomenology cannot be describable other than saying phenomenology goes with *seeing* that propositions are true. Some other philosophers and psychologists, such as Jennifer Nagel, think that intuition is a belief state that is generated *spontaneously* or *unreflectively*.[18]

Nonetheless, both reductionists and non-reductionists agree that 'philosophical intuitions' are paradigm examples of what an account of intuitions needs to cover.[19] Accordingly, I continue to discuss what the 'philosophical intuition' is when philosophers use it as *evidence* in their popular theorizing, for example, *thought experiments*.[20] In the meantime, I will articulate two main rival theories, for example, the reductionist and the non-reductionist theories of intuition, along with their criticisms and replies. I conclude by offering a seeming account of intuition, for example 'intellectual seeming'. Following Bealer (1998), Huemer (2005), Bedke (2010), Stratton-Lake (2016a, 2016b) and Bengson (2015), I believe that the seeming account of intuition can better capture how intuitions are intractable and why it is hard to find a rule governing our different intuitions.

2.1 Intuition pumps: A reductionist account of intuition

There are some philosophers who employ 'philosophical intuitions' (or just 'intuition' when there is no harm) as evidence in the context of philosophical thought experiments.[21] According to these philosophers, we use intuitions about various philosophical issues when we consider thought experiments, for example, Searle's Chinese Room, Parfit's mishaps in teletransportation or Putnam's Twin Earth.[22] Although these thought experiments use intuitions as a tool, they aim at a view about some theory that in itself is not intuitive. In his book, *Elbow Room*, Daniel Dennett used the term 'intuition pump' to refer to thought experiments that facilitate understanding complex philosophical subjects. He writes,

> A popular strategy in philosophy is to construct a certain sort of thought experiment I call an *intuition pump* [. . .]. Intuition pumps are cunningly designed to focus the reader's attention on 'the important' features, and to deflect the reader from bogging down in hard-to-follow details. There is nothing wrong with this in principle. Indeed one of philosophy's highest callings is finding ways of helping people see the forest and not just the trees. (1984, 12)[23]

Philosophical intuitions can be reached, with no conscious inference, from reflection on hypothetical thought experiments. Following Dennett's 'intuition pump', to get an understanding of what philosophical intuitions are, let us review what philosophers intended when they were telling stories such as the Gettier cases, philosophical zombies or Mary, the colour scientist. This might help us to interpret some thought experiments as appealing to intuition. For instance, in Jackson's thought experiment,

> Mary is a brilliant scientist who is, for whatever reason, forced to investigate the world from a black and white room *via* a black and white television monitor. She specializes in the neurophysiology of vision and acquires, let us suppose, all the physical information there is to obtain about what goes on when we see ripe tomatoes, or the sky, and use terms like 'red', 'blue', and so on. (. . .) What will happen when Mary is released from her black and white room or is given a colour television monitor? Will she *learn* anything or not? It just seems obvious that she will learn something about the world and our visual experience of it. But then it is inescapable that her previous knowledge was incomplete. But she had *all* the physical information. *Ergo* there is more to have than that, and Physicalism is false. (1982, 130)

What is Jackson's intention in telling this story? In one interpretation, he aims to elicit the belief that Mary will learn something new about the world, so physicalism is false. He considers this belief to be justified by reflection on the story told. In fact, the *belief* that we directly obtained and hold to be justified based on Jackson's story is our *intuition*.

The same interpretation can be made for the 'Gettier case'. Edmund Gettier famously described a situation in which Smith is completely ignorant of Brown's location, while he believes on strong evidence that Jones owns a Ford. He writes:

> But imagine now that two further conditions hold. First, Jones does not own a Ford, but is at present driving a rented car. And secondly, by the sheerest coincidence, and entirely unknown to Smith, the place mentioned in proposition (h) [i.e. Either Jones owns a Ford, or Brown is in Barcelona] happens really to be the place where Brown is. If these two conditions hold, then Smith does not know that (h) is true, even though (i) (h) is true, (ii) Smith does believe that (h) is true, and (iii) Smith is justified in believing that (h) is true. (1963, 122f)

Gettier concludes that Smith is justified in believing the proposition (h), that is 'either Jones owns a Ford, or Brown is in Barcelona', although, Gettier maintains, Smith still does not have knowledge. Gettier's story leads us to *believe* that Smith has a justified true belief that (h) but does not know (h).[24] Again, in one interpretation, the belief that we acquired and justified based on this story is our *intuition*.

If it is true to interpret thought experiments as appealing to intuition, at this stage, I think, we are able to provide a response to the question that this chapter started with: What is 'intuition'? The thought experiments that philosophers use in their theorizing can help us to have straightforward psychology of 'intuition'. In other words, since thought experiments ('intuition pump') lead us to believe something, they can give us an explanation of 'what intuition is' by reading intuition in terms of familiar mental states such as belief. In fact, these philosophical thought experiments give us at least *prima facie* reason (motivation) to support what I call

> *The Reductionist Account of Intuition (doxastic view): Intuitions are belief-like states. To have the intuition that p is to have the non-inferential, pre-theoretical and firm belief that p.*[25]

But we are not entitled to say that any sort of belief is intuition. For example, if I were now to have the belief that I am on a train, this would be a belief and not an intuition; it is an observation of location. There are certain philosophers who offer a reductionist account as a way of understanding intuitions. Lewis, for example, writes,

> Our 'intuitions' are simply opinions; our philosophical theories are the same. Some are common-sensical, some are sophisticated; some are particular, some general; some are more firmly held, some less. But they are all opinions. (1983, x)

In this passage, Lewis reduces intuitions to opinions. For him, opinions are not different from beliefs. To understand intuition in terms of beliefs has the same connotation as 'S has the intuition that p iff S believes that p'. Adopting this account has different characteristics:

First, it explains what intuitions are without introducing a new mental state or phenomenon; that is, it explains intuition in terms of an already *familiar* mental state—*belief*.

Second, the reductionist account attempts to make a demarcation between defining intuition in terms of the cognitive state of belief and intuition in terms of the phenomenal state of, say, feeling of conviction. The reductionists' account, however, endorses defining intuition in terms of the cognitive state of belief.[26]

Third, advocates of this account often think that intuitions under this account can be of two forms: dispositional and occurrent.[27] A dispositional claim or state is not about anything that is actually occurring at the time. Rather, it is about some particular thing that is prone to occur. The reductionists believe that they can support these two ways in which intuitions figure in our mental lives. For example, in the Gettier case, when we become convinced that Smith lacks knowledge, our intuition appears in our conscious thinking. This entails that our intuition is in an occurrent cognitive state. However, we can retain this very intuition even when we do not think about Smith's situation. Here, intuition is used to denote a purely inclinational or dispositional cognitive state.[28] For example, Earlenbaugh and Molyneux write,

> [I]ntuitions are a subclass of inclinations to believe: Not all inclinations to believe are intuitions, but all intuitions are inclinations to believe . . . In particular, it explains why intuitions appear to be used, in philosophical methodology, as evidence, without conceding either that they are evidence or even that they are really treated as such. (2009, 89–90)

However, the primary account of intuition wants to explain what intuitions are when one is occurrently in the relevant conscious psychological state. But the purely dispositionalist account of intuition can hardly capture the occurrent conscious character of intuitions which philosophers have interests in. It seems very odd to say that we are consciously having philosophical intuitions all the time! Could one say that we have intuitions when we are asleep? We are not having intuitions when asleep as they are generally held to be conscious and occurrent states. It is very hard to theorize about our philosophical intuitions when we are asleep. If it is true that we are still disposed to believe certain things when we are asleep or unconscious, then on that view, we have to include mystical intuitions that mystics experience in their ecstasy in our account of intuition. However, philosophers do not need to theorize about mystics' intuitions. We might be disposed to believe certain intuitive propositions when we are asleep, but if we do not have intuitions when we are asleep, that looks like an argument that intuitions do not equal purely dispositions-to-believe.

Furthermore, as I claimed at the beginning of the chapter, the primary notion of intuition that I am working within this book is a notion that someone has an intuition that p only when S is occurrently in the relevant conscious state. But a pure disposition-to-believe is not an occurrent and conscious mental state. If so, any purely dispositional intuition might fail to capture the occurrent conscious character of intuitions.[29]

If I am right, then intuitions are conscious and occurrent states. If intuitions are conscious and occurrent states, then we should reject the purely dispositional or inclinational account of intuition. Although I believe that this argument works against the purely inclinational or dispositional account of intuition, at the end of this chapter, I will return to mere belief and inclination or disposition-to-believe accounts to discuss whether they are as attractive as the non-doxastic account of intuition, that is, the seeming account.

Yet, some of those who support the dispositional account might reject this *purely* dispositional account, as there are some limitations on these dispositions. Ernest Sosa (1998), for instance, claims that a plausible account for the advocates of intuitions as dispositions-to-believe is to read intuition as disposition-to-believe merely on the basis of adequate understanding. This implies if one has the intuition that p, one is disposed to believe p merely on the basis of adequate understanding of p. Such an account of disposition, unlike a purely dispositional account, would allow that intuitions are propositional attitudes and can also explain one's believing p on the basis of adequate understanding.

Related to that point, some advocates of the dispositional or inclinational view, for example, Sosa (1998, 2007), hold that if we read intuition in terms of 'felt inclination' or 'attractions to assent' based on an adequate understanding, we can claim that it is an occurrent state. That is, although the pure disposition or inclination account of intuition does not provide the occurrent nature of intuitions, we can have an understanding of the disposition or inclination view that might provide the occurrent nature of intuitions. This understanding of the disposition or inclination account might be compatible with my view that philosophical intuitions are occurrent and conscious states. However, I will argue later in this chapter that the seeming account is superior to the disposition or inclination account of intuition, whether or not the disposition or inclination account can make room for the occurrent nature of intuitions.[30]

Nevertheless, why adopt the reductionist view? It would be necessary to have some defence of the reductionist view in mind before discussing its rival. One reason to adopt the reductionist view might be that there is a clear link between intuitions and beliefs in some cases, so one can typically believe the contents of an intuition. Another reason is that the reductionist view is more parsimonious ontologically. If intuitions are beliefs or inclinations-to-believe, we do not need to accept a new kind of psychological state. To defend the reductionists' core idea, we can repeat Peter van Inwagen's observation when he writes that

> Our 'intuitions' are simply our beliefs – or perhaps, in some cases, the tendencies that make certain beliefs attractive to us, that 'move' us in the direction of accepting certain propositions without taking us all the way to acceptance. (1997, 309)

That will suffice for reductionism. I introduced and gave some defence of the reductionist view. I will not say more about the reductionist account at this stage, as I think we are sufficiently familiar with mental states such as belief-like states. Therefore, I turn now to the non-reductionist (non-belief) account and explore what intellectual seemings are.

2.2 Intellectual seemings: A non-reductionist account of intuition

Although the reductionist account of intuition provides a commonsensical understanding of philosophical intuitions, some philosophers prefer to embrace the rival account of intuitions espoused most prominently by Bealer, who writes that

> Intuition is the source of all a priori knowledge – except, of course, for that which is merely stipulative. The use of intuitions as evidence (reasons) is ubiquitous in our standard justificatory practice in the a priori disciplines – Gettier intuitions, twin-earth intuitions, transitivity intuitions, etc. By intuition here, we mean seemings: for you to have an intuition that A is just for it to seem to you that A. Of course, this kind of seeming is intellectual, not experiential – sensory, introspective, imaginative. (2002, 73)

To give an account of intuition, Bealer points to 'seemings' rather than beliefs.[31] In the discussion of intuition, he starts off by distinguishing between the intuitions of primary interest in philosophical inquiry and other states.[32] He claims that philosophical inquiries are typically based upon 'rational intuition' or 'a priori intuitions'. Rational intuitions *might* present themselves as necessary, although they are not *necessarily* true (1998, 165). They might turn out to be mistaken after reflection. Bealer, for example, writes that

> When we have a rational intuition – say, that if P then not not P – it presents itself as necessary: it does not seem to us that things could be otherwise; it must be that if P then not not P. (1998, 207)

He believes that rational intuition cannot be overlapped with what we experience in scientific experiments. For there are many things that can seem to us intellectually to be so but they cannot sensorily seem to us to be so and vice versa. He writes that

> [It cannot] seem to you intellectually (i.e. without any relevant sensations and without any attendant beliefs) that there exist billions of brain cells; intuition is silent about this essentially empirical question. (1998, 208)

Bealer also distinguishes between *intellectual* and *experiential* seemings and defines rational intuitions in terms of *intellectual seemings*. That is, rational intuitions are intellectual seemings, not sensory seemings. He elsewhere stresses that 'seeming' is to be understood not in its cautionary or hedging sense but as marking off a 'genuine kind of conscious episode' (Bealer, 1998, 207). I call this account of intuition

> *The Non-Reductionist Account of Intuitions-As-Seemings (non-doxastic view):* Rational intuitions are intellectual seemings. To have the (rational) intuition that p is to have the intellectual seeming that p.

Understanding intuition in terms of seemings has the same connotation as 'S has the intuition that p if it seems to S that p'. Bealer maintains that the intellectual seeming account can cover everything that 'rational intuitions' cover.[33] A rational intuition, in the case of, for instance, mathematics, happens when it seems to us that a mathematical proposition (e.g. 2+2=4) must be true.

Bealer tries to defend the kind of intuition that we use in philosophical arguments as evidence. His argument, briefly, is that our intuitions are based on our abilities to understand concepts, and this is what we need to attend to as evidence in philosophy. As for characterizing what exactly the nature of intuition is, Bealer talks about the psychology of intuition, that is, what it is like to have an intuition:

> We do not mean a magical power or inner voice or special glow or any other mysterious quality. When you have an intuition that A, it seems to you that A . . . a genuine kind of conscious episode. (1998, 207)

Bealer's psychology of intuitions is mainly negative and against reductionists who reduce intuition to other mental states or phenomena. For example, Bealer thinks that intuitions are not beliefs, inclinations-to-believe, guesses or hunches, commonsense opinions, linguistic intuitions or judgements.[34]

In the following, I will try to expound upon two important features of the intellectual seeming account that *may* need more attention. The reason is that commentators believe that Bealer has expressed different and, to some extent, inconsistent views about intuition in different years (i.e. 1992–2002). However, I try to explain and defend Bealer's account in light of different criticisms. I then focus on one of Bealer's arguments against the reductionist account, that is, the argument from intuition without belief. He rightly undermines the idea of the reductionists who think that intuitions are *mere* beliefs.

(i) The seeming account defines (rational) intuitions as seemings, or as Bealer says, 'when you have an intuition that A, it seems to you that A' (1992, 101).

This kind of seeming is also intellectual rather than perceptual, sensory or introspective, for one can have a certain intuition without having perception or introspection at all.[35] Thus, when S intuits that p, it intellectually seems to S that p.

Bealer's seeming account advocates a special phenomenology of rational intuition when he writes: 'it presents itself as necessary'. Interpreting Bealer, Pust writes that

> S has a rational intuition that p if and only if (a) S has a purely intellectual experience ... that p, and (b) at t, if S were to consider whether p is necessarily true, then S would have a purely intellectual experience that necessarily, p. (2000, 39)[36]

Although Pust, like Bealer, holds that intuitions are seeming states, he disagrees with Bealer that seeming involves *necessity*. Pust believes that Bealer's phrase expresses the mistaken idea that all rational intuitions are 'phenomenologically like seeing that *p must be* true' (2000, 36). Pust denies (not only that rational intuitions *must* be true but also) that rational intuitions' modal character must be obvious to the person who has the intellectual experience of a rational seeming. For the avoidance of this mistake, Pust introduces the concept of *reflection* and suggests that one of the charitable readings of the *modal* character of rational intuitions is that this modal character must be apparent on reflection.[37] Therefore, we might have the rational intuition that p, although it does not seem to us that *p must be* true. When we reflect on the matter, the *modal* character will appear.

Bealer is not clear enough about whether people can have rational intuitions without actually having any thoughts about necessity. To say that rational intuitions *present* themselves as *necessary* truths seems to imply that anyone who has a rational intuition has the intellectual experience of some proposition's seeming to be not only true but also necessarily true. If Bealer does really go so far as to think that every rational intuition is a seeming of the necessary truth of a proposition, then he really is stuck with the problem, Pust identifies. But perhaps Bealer himself does not go so far. What is important here is that whether or not he did go that far, he definitely should not have. It is not the case that all rational intuitions are intuitions of necessity.

In fact, there are two issues here. One is whether rational intuitions can be defined as intuitions of necessary truths. The second is whether such truths must present themselves as necessary for an intuition to count as rational. I think it is a mistake to define rational intuitions as intuitions of necessary truths since I believe intuitions are fallible seemings. Something can seem to be necessarily true even though it is not true. Furthermore, suppose I have an intuition that

2+2=4 and a different intuition that necessarily 2+2=4. The former looks like an *a priori* intuition because it is an intuition of a necessary truth even though it does not present itself as necessary. So, it looks false to say that intuitions *always* present themselves as necessary truths.

(ii) The seeming account emphasizes the *episodic* character of rational intuitions.[38] Bealer points to the episodic character of intuition and rejects the idea that intuitions are inclinations-to-believe. Bealer goes so far as to hold that intuitions are *essentially* episodic. He claims that whenever someone has an intuition, 'a *sui generis* cognitive episode must occur' (1998, 209). However, some commentators, for example, Nimtz (2010), argue that taking intuitions to be *essentially episodic* can cause a problem for Bealer. For *perceptions* are entirely episodic, and one can think that there is a corresponding equivalency between intuition (intellectual seeming) and perception. But, as we do not have the perception that, for example, the wagon is red unless we *accurately* perceive the redness of the wagon, in much the same vein, one can hold that you do not have the intuition that a kind of act is wrong unless you accurately intuit the wrongness of that kind of act. In other words, Nimtz's argument against Bealer is an argument by analogy: since Bealer holds that intuition is like perception in being episodic, Bealer must hold that intuition is like perception in being accurate (factive).

Nimtz's argument against Bealer's episodic characteristic is not convincing. First of all, we should be careful in how we understand Nimtz's analogy. I assume here that what he must have meant is an analogy not with perception but with perceptual experience because perception is factive, and Bealer clearly does not hold that intuition is factive. Second, all things considered, Nimtz's reading of Bealer is not right. Although Bealer believes that intuitions are episodic-like perceptions, he does not mean by this that intuitions are similar to perception in *all* respects. He merely draws a parallel between intuition and perception in terms of being episodic and nothing more. At some points, Bealer clearly says that intellectual seeming (intuition) is *not* like perception. For example, he argues that it is assumed perceptual experiences have sui generis distinctive, phenomenally conscious aspects presenting what is perceived. However, proponents of the intellectual seeming account seem to agree that episodic intellectual seemings do not have a distinctive phenomenal character.[39] Thus intuition is not like perception in this respect, or as Bealer writes,

> [M]y view is simply that intuition is a *sui generis*, irreducible, natural propositional attitude which occurs episodically. That is all, no 'glow' or other 'positive' element. (1996a, 169)

Nimtz also criticizes Bealer that it is far from clear whether we do have intellectual seemings. In Nimtz's view, we, of course, do have sensory seemings. For example, we open our eyes and find ourselves having experiential states with a specific sensory phenomenology. But do we have any intellectual seemings like what Bealer describes? It is difficult to say that activities such as judging, imagining, inferring, etc. actually belong to the distinctive kind of intellectual seeming which constitutes a kind of conscious episode, according to Nimtz.

He is again wrong, I believe. Yes, we are familiar with mental states such as belief; but this does not entail that we are not entitled to introduce a new mental state. Reducing any new phenomena to an already familiar mental state might be problematic. Moreover, we have clear examples of intellectual seemings. For example, one can think about 'Dick Cheney's faking the evidence of Iraqi weapons of mass destruction' or 'his mandating torture of prisoners' and, inasmuch as one adequately understands the conceptual constituents, one can be struck by the seeming wrongness. One's consciousness of this seeming wrongness lasts for as long as one *thinks* about these matters. So here we have a clear example of an episode of intellectual seeming.

Nimtz states that Bealer's intellectual seeming account, generally, suffers from an inconsistency. Perhaps this is because Bealer has different papers elaborating on the phenomenology of intuition. On the one hand, as Bealer thinks, the seeming account points to the states of intellectual seemings, a 'genuine kind of conscious episode' (1998, 207) and similar to perceptual experiences. However, on the other hand, they are in the intellectual mode. Or, as Pust elaborates, they are 'purely intellectual experience' (2000, 39). How is it possible to have states that are at the same time experiences, that is to say, they belong to a category of states with a distinct phenomenology, but they are also purely intellectual and hence non-perceptual, and thus they do not have a distinct phenomenology? This tension, Nimtz thinks, leads us to be more cautious about Bealer's claim that having non-perceptual experiences is a distinct mental category.

As I explained earlier, I do not see any tension in Bealer's claim that seeming states are intellectual and, at the same time, similar to perceptual experiences. He seems to think that intuitions are episodic. When Bealer wants to explain the psychological aspect of intuition, he refers to perceptual experiences. However, of course, he does not hold that intuition and perception are alike in *every* respect. Besides, when we think that 'The boiling point of water is 100 degrees Celsius', do we not have the *experience* of thinking this? We can think of an infinite number of other abstract propositions, including moral ones. Why are not all of these thoughts examples of non-perceptual experiences? They certainly *seem* to be non-perceptual experiences.

In the face of this appearance, we would need a very good argument to persuade us that there are no non-perceptual experiences. And if there are non-perceptual experiences, intellectual seemings seem obviously to be examples. Therefore, we should accept intellectual seemings as non-perceptual mental states.[40]

So far, so good. We have investigated two main rival intuition theories, that is, the reductionist and the non-reductionist account of intuition. I have also given some defence of both the reductionist and the non-reductionist views. It is now time for a more comprehensive evaluation. In the next section, I evaluate which of these two accounts is superior.

3 Why is the non-reductionist account of intuition superior to the reductionist account? Spelling out the argument from intuition without belief

Adherents of the non-reductionist account of intuition, such as the intellectual seeming account, need to refute the rival reductionist account. Here is Bealer's criticism of the reductionist account of intuition:

> I have an intuition – it still *seems* to me – that the naive comprehension axiom of set theory is true; this is so despite the fact that I do not believe that it is true (because I know of the set-theoretical paradoxes). There is a rather similar phenomenon in sense perception. In the Müller-Lyer illusion, it still *seems* to me that one of the arrows is longer than the other; this is so despite the fact that I do not believe that one of the two arrows is longer (because I have measured them). In each case, the seeming persists in spite of countervailing belief. (1998, 208)

The argument Bealer appeals to in this paragraph is what can be called *the argument from intuition without belief*. He supports his argument by drawing an analogy with perceptual experiences (e.g. the Müller-Lyer illusion). The point here is that just like perceptual experiences, which allow us to have sense perception without belief in the advent of optical illusion, intellectual seemings allow us to have intuition without belief. In fact, when we look at the Müller-Lyer picture, the inequality of the two lines is *presented* to us, although we believe that they are equal. Let me explain with some examples.

Perceptual illusions generally help us to see that there is a gap between *appearance* and belief. For instance, let us take Adelson's checker shadow illusion

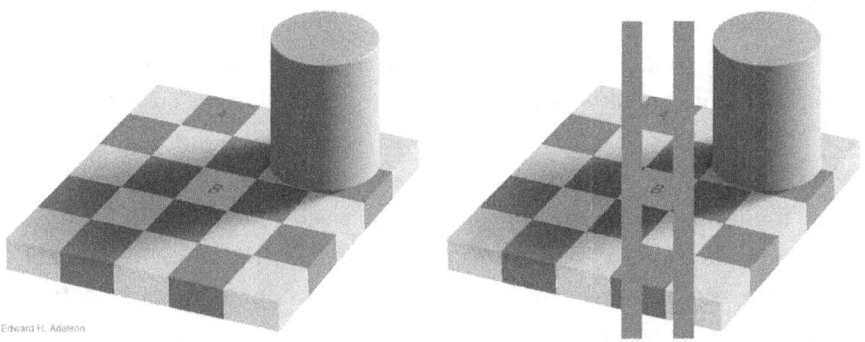

Figure 2 Adelson's checker shadow illusion. ©1995, Edward H. Adelson. The image is derived from: http://persci.mit.edu/gallery/checkershadow.

(Figure 2). When we look at the left-hand picture, square B seems to be brighter than square A. However, the two squares are, in fact, the exact same colour, as can easily be seen in the right-hand picture. Square B seems to us brighter than A, although we know that it is not.

As another example, there are some philosophers who, following Tamar Gendler (2010, Ch. 13), refer to a mental state called 'alief' as an automatic or habitual belief-like attitude, particularly when it is in tension with one's explicit belief.[41] For instance, suppose someone stands on a transparent balcony. One might believe that it is safe, but at the same time, one's alief is that it is dangerous. Or suppose someone believes in racial equality. However, one might have an alief that makes one treat people of different racial groups in different ways. Alief states can help us to explain some psychological phenomena such as certain religious beliefs and psychiatric disturbances (e.g. phobias and obsessive-compulsive disorder). Although Gendler does not mention intuition in her paper, it seems plausible to say that the mental state we experience as alief is similar to intuition in terms of intellectual seeming since both are defined as opposed to one's explicit belief. Thus, there are intuitions and aliefs that are different, although similar in certain respects.

Daniel Kahneman also refers to such belief-like states that are defined as opposed to one's explicit belief as 'lazy system' or 'fast thinking' (2011, 44). In experiencing such states, we find it hard, according to him, to manage to resist the automatic and spontaneous reaction that comes to mind. He believes that intuitions, in the case of, for instance, intellectual illusion or puzzle, should be understood as a subset of this category.[42] Hence, intuitions are different mental states than beliefs.

Nonetheless, what, then, is the argument from intuition without belief? The argument seeks to find a reason to show that intuitions are not beliefs. So those reductionist accounts of intuition, which rest entirely on this claim, should be discarded. Of course, the rejection of one reading of the reductionist account that equates intuition with *mere* belief does not make room for the proof of the non-reductionist account of intuition, that is, non-belief-like states.[43] The reason is that we still need more arguments to undermine another version of the reductionist account, that is, inclination or disposition-to-believe account.

The argument from intuition without belief simply states that since we have the intuition that p and at the same time we believe that not-p, intuitions are not, therefore, *mere* beliefs. However, this argument can only work if we do not have two inconsistent beliefs. So, in the examples I put forward in the following, I show that we do not have two inconsistent beliefs in such cases. The argument hinges on the three claims that can be formally articulated as follows:

(P1): if intuitions are beliefs, then when S has the intuition that p, S must have the belief that p.
(P2): there are clear cases where S has the intuition that p, but S lacks the belief that p. Indeed, there are cases where S has the intuition that p, but S has the belief that not-p.
(P3): in many of these cases, S does not hold contradictory and inconsistent beliefs.
(C): therefore, intuitions are not (mere) beliefs.

It seems that the argument is valid, that is, the premises entail the conclusion. But are the premises true? What can be said about P1–P3? Let me evaluate each premise in turn.

P1, clearly, is a conditional claim that adherents of one model of the reductionist account of intuition presuppose. So if intuitions are (mere) beliefs, then P1 is true.[44]

P2 is very well supported. Certainly, as I have already given examples earlier, there are clear cases where *S has the intuition that p but lacks the belief that p*. However, as a straightforward *moral* example, suppose one who believes in divine command theory might have the intuition that 'abortion is permissible' but does not believe that this is so because one believes abortion is not permitted by the *correct* moral theory. In case that example seems unconvincing, I provide two more in the next two paragraphs.

(1) Sarah has the intuition that whatever gives us pleasure is always (because necessarily) right. Then she comes to accept natural law theory or deontological pluralism as the correct moral theory and sees that her moral theory implies that whatever gives us pleasure is not necessarily right. So, although Sarah still has the intuition that whatever gives us pleasure is necessarily right, she does not have the belief that it is. This entails that while one does not hold two contradictory beliefs, one's intuition is not the same as one's belief.

(2) Joe has the intuition that morality is necessarily restricted to how one treats others. If that intuition were correct, then behaviour that has no impact on others cannot be morally required or morally forbidden. But then Joe comes to believe in act-utilitarianism, which counts the benefits and harms to the agent for no less than the benefits or harms to anyone else. Once Joe accepts act-utilitarianism, he can no longer believe that morality is necessarily restricted to how one treats others since his act-utilitarianism forces him to concede that when facing a decision that will have no impact on others, one is morally required to choose what is most beneficial to oneself. Thus, Joe's intuition about morality is not mirrored by his belief, even though he does not have two contradictory beliefs. Again, this entails that one's intuition is not one's belief at the same time.[45]

Less certainly, there are cases where *S has the intuition that p but believes that not-p*. For instance, many people might have the undying intuition that X is wrong and yet believe that it is not true that X is wrong. For example, when we encounter hard-to-solve (or unsolved) paradoxes, that is, the Lottery Paradoxes or the Preface Paradox and come to believe that one of the premises p is false, we sometimes keep the intuition that p.[46] Furthermore, suppose the reductionist account is correct. So, if 'S has the intuition that p, and the intuition that q, and the intuition that r' is true in a paradox case, it is also true that S has the belief that p, and the belief that q, and the belief that r. But if S believed p, q and r altogether, S would be irrational. However, we are not irrational if a set of contradictory propositions is intuitive to us.[47]

Bealer (1996a, 123) also provides different cases of intuition without belief, such as the naive comprehension axiom in mathematics. Bealer says that although the naive comprehension axiom is mistaken, our intuition goes differently. This entails that the axiom is false despite seeming true.[48]

In the cases described earlier, I showed that there is a pre-theoretical intuition as opposed to, say, a belief. However, one might object that many of these cases can be handled by allowing that one can believe p and believe not-p, for different reasons. So, to justify our argument, we need to defend that one does not hold two contradictory beliefs in these cases. This is where P3 comes in.

P3 appears to be true. It is true that we often express inconsistent and conflicting beliefs by saying: 'I believe that not-p, but I still have the intuition that p.' These cases of intuition with belief, that is, cases where 'intuition' is to be read simply as 'belief', do not challenge the reductionist account of intuitions with mere belief. However, there are some cases where we do *not* express inconsistent and conflicting beliefs by saying: 'I believe that not-p, but I still have the intuition that p.' These cases of intuition are at stake here. For example, we sometimes cannot shake our intuition that 'every property defines a set', even though we know that this is false. This can happen without creating an inconsistency in our system of belief.

However, reductionists might object that inconsistent beliefs can be just a case of a belief that p plus a belief that it looks like not-p, based on how things look. After all, the intuition must generate a belief, for example, about how things seem, so it can be more parsimonious and less obscure to eliminate the intuition and just posit an appearance and a belief based on the appearance.

Reductionists are right that we can posit an appearance and a belief based on that. This can even work in the case of intellectual examples. Huemer, for example, talks about 'intellectual appearances' when he refers to seemings. But talking about appearance instead of intuition is just changing our wordings. It is not parsimonious, as once again, we need to ask what appearance is, and then we need to have a philosophical theory about it, just like what I did about seeming.

Hence, if P1–P3 are true, C must be true. So, intuitions are not (mere) beliefs after all. If this argument works, which I think it does, at least one version of the reductionist-doxastic account of intuition (which identifies intuition with mere belief) should be disqualified because it cannot support many philosophical intuition cases.

Even so, the earlier argument does not rule out the inclination-to-believe or disposition-to-believe account since the argument does not apply. In the following section, I argue that, although the inclination or disposition account of intuition is superior to the mere belief account, it cannot stand against the chosen account of this book, that is, the seeming account.

3.1 Why is the seeming account of intuition superior to the inclination or disposition account?

Although I argued against the disposition or inclination account of intuition before, there is still a question which I have not dealt with so far and which we should be clear about before going to the next chapter: Is the inclination or disposition account superior to the seeming view advocated here? Can the disposition or inclination account of intuition explain different phenomena better than the seeming account?

Some philosophers have argued against the inclination or disposition-to-believe account of intuition (Bealer, 1992, 1998).[49] I do have an argument of my own to challenge the inclination or disposition account of intuition and show that it is inferior to the seeming account. Here is my argument.

It *seems* to me that my friends and family are objectively more important than other people, that is, not only more important to me but also more important objectively considered. I care more about my friends and family than I do about (the same number of or even more) other people. That is a fact about the pattern of my subjective concern. Another matter is how objectively important other different people seem to me. Well, to me, my friends and family seem objectively more important than other people, and I find it slightly surprising that other people cannot see how important the people who happen to be my friends and family really are. I am not making the preposterous suggestion that these people really are objectively more important merely because they are my friends and family. Rather, I am saying that people who happen to be my friends and family have other qualities that make them appear to me to be more important, objectively considered, than other people.

But am I inclined to believe or disposed to believe my friends and family are objectively more important? Well no. The reason I am NOT inclined to believe NOR disposed to believe my friends and family are objectively more important than others is that I really do know this is not true. But knowing it is not true does not prevent its seeming to me to be true. So here is a *seeming* that is not mirrored by a disposition or inclination-to-believe. In this example, the 'intuition' that my friends and family are objectively more important cannot be a disposition or inclination-to-believe. This argument shows why intuitions could not be thought of as a certain kind of disposition or inclination-to-believe. The reason why is that there are at least some examples where an intuition clearly is a seeming, not some kind of disposition or inclination-to-believe.[50]

Even if my argument does not work, I believe that the seeming account looks more fundamental than the disposition or inclination account in explaining different phenomena. Although we can remain open-minded about whether there are some cases that the inclination or disposition account explains best, the seeming account can do a better job. The reason is that we can explain why we are inclined (disposed) to believe various things by saying that they *seem* true to us. In other words, even in cases where we are inclined (or have disposition) to believe something, we are actually inclined (or have the disposition) to believe it because it *seems* true to us. In other words, that p seems true to me is a decent reason for my believing p. In contrast, that I am disposed or inclined to believe p is not a decent reason for me to believe p.[51]

Before concluding this chapter, let me touch upon an issue that I did not cover before. This chapter tried to answer the question, 'What are intuitions?' From the way the question is posed, it is clear that I assumed there are non-linguistic entities, which are intuitions, and that there can be multiple theories about what these things are. I treated intuitions as univocal and focused on criticisms that are also tangled up in the idea that 'intuition' is univocal in meaning. The chapter examined two theories, the doxastic theory and the non-doxastic theory, and tried to show that the doxastic theory is incorrect. This left the non-doxastic theory in possession of the field.

But it seems that there is a prior question to be faced as to whether the word 'intuition' is equivocal. It might have two meanings, meanings so diverse that no third theory takes the two in. In that case, it might be that intuitions, doxastically construed, are one kind of thing and intuitions, non-doxastically construed, are a different type of thing. If this is so, then counterexamples presented to the doxastic theory misfire: they only show they are motivated by a different sense of 'intuition'. Let me explain.

Let us consider the doxastic sort. Someone says, 'I think England will win the world cup next year.' Someone says, 'How do you know that? They never win. Germany is obviously better, etc. etc.' The first person says, 'I just have an intuition about this.'

It perhaps strikes us that this is a common and acceptable use of the word 'intuition'. Notice that it is directed towards a future physical event, so it is not the intellectual intuition Bealer talks about. But I do not think that this sort of intuition is to be despised. It is not a matter of blind faith: the intuition could be based on unconscious processing of a lot of information. It is just that, at the moment, the speaker does not have the information at hand and may not even know how he has processed it.

Now consider the non-doxastic sort. Someone says, 'I feel that it is more immoral to push the fat man in front of the trolley than to flip the trolley switch, but I don't have an argument that this is so. It's just my intuition.' Here we have an intuition about the normative features of an act, so I guess the intuition describes a kind of relation between the mind and its object, and the intuition is not merely backing up a belief. This, too, is a common and acceptable use of 'intuition', particularly as in 'moral intuitions'.

I tried to explicate these non-doxastic intuitions by recourse to the word 'seeming'. However, one might object that the sentences containing this word are not helpful. Typically, when we use the words 'seems', we intend 'seems so, but isn't so'. But the intellectual intuitions that we have, in ethics, do not present themselves as 'seems so, but it isn't'. They usually are 'seems so, and is so'. Now and then, in ethics, something seems so and then turns out to be wrong. But that is the exceptional case.

The rest of the book deals with the psychology and epistemology of *moral* intuitions. I will show how seeming states can explain the recalcitrant nature of moral intuitions well.

4 Conclusion

Let me conclude this chapter with a section that summarizes. I started by distinguishing between two main categories of theories about intuition. Supporters of intuition theories who believe that intuitions are a sui generis mental state I called non-reductionists, and adherents of intuition theories who think that intuitions are not a sui generis mental state I called reductionists. I then introduced and explained different subcategories of the reductionist account, for example, mere belief and inclination or disposition-to-believe. I undermined the first mode of the reductionist account, that is, mere belief states. The argument from intuition without belief casts doubt on the claim that intuitions are mere beliefs. What was left, then? At least a version of the reductionist account and the non-reductionist account remained on the table. At the end of the chapter, I argued that the seeming account is superior to the inclination or disposition-to-believe account. Although my position in this chapter was quite close to Bealer's account of intuition, I attempted to rebut criticisms against Bealer to save the non-doxastic account of intuition.

All in all, since the seeming account of intuition could fundamentally explain our beliefs in something better than doxastic accounts of intuition, for the rest of this book, my 'intuition' goes mostly with the seemings.

2

Moral intuition's mental ontology
Shifting from philosophical to moral intuition

1 Introduction

Epistemological moral intuitionism is ordinarily thought of as an account of non-inferentially justified *moral* intuitions. In this chapter, my main task is to deal with *moral* intuition's mental ontology. I will, however, need to discuss some epistemological issues at some points. I will start by defending the quasi-perceptualist account of *philosophical* intuition, which understands intuitions as *intellectual seemings*. This will help me to shift from philosophical to moral intuition. According to this account, to have an intuition that p is to have the intellectual seeming that p. I will say more about intellectual seemings and certain shared phenomenological features between intuitions and perceptual experiences. In order to do so, I appeal to John Bengson's view about intuition. Following Bengson (Dissertation), I explain intellectual seemings in terms of 'presentation' and 'translucency'. Although Bengson echoes almost all that George Bealer (1998) believes, Bengson labels his account of intuition 'Quasi-Perceptualism'. Bengson puts more weight on the shared phenomenological features between intuition and perceptual experience than Bealer did, and Bengson claims that intuition is fundamentally just *like* perceptual experience but is still not *sensory* experience.

Although in this chapter I rely on Bengson's view to outline a quasi-perceptualist account of philosophical intuition in terms of intellectual seemings, he argues in his paper, 'The Intellectual Given' (2015), that his perceptualist account differs from a seeming account of intuitions, for example, Bealer's seeming account. For example, Bengson argues that presentations are different from seemings on non-phenomenal grounds and that seemings are not non-voluntary, compare to presentations discussed in core quasi-perceptualist theses. Or, while a seeming is explicit, that is, its content is available when the content seems true, presentations in core quasi-perceptualist theses can be inexplicit.[1] In this chapter, however, I assume that what Bengson considers core quasi-perceptualist theses can be applicable to intellectual seemings. For the sake of argument, the distinction between core quasi-perceptualist theses and the seeming view is not at stake. I believe Bealer's seeming account and Bengson's quasi-perceptualist theses can give us important features to explain how moral intuitions work in terms of seeming.

After understanding what philosophical intuition is in terms of seeming, I then shift from philosophical intuition to moral intuition. I will say about Audi's doxastic account of moral intuition and, alternatively, explain moral intuitions in terms of the quasi-perceptualist account, which understands moral intuitions as intellectual seemings. In the meantime, I argue that the intellectual seeming account of *moral* intuition is superior to the doxastic account of moral intuition.

2 Quasi-perceptualist seeming account of intuition[2]

In this section, I discuss some similarities between intuition and perceptual experiences. In my discussion of perceptual experiences, I will be assuming the standard representational theory of perception. According to this view, to have a perception of an object O as having a property F is to be in a perceptual mental state with a phenomenal character which represents O as having the property F, that is, it has representational content that O is F.

Perceptual experiences should be distinguished from *inference*. In making inferences, we often actively practice a number of steps of explicit reasoning, whereas in perceptual experiences, something simply comes to us passively. Yet, we can use some inferences to explain why we have a particular perceptual experience. Thus, perceptual experiences, in this sense, give us a sense of directness, 'givenness' and vividness. Perceptual experiences are examples of non-doxastic states, so essentially can involve grounding non-inferential justification for our beliefs.[3]

Bengson is impressed by certain phenomenological features shared between intuition and perceptual experiences.[4] Of course, there are several differences between perceptual experience and intuition. For instance, intuition lacks the rich sensory phenomenology that most perceptual experiences have.[5] Also, perceptual experiences are only of particulars, while intuitions can be of the particular or the general.[6]

However, there are some abstract similarities between them that might be helpful in giving an account of the nature of intuition. For example, both perceptual experiences and *some* intuitions are direct, contentful and non-factive states.[7] Suppose I have a sensory experience that there is a pen on the table in front of me. So, I am in a state with the direct content that there is a pen on the table. But the experience might be non-veridical, that is, not coincide with reality. Even more so, some of our intuitions, especially in moral cases, often fail to be correct. This must be true since they so often contradict one another. And when one person's moral intuitions contradict another person's, at least one of these people must have incorrect moral intuitions.

What more can be said about abstract similarities between intuitions and perceptual experiences? If intuitions and perceptual experiences are, in a certain way, similar, what sort of mental state is intuition?[8]

We can make a distinction among different contentful states in terms of representationality and presentationality. Some states such as beliefs, perceptual experiences and intuitions are representational in the sense that they represent the world in a certain way as if their content were true. For example, the belief that 'Everest is the highest mountain in the world' *represents* the world in a certain way that its content is true. Or one's moral belief that p, for example, 'surrogate motherhood is wrong', *represents* the world as being such that p is true, that is, it is not permissible to obtain or be a surrogate mother. However, some states such as hopes, desires and wishes do not represent the world in a certain way as if their content were true, although they are contentful since they do not aim to describe the world. For example, my hope that 'World War III does not happen' does not represent the world in a way that its content describes the world. Spelling it out in terms of 'direction of fit', we can say that beliefs aim to fit the world, but desires, hopes, intentions and so on aim for the world to fit them.[9]

There are also some contentful representational states that are also presentational, in the sense that not only do they represent the world in a certain way, but also they *present* the world in a certain way.[10] For example, when I have a perceptual experience that there is a book in front of me, the world is represented to me in a certain way that it is true that there is a book in front of me. Furthermore, while I have this perceptual experience, it is presented to me (non-inferentially) that there is a book in front of me. In fact, I have the (non-inferred) impression or feeling that there is a book in front of me. Of course, we can have this (non-inferred) sense that there is a book in front of me even if it turns out that this is not so. For example, Jim Pryor writes about the presentationality of perceptual experience as the peculiar 'phenomenal force' or way our experiences have of presenting propositions to us. Our experience represent propositions in such a way that it 'feels as if' we could tell that those propositions are true – and that we're perceiving them to be true – just by virtue of having them so represented. (2000, 547)

William Tolhurst (1998, 298–9) also has the same idea in his mind when he writes about seeming states as 'felt givenness':

> The real difference between seemings and other states that can incline one to believe their content is that seemings have the feel of truth, the feel of a state whose content reveals how things really are. Their felt givenness typically leads one to experience believing that things are as they seem as an objectively fitting or proper response to the seeming.

Consider now again the famous image of the Müller-Lyer (Figure 3). Although the inequality of the two lines is non-voluntarily *presented* to us, we still believe that they are equal as they *represent* to us in another way. In such cases where it is as if something has come to us, we are actually in a state that is presentational. This entails that, unlike representational states, presentational states do not simply represent the world as being a certain way. Yet, they present the world as being that way, as if things are so.

Presentational states have at least three characteristics: they are gradable, non-voluntary and compelling.[11] They are gradable in the sense that their quality may vary from one situation to another, depending upon the way in which

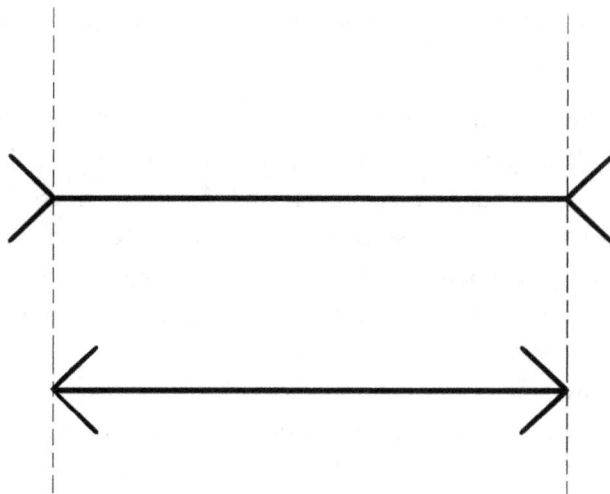

Figure 3 Müller-Lyer illusion.

they are presenting. They are non-voluntary in the sense that, unlike decisions (which are active), presentational states are passive and happen to us.[12] They are compelling in the sense that it is hard to resist assenting to their contents when they are presented.

Having understood the difference between presentationality and representationality, we can agree that the presentationality of perceptual experience is not a very challenging idea. We should accept that perceptual experiences are presentational states.

However, what about intuitions? Are they presentational states? There are some reasons, I believe, to think that intuition is a presentational state – a state that presents its content as being so. For instance, suppose that we have an intuition that it is not possible that both p and not-p. When we have this intuition, it is not simply to say that we are in a state that *represents* the world as if the principle of non-contradiction is true. We can have just the *sense* or *impression* that this principle is so.[13] And just like a perceptual error that an object x can present itself as a y, in the case of intuitional error, p can present itself as not-p or vice versa. For example, we might have an intuition that p because it seems to us that p. But after further reflection or getting confirmation from a third party, we find that we were wrong.

Thus, although intuition and perceptual experience are different and have different properties, they have some similarities and can be the same kind of state in terms of *presentations*. Following Dancy (2014b) and Bengson (2015), I call this

> The First Quasi-Perceptualist Thesis: (i) Intuitions are akin to perceptual experiences in being presentational.

Formulating intuitions in terms of presentationality has different virtues. First of all, this thesis simply makes a distinction between intuition and some other mental states such as guesses, hunches, hypotheses, conjectures or beliefs that are merely *representational*. Just as perceptual experiences are typically non-voluntary, intuition is a non-voluntary state and can oppose what we believe or are inclined to believe. Hence, insofar as intuitions are akin to perceptions in being presentations, they are *belief-independent*.

Moreover, by appealing to the first quasi-perceptualist thesis, we reveal another difference. We can make a distinction between intuition and *dispositions* or *inclinations* such as attractions and temptations. Intuitions are presentations, but inclinations are not. As happens in the case of wishful thinking, it is possible to have a feeling of being inclined to believe that p; however, p is not presented to one as true. Thus, the first quasi-perceptualist thesis identifies a difference between intuitions and other phenomena in terms of non-presentationality and presentationality.

As a second virtue, the first quasi-perceptualist thesis can provide us with an account of the *psychological* roles of intuition. In fact, the thesis *explains* how intuitions help us to come to believe something or form our beliefs. For example, in Jackson's thought experiment, we may form our *belief* that Mary does learn by having the *intuition* that she does learn. In this sense, intuition has the *explanatory* power with respect to beliefs, that is, intuitions explain beliefs. For in different situations, we can say, 'I believe that p on the basis of the intuition that p.' Why do we believe that, for example, Mary does learn? Simply because it *strikes* us that Mary does know, or we have the intuition that Mary does learn. Therefore, the thesis may explain why we have the corresponding intuitive belief. That intuitions are presentations helps us to explain why intuitions are explanatory of belief.[14]

Perceptual experiences also have another characteristic shared with intuition, namely, *translucency*. Bengson explains the idea of translucency in this way:

> Let us call a presentational state σ of x *translucent* iff, in having σ, it is presented to x that p is so, and there is no content q (where q ≠ p) such that it seems to x that p is presented as being so by q's being presented as being so. (Dissertation, 38)

Yet, what does it mean when we say a mental state is translucent? According to Bengson, calling intuitions translucent is a way of saying that intuitions are direct (or non-inferred). However, there is a distinction in the philosophy of perception between 'translucent' and 'transparent'. The distinction picks out as translucent a class of experiences that are not completely direct or non-inferred. Contrast this with transparent experiences, where this is not so. For example, when I look at a tree or when I introspect my visual experience, my experience is transparent to me.[15] What Bengson must mean by translucent experiences is transparent, direct (or non-inferred) experiences.[16] Let me explain.

Suppose one is sitting in front of a table and there is a pen on the table. One's vision of the pen directly presents the fact that there is a pen on the table. Contrast this with the situation that one suddenly notices that the pen's ink is empty by seeing that the pen does not work. It may be presented to such a person that the ink is empty even though she lacks perceptual experience of the ink (suppose the ink tank is covered up). That the pen is not working serves as her 'perceptual guide'.[17] Most likely, in such a case, one infers that the ink is empty from the fact that the pen is not working. One thinks that the best explanation for the pen's not working is that the ink has run out, and so one makes the inference about the ink. This entails that the presentation of the pen as being out of ink is not direct (translucent).[18]

We can think of this distinction between direct or translucent presentation and indirect presentation, in the *intellectual* cases, as well. Consider the intuition that 'rape is wrong'. This intuition is *translucent* in the sense that it is *presented* to one as being the case that rape is wrong. It does not present to one as being so by something else (other propositions) being presented so. It seems that one can 'just see' *directly* that it is so. However, there are intuitions that do not have this *directness* or are not *translucent*, especially in cases in which one may be presented with multiple contents, some of which hold in virtue of the others. In effect, translucency has two components: *presentation* and *directness*, which bring the *epistemic* status of being *un-inferred*. Note: that some presentation is translucent and thus un-inferred does not imply that its content *cannot* be inferred as well.

In the light of the discussion of translucency, we can now add another constituent to the quasi-perceptualist thesis. Let's call this:

> *The Second Quasi-Perceptualist Thesis: (ii) Intuitions are intellectual translucent states.*

But how is this 'intellectual' state generated? Why do not we postulate intuitions as sensory or perceptual states? One might even object that intellectual states are *completely non-sensory* because they do not involve sense data. If this is the case, it seems that all we have said so far about the certain shared phenomenological features between intellectual seemings and perceptual experiences is redundant.

The answer is that, although intuitions are similar to perception in terms of translucency and presentation, intuitions *cannot* be just sensory-perceptual states. We can also think of two negative and positive readings of an intellectual state: a negative reading of an intellectual state equates 'intellectual' with *completely non-sensory*. However, a positive conception reads an intellectual state as a state that involves the *deployment* or *exercise* of *concepts*. The quasi-perceptualist does not need to choose between these two readings. Therefore, the quasi-perceptualist thesis is 'neutral' on this issue.[19]

Hence, combining the two constituents of the quasi-perceptualist thesis, that is, (i) and (ii), yields the core idea of quasi-perceptualism about intuition. This can be formulated as

> *The Quasi-Perceptualist Theory of Intuition: Intuitions are translucent intellectual presentations.*

Although quasi-perceptualism explains intuition with terminology different from that used by Bealer, I think they are both saying the same thing. In other words, Bengson tries to elaborate on what Bealer means when he uses intellectual seemings. And by seemings, in Bengson's terminology, Bealer means something direct or translucent and presentational.

We should bear in mind that nothing we have said implies that intuitions must be *unreflective* or *gut feelings*.[20] Rather, a translucent intellectual presentation with certain content may occur in the case of *substantial reflection*. But through this reflection, intuitions do not need to make a *transition* from one proposition to the second one because they are translucent.[21] However, an account of how substantial reflections work is needed as one might be puzzled by how intuitions can involve reflection without making inferences. In Chapter 5, I will discuss my account of reflection and explain how reflection can bring us non-inferential justification.

So far, I have given an explanation – and to some extent justification – of what a quasi-perceptualist account of philosophical intuition is. It is now time to examine whether the quasi-perceptualist account of philosophical intuition in terms of seemings is applicable to moral intuition. I argue we can have a seeming account of moral intuition as well.

3 Shifting from philosophical intuition to moral intuition: The seeming account of moral intuition

Having discussed what *philosophical* intuition is, we now direct our focus to what *moral* intuition is. Jennifer Nado (2014) distinguishes between *epistemological* intuition and *moral* intuition and argues that the mental states falling under the category of intuition are quite heterogeneous. In almost the same manner, I assume here that it is plausible to think of two separate types of intuition with different content as 'philosophical intuition' and 'moral intuition'. However, I do not believe that philosophical intuition and moral intuition are not two different types of mental state. For having different content does not make something a different mental state. The nature of moral intuitions and philosophical intuitions and how they work to justify our beliefs are the same. Thus, the characteristics that we attribute to philosophical intuitions can also be attributed to moral intuitions. Yet, we can make a distinction between philosophical and moral intuition in terms of their different content, and this distinction between philosophical and moral intuition helps us focus solely on moral intuition. This chapter will examine whether our theory of philosophical intuition (i.e. the seeming view) can be applied to moral intuition.

Let us start with the first task, that is, the nature of moral intuition. The term 'ethical intuition' or 'moral intuition' has often raised difficulties in the history of moral philosophy. Some moral philosophers think that the term 'moral intuition' refers to a moral judgement shared by philosophers and scholars. Some of these philosophers think that moral intuition is just immediate or non-inferential moral judgements. Some others think of moral intuition as a pre-theoretical judgement. Another understanding refers to philosophers who think about moral intuitions as apparent and self-evident truths.[22] For example, notably, Robert Audi describes moral intuition as a doxastic state about a self-evident proposition.[23]

I will delineate Audi's doxastic account of moral intuition to argue that the seeming account of intuition is better than the doxastic account of intuition as follows. I will partly argue against Audi's account of moral intuition that the seeming account of moral intuition can do better a job than his doxastic account. I then discuss an alternative.

4 Audi on the nature of moral intuition

According to Audi, a moral intuition should have at least four conditions (listed as follows). Although Audi talks about four conditions, it seems to me that the 'pre-theoretical' condition entails the 'directness' condition.

> (1) First, a moral intuition must be non-inferential (*directness requirement*). This means that 'the intuited proposition in question is not – at the time it is intuitively held – believed on the basis of a premise' (2004, 33).[24] (2) Second, moral intuitions must be firm cognitions (*firmness requirement*). This means that 'intuitions are typically *beliefs*, including cases of knowing'; however, '[a] mere inclination to believe is not an intuition' (2004, 34). A moral intuition must have some degree of epistemic weight, that is, conviction.[25] (3) Third, a moral intuition must be shaped by an adequate understanding of its propositional object (*comprehension requirement*). An adequate understanding of a belief 'tends both to produce cognitive firmness and to enhance evidential value' (2004, 34–5).[26] (4) Fourth, moral intuitions must be pre-theoretical (*pre-theoretical requirement*). Moral intuitions are not like theoretical hypotheses, nor do they depend on being inferred from theories. So, 'an intuition *as* such . . . is held neither on the basis of a premise nor as a theoretical hypothesis'. (2004, 35)[27]

Nevertheless, moral intuitions are defeasible. They can be defeated by some theoretical results that are incompatible with moral intuition.[28] By accepting the defeasibility of moral intuitions, Audi tries to distinguish between *reliable* and *unreliable* moral intuitions through entering the notion of *justification*.[29] According to him, reliable moral intuitions are those that 'we can rationally hope will remain credible as we continue to reflect on them' (1996, 121). Of course, Audi does not suggest that what makes certain moral intuitions reliable is that we rationally hope they will remain credible as we reflect on them. What he must have meant is that we rationally hope that the moral intuitions that are reliable will remain credible as we reflect on them. For a moral intuition to remain credible as we reflect on it is for it to be 'stable under reflection'. Reliability and stability under reflection are different things. In Audi's view, what makes a moral intuition reliable is that it normally or nearly always leads to the *truth*. In fact, some moral intuitions are reliable, as they have initial credibility and are *prima facie* justified. Audi says that insofar as moral intuitions

> are like certain perceptual beliefs (e.g. in being non-inferential, 'natural,' and pre-theoretical) – and perhaps more important – insofar as they are based on an understanding of their propositional objects, there is reason to consider them *prima facie* justified. (1996, 116)[30]

So understood, in Audi's view, moral intuition *simpliciter* can be reliable, has initial credibility and can be considered as *prima facie* justified, but on one condition: moral intuitions must be formed in light of an adequate understanding. If they are not based on sufficient reflection, we lack enough reason to consider them *prima facie* justified.[31]

Moreover, the pre-theoreticality of moral intuitions does not imply that the propositional content of moral intuition is not capable of proof and inferential justification. It is not true that a non-inferential cognition cannot be believed as a theoretical hypothesis.[32]

In Audi's view, to give a plausible account of moral intuition, we need the idea of 'reflection'. In order to do that, he distinguishes between a *conclusion of inference* and a *conclusion of reflection*. A conclusion of inference is 'premised on propositions one has noted as evidence' (1998a, 19). Simply put, a conclusion from one or more evidential premises is a conclusion of inference. In contrast, a conclusion of reflection 'emerges from thinking . . . but not from one or more evidential premises' (1998a, 19). To give a better idea of what the conclusion of reflection is, Audi compares it to looking at a painting or seeing a facial expression. When a conclusion of reflection emerges, one can obtain a view of the whole and characterize it.[33] Moral intuitions, Audi holds, should be known as conclusions of reflection.[34] The conception of moral intuition, then, is that moral intuition is a non-inferential cognitive capacity, not a non-reflective one.[35] However, as Audi rightly observes, this does not imply that '*every* intuitive moral judgment need be a conclusion of reflection' (Audi, 2007, 204).

It is clear from Audi's definition that moral intuitions have an epistemological feature as well as a normative one. A moral intuition is totally dependent on each person's level of understanding and is not necessarily obvious to all. Rather, it may be rejected or become clearer in the course of theorizing. Also, as Audi puts it, moral intuitions must be understood here in a cognitive sense.[36] Moral intuitions have an epistemic role in our judgements, and they have effects on our beliefs, that is, they lead us to know some moral principles and believe in them. To have a better understanding of the cognitive role of moral intuition, we can use Richard Boyd's terminology of 'epistemic access'.[37] Moral intuitions help moral agents to have epistemic access to some self-evident moral propositions or principles. I use this terminology to emphasize the epistemic role of moral intuitions in our daily moral judgements.

Most of what Audi has discussed here about moral intuition will be repeated in the discussion of moral self-evidence (*cf.* Chapter 5). This is because he sees a sort of connection between moral intuition and self-evident propositions. Audi believes that moral intuitions are typically our beliefs about some self-evident moral principles, and there are some self-evident moral principles that we have moral intuitions (beliefs) about.[38] For example, in Audi's view, the moral intuition that 'promise-keeping is permissible' is typically our belief about the self-evident principle that 'promise-keeping is *pro tanto* right'. Furthermore, we have a moral intuition about the self-evident proposition 'promise-keeping is *pro tanto* right', which is intuitively true. Of course, this does not entail that all moral intuitions are self-evident propositions.

Although adopting the doxastic account of intuition has different advantages, I believe the seeming account is superior. The seeming account of moral intuition can help us distinguish intuition from certain similar mental states, such as guesses, gut reactions, hunches and commonsense beliefs. As I argued before, I advocate the seeming account because it looks more fundamental than the doxastic account. We can explain why we believe various things by saying that they *seem* true to us. In other words, even in cases where we believe something, we actually believe it because it *seems* true to us. Although seeming p true to me is a decent reason for my believing p, believing p is not a good reason for me to believe p.

In Chapter 5, through the discussion of Audi's account of self-evidence, I will return to Audi's account of moral intuition and repeat some of his points. However, while my alternative account of self-evident propositions has some similarities with Audi's ideas about adequate understanding and the epistemic role of moral intuition, I depart from Audi in construing moral intuitions as seeming states rather than as beliefs. My account of reflection also is different from him. Now let us see how moral intuitions can be defined in terms of seemings.

5 Moral intuitions as seeming states: Can Bealer's and Bengson's accounts be applied to the moral domain?

Moral intuitionists like Michael Huemer understand intuition in terms of *seeming* states or as an 'initial intellectual appearance' (2005, 101–5). Moral intuition, on the basis of this understanding, is an initial intellectual appearance with moral content.[39] In what follows, I will focus on the psychology of moral intuition generally and try to answer the question of 'what are moral intuitions like' specifically.

Three main questions about moral intuitions can be distinguished, Sidgwick believes. One is a question about the existence (psychology). The second is a question about the validity (epistemology).[40] The third is a question about the origin. The question about existence is a psychological question asking whether it is possible for people to ever have a moral intuition. The question about validity is an epistemological question seeking truth in such moral intuitions. Finally, the question about the origin is a question of what the nature of moral intuition is and how moral intuition is developed.

Although an answer to the question about existence can be affected by what we think a moral intuition is, Sidgwick rightly thought that the question about existence and the question about moral intuition's nature should be kept separate. By listing some states of mind that can be confused with intuitions, Sidgwick directs our attention to the question of what exactly intuition, and specifically moral intuition, is. He starts by asking what the difference between moral intuition and blind impulses or vague preferences is. And he finally ends up talking about moral intuition as 'judgment or apparent perception that an act is in itself right or good' (1967, Book 3, Ch. 1, §4). However, he cannot endorse that this is the definition of moral intuition. For there are some examples that even Sidgwick knows of as fundamental intuitions, but they do not have such content! Consider his intuition that it cannot be right for person A to treat others in a certain way and not right for person B to treat others in that same way unless there is some relevant difference between A and B or their situations, beyond the bare fact that A is A and B is B. Another is his intuition that from the point of view of the universe, no one person's good can matter any more or less than any other person's good, apart from their effects on others. Neither of these intuitions holds that an act is in itself right or good.[41]

But, if it is true that moral intuitions are not judgement or apparent perception that an act is in itself right or good, what phenomenon, event or state is a moral intuition? As I discussed before, recent works in philosophical intuition by Bealer and Bengson understand philosophical intuitions as intellectual seemings. Intellectual seemings are similar to perceptual experiences, though important differences should be taken into account. For instance, perceptual experiences are conscious, contentful, non-factive and presentational. And since they are presentational, they differ from belief or judgement. In being presentational states, they are baseless, gradable, fundamentally non-voluntary and compelling. Bealer, whose works in this area are seminal, discusses philosophical intuitions only in four domains: the conceptual, the logical, the mathematical and the modal. Perhaps we do not need to determine whether Bealer's account of intuition is suitable for the four domains of philosophical intuitions he is interested in. Our question is whether his discussions are appropriate for intuitions in ethics. Bealer does not apply his account explicitly to ethics. Nevertheless, Bealer's four domains can be used as an argument for the view that moral intuitions can be treated as evidence, as I will explain as follows.

Bengson's work, which is a development of Bealer's ideas, also does not clearly discuss moral intuition's mental ontology. Although both Bealer and Bengson do not clearly apply their theory to ethics, I think Bealer's or Bengson's account of intuition can make space for the ontology of moral intuitions. In the next couple of paragraphs, I run through Bealer's and Bengson's accounts of the ontology of philosophical intuitions to provide an account of moral intuition.

Let's start with the psychological question about moral intuition. Borrowing Bengson's account of philosophical intuition, we can ask whether we have conscious, contentful, non-factive and presentational states with moral content. Do we have such mental states in ethics? The answer to these questions, I think, is simple. It is clear to us that at some point, we have conscious, contentful, non-factive and presentational states with moral content (e.g. promise-breaking is wrong). These are states with moral content that fit the general account of the presentational state.

Now, if moral intuitions so defined exist, what is the nature of moral intuition? According to Bengson's view, intuitions are intellectual seemings, or to put it more accurately, intuitions are translucent presentational states. But are moral intuitions intellectual seemings?

There is a decisive reason for believing in seemings with moral content, I believe.[42] We should admit that at least some moral intuitions are intellectual seemings. Consider, for example, the following propositions: 'it seems that killing innocent people for no reason is absolutely wrong'; 'it is wrong to torture someone for one's own amusement'; 'that an act would hurt an innocent person must count morally against it'; 'that an act would reduce the pain an innocent being is suffering counts morally in favour of it'. Insofar as one adequately understands the conceptual constituents, one can be struck by the seeming rightness of these propositions. Consideration of these propositions produces intellectual seemings with moral content. In effect, what makes an intuition a moral one is intellectual seeming with moral content.

Yet, one might object that what gets produced are beliefs. The reply should be that these propositions match the contents of the intellectual seemings. For example, suppose we have a proposition (P) and suppose further that the proposition seems to us to be true. Then the proposition matches the content of our intellectual seeming.

Moral intuitions are similar to philosophical intuitions in that they are seeming states but with different contents. And in so being, one might believe that moral intuitions can present a consideration as evidence (which provides reason). And to present a consideration as evidence (which provides reason) is to present it as favouring a response of a certain sort. On this account, some moral intuitions or intellectual seemings present propositions as true (facts) and generate evidence for this or that sort of response. The seemingness of moral intuition, associated with some phenomenological features such as a feeling or appropriateness, can provide evidence for us.

But if the seemingness of moral intuition can provide evidence, a plausible objection could be raised. The objection is that there is no difference between moral intuitions and emotions in presenting evidence (which provides reason) since at least certain emotions do this. So, if emotions seem to present the person who has them with evidence (which provides reason), are at least some moral emotions, in fact, moral intuitions? The answer is that moral intuitions are not emotions at all. This is because intuitions are purely intellectual seemings and hence truth-apt, yet emotions are not.[43]

Although (some) moral intuitions, in my view, are reliable, most empirical moral psychologists treat moral intuitions as completely non-epistemic states because they believe that moral intuitions, like emotions, are not reliable.[44] For example, they think that moral intuitions are like sensory gut feelings and emotional immediate-spontaneous responses caused by our 'fast thinking', as Kahneman labels it. Since moral intuitions are produced by our fast thinking, these psychologists consider moral intuition to be most dubious, epistemologically. Although psychologists might not be in the business of showing that our intuitions are epistemologically reliable, they can produce evidence that casts doubt on their reliability.

However, most philosophers treat intuitions as epistemic evidence. For example, Bealer (1992) famously writes about the three Cs to answer the question of whether intuition can be a source of evidence. Here are the three criteria: consistency, corroboration and confirmation. The consistency test explores whether one intuition is consistent with other intuitions. The corroboration test asks whether one person's intuition is corroborated by others' intuitions. And the confirmation test seeks to establish whether those intuitions are confirmed by observation or experience.

Philosophers also think that intuitions can be produced by our thinking and reflection, also termed 'slow thinking'. This huge difference between philosophers' and psychologists' accounts of intuition sometimes makes us think that they are not talking about the same phenomenon.[45] In Table 1, I show how these two groups think about intuition.

Understanding moral intuition with reference to seeming states, I think, can easily bring us at least some degree of justification.[47] For example, if you have seemings about p and there is no defeater against p, you are to some degree justified in believing p based on that seeming.[48] And if there is an explanation of how moral intuitions can serve as evidence in philosophy, this at least can give us a *prima facie* justification for using them.

6 Conclusion

I have investigated the nature of moral intuition. I started by explaining the quasi-perceptualist account of philosophical intuition in terms of seeming. I focused on Bengson's (and Bealer's) intellectual seeming account and elaborated on what the intellectual seeming is by appealing to Bengson's theory of quasi-perceptualism. Following Bengson, I considered presentational states as

Table 1 Views about intuition in philosophy and psychology[46]

		Type of mental state	Aetiology	Epistemic stance
Psychology		Gut feeling	Fast thinking/Lazy system	Unreliable/dubious
Philosophy	Doxastic view	Belief or disposition/inclination to believe	Sufficient understanding of the conceptual constituents	Is a source of knowledge/justifies beliefs
	Non-doxastic view	Seemings/presentation	Inasmuch as one adequately understands the conceptual constituents, one can be struck by the seemings	Forms and justifies belief, absent undermining defeaters

'immediate apprehensions' and allowed the notion of translucence to serve as an explanation of the notion of 'directness'. Consequently, I now have a conception of philosophical intuition as a kind of direct, immediate apprehension *akin* to perceptual experience, though it includes intellectual concepts. I also showed that intellectual seemings are translucent intellectual presentations. I then argued for reading moral intuitions in terms of Bengson's (and Bealer's) account of intellectual seemings. I showed that the quasi-perceptualist account of philosophical intuition, which understands intuitions as seemings, can be applied to moral intuition. Therefore, we now can have a conception of moral intuition in terms of intellectual seemings similar to perceptual experiences.

3

The use of intuition as evidence

1 Introduction

This chapter tries to explain how both moral and philosophical intuitions can be used as evidence. If intuitions, either philosophical or moral, do not provide evidence, as some psychologists maintain, what is the point of using intuitions in our philosophical enquiry? Let me discuss whether intuitions can serve as evidence. If our intuitions cannot provide evidence for us, they are useless for philosophical methodology (e.g. in ethics). Later, I will explain my account of evidence and argue that intuitions in general (i.e. both philosophical and moral) can be treated as evidence, and they can provide us at least *prima facie* reason for believing.[1]

After seeking the nature of moral intuition in the last chapter, this chapter's task is to argue whether intuitions, either philosophical or moral, in general, *can* be treated as evidence in our philosophical inquiry. This task helps us build a bridge between this chapter and the next chapter, which is about the epistemology of moral intuitionism. Arguing in favour of intuition, generally, as evidence, prepares us to discuss in more depth how moral intuition is supposed to work in the epistemology of moral intuitionism.

But before going on, I should mention that, in the entirety of this chapter, I will try to avoid talking extensively about whether intuition can 'justify'. This is because, first, this chapter focuses mainly, but not only, on the ontology of moral intuition. Second, most philosophers who question the use of intuition in philosophy prefer the term 'evidence'. So, instead of talking about justification, I would rather talk about intuition as 'evidence' where possible. However, we need to keep in mind that evidence per se does not justify us, but our knowledge and awareness of the evidence can do that. For example, if the concept of evidence refers to X that we want to endorse, the concept of justification refers to our knowledge or cognitive position about those X.[2] Since I do not use the standard conception of evidence as that which provides us justification, I need to elaborate my account of evidence when I refer to intuition as evidence. I will discuss my favoured account of evidence in this chapter, and I will also use it later when I discuss my account of self-evidence.³

2 Scepticism against using intuition as evidence

Timothy Williamson (2004) and Herman Cappelen (2012), notably, raised objections against using intuition as evidence in philosophical methodology. They believe that the thesis that (i) intuition can play a *central* role and (ii) can be treated as evidence in philosophical methodology is wrong because intuitions do not have positive epistemic status.⁴ Contemporary analytic philosophers who rely on intuition as evidence are also wrong. For example, Williamson writes,

> We should face the fact that evidence is always liable to be contested in philosophy, and stop using talk of intuition to disguise this unpleasant truth from ourselves. . . . In explaining why we have intuitions, analytic philosophy has a preference for explanations on which those intuitions come out true over explanations on which they come out untrue, but the justification for that preference remains unclear. (2004, 120)⁵

Cappelen labels the thesis according to which intuitions play a central positive epistemic role in philosophy as 'Centrality'. In his *Philosophy without Intuitions*, Cappelen, for example, writes that

> In this book I argue that centrality, on any reasonable interpretation, is false. If you share that view . . . [t]here's no urgency in figuring out what intuitions are and what epistemic status they have. (2012, 18)

Although Cappelen believes that philosophers do 'undeniably' engage in 'intuition-talk', he argues that such talk does not plausibly denote any mental state with positive epistemic status.⁶ In Cappelen's view, philosophers should be sceptical about using intuition as a tool. He concludes by saying that philosophers' use of intuition in their works does not provide a good reason for believing in 'Centrality', that is, treating intuition as evidence. So, the 'Centrality' thesis fails.⁷

However, I believe that this conclusion is false. To be clear, following Bengson (2014), I will argue that although much intuition-talk by philosophers and ordinary people cannot support the Centrality thesis, there is some special *technical* use of intuition on certain occasions by philosophers to which proponents of Centrality can refer. This *technical* use can be referred to as phenomenological or non-comparative use of seemings. I believe that the *technical* use of intuition in terms of phenomenological or non-comparative use of seemings can show how intuition can be evidence. However, we need to know what we mean by evidence when we support the claim that intuitions can be treated as evidence. Later, I explain my favoured account of evidence. Next, I will be focusing on whether intuition can play a central role by introducing two examples of the *technical* use of intuition by Chisholm and Kripke.[8] This might weaken Cappelen's claim against using intuition.

The account of evidence I favour and that I am working with, in this book, can be articulated as follows: evidence (e) for (p) is a mental state or proposition that raises the (epistemic) probability of (p) being true. In fact, the probability of (p) on (e) is higher than the unconditional probability of (p):[9]

$$P(p|e) > P(p)$$

In other words, evidence (e) for (p) is a mental state or proposition that makes p a probable truth. If (e) is evidence for (p), then (e) makes it more probable that (p) is true. So, in this conception of evidence, 'when philosophers produce evidence, they produce something truth-evaluable' (Williamson, 2007, 209). Evidence, in this sense, can consist of perceptual, introspective, memorial and intuitional experiences. For example, if I have a memory that I felt a pain in my stomach this morning, I have evidence for a belief about the past that I had a stomachache. When I have the intuition about the proposition that 'circles are not squares', depending on how I came to have that intuition, I have evidence for believing that proposition. Or a proposition like 'A is rectangular' gives us evidence to believe that the 'sum of angles of A is 360'.

Nevertheless, where is facticity? Are all evidence facts? Using 'fact' for 'something known to be true' or 'true proposition', one might think that evidence consists only of facts. Because the facts we are guided by are the facts that are our evidence. So, all evidence would be true, although not all truths are evidence.[10] However, this needs to be qualified as it might not work in some cases.

It is plausible to think that facts are evidence and some evidence are facts, but it is not the case that *all* evidence are facts. For example, when I have a perceptual experience that there is a pen in front of me, I have evidence to believe that there is a pen in front of me. But my perceptual experience that there is a pen in front of me is not a fact. Or a proposition such as 'there is no oxygen on this planet' is evidence for believing that 'nobody lives there', but it is not a fact. Furthermore, if intuitions are evidence, it is obvious that not all intuitions are true propositions. It might be that we have an intuition, although the content of the intuition is false. For instance, my intuition that 'it is permissible to kill one person to save four' gives me the evidence to believe this, but it might be wrong. But, how can our evidence turn out to be false? The answer is that sometimes what is offered to us as evidence is not evidence.[11] That is, it seems to be evidence, but it is not really. For example, one can think that 'the grass is green' is evidence for its being healthy. Although some evidence seems to us true at first, it might turn out to be false. So, evidence does not consist only of facts.

Having understood what we mean by evidence, we should know whether intuition can play a central positive epistemic role as evidence. Chisholm, for example, distinguishes between 'three uses of appear words'.[12] He believes that there are three possible uses of the term 'seem', which should be taken into account.

First, when a speaker says: 'It seems to me that General de Gaulle was successful' or 'This ship seems to be moving', she actually expresses an evidence-based belief or inclination-to-believe. This is the *epistemic* use of 'seem', which indicates tentative belief.

Second, when a speaker says: 'The railroad tracks seem to converge' or 'She seems just the way her uncle did 15 years ago', she makes a comparison between appearance and reality. This is the comparative use of 'seem'.

Third, when a speaker says, 'This seems white to me' or 'Though I don't believe these two lines are equal, it seems that they are', she describes how something appears to her or how things are presented to her rather than comparing or expressing an evidence-based belief. This is the non-comparative use of 'seem', which Jackson calls 'phenomenological' or 'phenomenal' use.

Both Chisholm and Jackson claim that we should distinguish these three uses of 'seem' and explain that it is only the non-comparative use of 'seem' that philosophers have a special interest in.[13] The non-comparative use of 'seem' may refer to a mental state which purports to play a positive epistemic role.

Chisholm's and Jackson's examples of 'seem' focus on the sensory cases. But the non-comparative use of 'seem' can be used for non-sensory states such as the state of intellectual seemings. The non-comparative use of 'seem' can show us how things are presented to us when we reflect on them. The intellectual sense of the non-comparative use of 'seem' interests most contemporary theorists of intuition such as Kripke, Bealer, Pust, Huemer and others.[14]

Saul Kripke's seminal work, *Naming and Necessity*, can be another important example of using intuition as evidence in philosophy to support the Centrality thesis. There are different instances where Kripke engages in intuition-talk, although he did not use the term 'intuition'. He writes that

> On the view in question, then, . . . since the man who discovered the incompleteness of arithmetic is in fact Schmidt, we, when we talk about 'Gödel', are in fact always referring to Schmidt. But it seems to me that we are not. We simply are not. (1980, 84)

And

> [I]t is supposed to be a contingent property of the state that it is a mental state at all, let alone that it is something as specific as a pain . . . this . . . seems to me self-evidently absurd. (1980, 147)

More importantly, although Cappelen refers to Kripke at some point, it seems that he ignores the following quotes by Kripke:

> Of course, some philosophers think that something's having intuitive content is very inconclusive evidence in favour of it. I think it is very heavy evidence in favour of anything, myself. I really don't know, in a way, what more conclusive evidence one can have about anything, ultimately speaking. (1980, 42)

And

> My main remark, then, is that we have a direct intuition of the rigidity of names, exhibited of a scenario in our understanding of the truth conditions of particular sentences. In addition, various secondary phenomena, about 'what we would say'. . . give indirect evidence of rigidity. (1980, 14)

These passages from Kripke and Chisholm's three distinctions, all together, show that analytic philosophers do rely on intuition for evidence, and there is a place for them to use intuition (construed as seeming) to provide positive epistemic status.

The examples that Kripke and Chisholm have focused on are mostly particular kinds of examples of intuitions as evidence. However, we should make a distinction between particular and general intuitions. For instance, having an intuition about Dick Cheney's mandating torture of prisoners is a particular intuition about a particular situation. But this does not entail that we cannot have general intuitions as evidence. For example, having an intuition that promise-keeping is right, ceteris paribus, is a general intuition for every situation. If this is the case, we can have both general and particular intuitions as evidence.

Following Pust (2000, 11–12), I think we can talk about three different forms of *intuition-usage*. One can treat particular intuitions in particular cases as evidence and form a general theory based on them. This is 'particularist' intuition-usage. In contrast, one can treat only general intuitions as evidence and find general intuitions more compelling. This can be called 'generalist' intuition-usage. However, by adding these two kinds of intuition-usage together, one can treat both particular and general intuitions as evidence to provide *prima facie* justification for believing further claims. This is 'global' intuition-usage. For example, in the case of Rawls's 'reflective equilibrium', both particular and general intuitions are treated by this philosophical methodology as basic evidence.[15] In Chapter 7, I will come back to this idea to form three different kinds of moral intuitionism.

What is currently happening in different branches of analytic philosophy (especially in epistemology, philosophy of mind, value theory, decision theory, metaphysics and philosophy of science) shows that different philosophers are, in fact, making evidential appeals to intuitions. Analytic philosophers' current practice, for example, using thought experiments as intuition pumps, is to treat intuition as evidence for various conclusions. As Bealer put it:

> To see the prevalence of the use of intuitions in philosophy recall some standard examples . . . Chisholm's abnormal conditions refutation of phenomenalism, Chisholm and Putnam's refutations of behaviorism, the use of multiple-realizability in refuting narrow identity theses, the Twin-Earth arguments for a posteriori necessities and externalism in mental content, Burge's arthritis argument for anti-individualism in mental content, Jackson's Mary example, and so on. . . . As the examples illustrate, it is intuitions about concrete cases that are afforded primary weight by our standard justificatory procedure. (1998, 205)[16]

Yet, one might object that if the only way intuitions can be evidence requires a *technical* sense of intuition, then there is not much left for intuition as evidence. In response, first, I did not claim that my account of evidence is the only way that intuitions can be evidence. Second, if this objection entails that my account of intuition as evidence leaves only a small space to use intuition in philosophy, this is not necessarily a big challenge. Because in my view, it is not true that all intuitions are evidence in philosophy. Rather intuitions are evidence for when the use of intuitions is taken to refer to phenomenological or non-comparative use of seemings.

So far, I have shown that much analytic philosophical inquiry sees intuition (construed as seeming) as evidence. However, how intuitions should be treated as evidence is a different question, which needs to be discussed.

The phrase 'the intuition that p' can have two meanings: one interpretation would be that a person's *intuitings* provide some kind of evidence. In that case, the claim that 'the intuition that p is treated as evidence for believing p' is similar to the claim that '*the fact that one had an intuition that p* served as the evidence for believing p'. Another interpretation would be that the *intuited* or propositional content of the intuition is evidence. So, the claim that 'the intuition that p is treated as evidence for believing p' is similar to the claim that 'the propositional content of the intuition serves as the evidence for believing p'.

Treating intuitings as evidence is a sort of psychologizing philosophy.[17] However, in the second interpretation, that is, treating the intuited as evidence, the content of the intuitings is at stake. Each of these interpretations, that is, intuitings and intuited, has some advantages and disadvantages.[18] Yet, the second interpretation looks implausible because treating intuited as evidence entails that the content of the intuition can be evidence for itself. This makes our belief in the intuition inferential (if their contents are not the same) since the content of intuition can figure in a justification or argument for the content of belief. So, my view is closer to the first interpretation.

It is the *intuition* that p that is evidence for p, not the content. To say that intuitions are evidence in philosophy is to say that intuitions (construed as seemings) raise the (epistemic) probability of a proposition, and our justification for believing a proposition can consist in our having intuitions (intuitings). To put it more accurately, intuiting a proposition provides us with *prima facie* justification for believing the proposition and for believing theories that provide the best explanation of that proposition. To say that S has the intuition that p is to say that S's intuition *prima facie* justifies S in believing that p and counts against theories that cannot accommodate it.[19] We can respect many core philosophical questions by adopting this explanation of how intuition should be treated as evidence. This explanation can also bring us a justification for using intuitions as evidence in philosophy.

3 Conclusion

I attempted, in this chapter, to answer a case against the 'Centrality' thesis made by Cappelen and Williamson. The Centrality thesis is the view that intuitions are central sources of evidence for philosophy. The topic is thus the methodology of philosophy, and my nominal opponents argue that there is no notion of intuition that all or most present-day analytic philosophers accept and use in their work.

Unchallenged talk of intuitions gives an illusion of an accepted methodology for the discipline of philosophy, they argue. But when one examines how the philosophers characterize and use the so-called intuitions, we do not find that philosophy has a single and reasonably clearly understood method.

I, however, discussed two main points against the anti-intuition case: one is that some good philosophers, such as Kripke, Chisholm and Pust, treat what they call intuitions as evidence for philosophical theses and as evidence for more elaborate philosophical theories too (Rawls). But anti-intuitionists might object that no one on the anti-intuition side of this dispute would deny that. It is the lack of an agreement on what counts as an intuition and how it may serve as evidence that is claimed.

To answer this objection, I discussed my second point. I defended the notion of an intuition by describing a favoured version and defending it against alleged problems, letting the claims of an already functioning and widely accepted method go.

This is the end of Part I. Let me draw your attention to what I tried to argue for so far in the last chapters. I invite readers to keep this point in mind as we progress. I believe that treating philosophical and moral intuition as evidence can only be acceptable if we assume that the intuition that p is not the belief that p. The reason for this is that the belief that p cannot be evidence for the belief that p. Otherwise, the content would have to be evidence for itself, which would obviously be absurd. So, given that intuitions can be evidence when one claims that 'I believe that p on the basis of my intuition that p', this can work only if intuitions are distinct states from beliefs.[20]

I now turn the discussion from moral intuition to moral intuitionism focusing on the epistemology of moral intuitionism. In the following two chapters (Part II), I will discuss the tradition of moral intuitionism and how its epistemology can be developed. After spelling out the idea of self-evidence in the intuitionist epistemology, I will be examining the relationship between 'intuition' and 'self-evidence'. This will help lay out grounds for thinking that intuitions justify and reasons to suppose that some moral propositions are self-evident.

Moreover, I will consider whether the picture that I have given here of moral intuition can be applied to moral intuitionist epistemology. To determine whether this is so, I elucidate that we do not have one, and only one, moral intuitionism; rather, there are different sorts of intuitionism that can accommodate the picture of moral intuition presented here.

Part II

Epistemology

4

Shaping classic moral intuitionism
An examination of H. A. Prichard's and W. D. Ross's ideas

1 Introduction: Historical evolution and classifications

The traditional and classical expression of moral intuitionism can be found in the work of some British moral philosophers of the seventeenth and eighteenth centuries. The term 'moral intuitionism' may be used to pick out sentimentalist and rationalist (either monist or pluralist) moral philosophers. For example, Shaftesbury and Hutcheson are sentimentalists, Sidgwick and Moore are rationalists–consequentialists (monists), and Prichard and Ross are rationalists–pluralists.[1] This diversity often makes it hard to gather all of these people under one umbrella. As Thomas Hurka writes,

> [T]here is no satisfactory name for this school. They are often called 'non-naturalists' or 'intuitionists'. . . . But these labels ignore their equally important shared views in normative ethics. . . . One could try calling the school 'underivativists', 'primitivists', or even 'quietists' . . ., but those names again highlight just some of their shared beliefs . . . they may have to be just the school of moral philosophers from Sidgwick to Ewing. (2011, 1)

What is at stake in this book and distinguishes these intuitionists from each other is their moral epistemology. Although the sentimentalists' epistemology, that is, believing that moral judgements express our sentiments and feelings, has important implications for contemporary intuitionists, I will put it aside for other research and focus here on the rationalists' epistemology.

Later, I will delineate – but will not necessarily argue for – the history of moral intuitionism and its different classifications. In the meantime, I will focus on the ideas of two significant classic intuitionists, that is, Prichard and Ross. However, in describing their views, I will keep my comments to a minimum. I invite the reader to keep the ideas in mind, although I will repeat some of them as we progress. Next, following the Wittgensteinian idea of 'family resemblance' and the example of 'game', I will argue about different kinds of moral intuitionism and marks of moral intuitionism. I reason that although there are many moral intuitionisms, this does not preclude us from having a definition of moral intuitionism. We can meaningfully employ and refer to moral intuitionism in different contexts.

British moral philosophers of the seventeenth and eighteenth centuries, such as John Balguy, Samuel Clarke, Richard Price, Ralph Cudworth and Thomas Reid, began to shape the intuitionist tradition by focusing on the idea that there are at least some basic moral truths that can be known non-inferentially or intuitively.[2] In the last quarter of the nineteenth century, Henry Sidgwick was the first to discuss intuitionism at length. The tradition of intuitionism in moral philosophy was taken further by his student G. E. Moore and was systematized in the hands of W. D. Ross.[3] However, at least three kinds of moral intuitionism through its tradition can be distinguished from each other with respect to 'history' and 'epistemology'.

We can consider Second World War (1939–45) to be a 'historical' turning point for moral intuitionism in the sense that the pre-Second World War period belongs to 'classic moral intuitionism' and the post-Second World War period belongs to 'contemporary new moral intuitionism'.[4] Meanwhile, we can distinguish each of these categories as far as the 'epistemology' is concerned. In the classic tradition of moral intuitionism, two kinds of epistemology, that is 'strong classic moral intuitionism' and 'modest classic moral intuitionism', can be distinguished.[5] On the other hand, regarding the epistemology of the contemporary new moral intuitionists, we can call their epistemology 'moderate moral intuitionism' – a terminology offered by Audi (cf. chapter 5).

In terms of epistemology, strong classic intuitionism is a version of moral foundationalism. In this view, some moral beliefs are epistemologically basic in the sense that they are *not* capable of inferential justification from each other or from non-moral beliefs. These moral beliefs are infallibly justified by indefeasible intuitions.[6] Modest classic moral intuitionism, however, argues that there are at least some moral beliefs that are fallible, and their non-inferential or intuitive justification is defensible.[7] Although strong and modest classic moral intuitionists have different beliefs about (in)defeasibility and (in)fallibility of moral intuition, they both believe that some moral beliefs are basic in the sense that they are non-inferentially or intuitively justifiable.

The principal figures of classic moral intuitionism (both strong and modest), almost all of whom are British moral philosophers between the 1870s and the 1950s, are Henry Sidgwick, Hastings Rashdall, J. M. E. McTaggart, G. E. Moore, H. A. Prichard, E. F. Carritt, W. D. Ross, C. D. Broad and A. C. Ewing. They all taught at Oxford or Cambridge.[8] The peak of the influence of classic intuitionism was roughly from 1900 to 1940 and faded after Second World War under the influence of Austin and Wittgenstein at Oxford and Cambridge. Also, in the mid-1930s, classic moral intuitionism was challenged by various forms of emotivism, developed by A. J. Ayer and C. L. Stevenson.

Let me discuss Prichard's moral epistemology as an example of strong classic moral intuitionism. This can help us to have a clear idea of the difference between strong classic intuitionists, modest classic intuitionists (e.g. Ross) and moderate new contemporary intuitionists (e.g. Audi), which will be discussed afterwards.

1.1 Prichard's moral epistemology as a representative of strong classic moral intuitionism

In his famous article, 'Does Moral Philosophy Rest on a Mistake?' Prichard says that moral philosophy rests on 'the mistake of supposing the possibility of proving what can only be apprehended directly by an act of moral thinking' (1949, 16). According to Prichard, through our intuition – which is not peculiar to morality – we become aware of what is right or obligatory. No argument can give us justification, according to Prichard, for holding our moral knowledge. Rather, in order to be justified in holding our moral knowledge, all we can do and need to do is to have intuitively justified moral knowledge. We presumably can put ourselves in a situation (through imagination) in which our moral capacity of thinking yields intuitively justified moral knowledge.[9] In this vein, Pritchard writes,

> Suppose we come genuinely to doubt whether we ought to pay our debts, owing to genuine doubt whether our previous conviction that we ought to do so is true, a doubt which can, in fact, only arise if we fail to remember the real nature of what we now call our past conviction. The only remedy lies in actually getting into a situation which occasions the obligation, or if our imagination be strong enough, in imagining ourselves in that situation, and then letting our *moral capacities of thinking* do their work. (1949, 16, italic added)

But what can be revealed through 'our moral capacities of thinking'? Simply put, Prichard believes that by carrying out an activity of moral thinking, we can immediately detect the truth of moral judgement (moral proposition).[10] We reflect on the nature of the judgement by moral thinking, and this reflection *alone* can yield intuitive knowledge. Hence, if this is the case, we can discern a moral judgement's truth without appealing to an argument. More precisely, Prichard claims that by reflecting on the moral judgement's nature, there is no *need* to appeal to an argument to apprehend what is 'self-evident'. To explain the nature of moral reflecting, for instance, he writes that

> This apprehension is immediate, in precisely the sense in which a mathematical apprehension is immediate, e.g. the apprehension that this three-sided figure, in virtue of its being three-sided, must have three angles. Both apprehensions are immediate in the sense that in both, insight into the nature of the subject directly leads us to recognise its possession of the predicate; and it is only stating this fact from the other side to say that in both cases the fact apprehended is self-evident. (1949, 8)

Prichard concludes that, since moral philosophers try to prove what is right (wrong) and obligatory (prohibited) by appealing to a kind of inferential reasoning that contains some premises about the goodness or badness of actions, moral philosophy rests on a mistake. He thought that it is impossible to do that. What is right or wrong, he says, 'can only be apprehended directly by an act of moral thinking' (1949, 16).

In Prichard's view, it is not justified to hold moral beliefs about what is right or obligatory by referring to the good and bad consequences of the act in question. To answer the question of 'what makes an act either right or wrong?' Prichard claims we need to know the nature of the act and what Prichard calls 'a definite relation' between the agent and those whose interests and rights are promoted or honoured by the act. In one interpretation, Prichard wanted to show that an act cannot be made right by its consequences.[11] This is because, as he argues, consequences alone cannot be sufficient to make an act right.[12]

On the other interpretation, although Prichard holds that good and bad consequences are not at stake, he believes that these are preconditions for apprehending the truth. So, it seems that he thinks there is a truth to consequentialism. Prichard says, for example, that 'unless the effect of an act were in some way good, there would be no obligation to produce it, i.e. the goodness of the thing produced is a presupposition of the obligation to produce it' (2002, 2). In the same vein, he writes that

> At best it can only be maintained that there is this element of truth in the Utilitarian view, that unless we recognised that something which an act will originate is good, we should not recognize that we ought to do the action. (2002, 10)

And yet, perhaps, according to Prichard, there is an unbridgeable gap between good and right because it is always possible to believe that something is good but at the same time reasonably ask: 'But why should I bring it about?' Following early Moore in *Principia Ethica*, Prichard maintains that one cannot prove something is morally right simply by showing that it is morally good. There is always a further step that must be taken. Prichard writes,

> [W]e do not come to appreciate an obligation by an argument, i.e. by a process of non-moral thinking, and in particular we do not do so by an argument of which a premise is the ethical but not moral activity of appreciating the goodness either of the act or of a consequence of the act, i.e. our sense of the rightness of an act is not a conclusion from our appreciation of the goodness either of it or of anything else. (2002, 13–14)

Prichard's argument is similar to Moore's 'open question argument' against moral naturalism, although Moore appeals to the argument to show that there is a gap between good and other moral or non-moral properties of what is good.[13] In his classic book, *Principia Ethica*, Moore claims that while good cannot be defined in terms of other moral or non-moral properties, right can be defined in terms of good, and therefore there is no gap between right and good. However, Moore changed his mind in his later book, *Ethics*, about the relation between goodness and rightness and accepted Prichard's position that right is indefinable.[14] But he never accepted Prichard's pluralism about right.

To elaborate on what Prichard is saying, suppose one is asked whether one's belief that you ought to pay your debts or to tell the truth comes from the belief that in doing so, you should be producing something good. One probably would immediately and without hesitation answer 'no'.[15] However, although Prichard did not talk about it clearly, we should be aware that this does not entail that one's moral beliefs about what is right and wrong are not justifiable or *capable* of inferential justification. That right cannot be inferred from good does not entail it cannot be inferred from something else, for example, Kant's Categorical Imperative.

Although Prichard accepts that there might be some relations between the consequences of action and moral obligation, he insists that this relation is known intuitively. That is, by reflecting on the relevant features of the action, including its consequences, this reflection is enough for one to discern the moral truth. He says that

> we do not come to appreciate an obligation by an *argument* . . . and that, in particular, we do not do so by an argument of which a premise is . . . the goodness either of the act or of a consequence of the act. (1949, 9)

What is important in Prichard's epistemology is his attack on a kind of moral evidentialism or inferentialism. 'Evidentialism' or 'inferentialism' generally is the view that a belief is justified when it is based on good evidence. Evidence is supposed here to be another belief that is epistemologically justified and is related to the first belief through a logical inference. Evidence sometimes logically implies what it is evidence for. Moral evidentialism, or moral inferentialism, then, is the view that moral beliefs are not basic and stand in need of inferential justification.[16] According to this view, a moral belief is justified when it is based on, and logically inferred from, another moral or non-moral belief that is independently justified.

One of the questions Prichard dealt with is whether a certain state of mind is knowing or merely believing. He writes that we need 'a principle by applying which we can show that a certain condition of mind was really knowledge' (1949, 2). Prichard thought that appealing to inferential reasoning to prove something that is not provable or does not need any proof is the mistake of epistemologists and ethicists, for this cannot bring us a form of moral knowledge. The idea of self-evidence comes in here. Prichard believes that there are some self-evident moral principles that cannot be proved or do not need any further justification. The idea of self-evident propositions is the central theme in the epistemology of the classic intuitionists, although moral intuitionists such as Sidgwick, Moore, Prichard and Ross have to some extent different views about it.

I do not have enough space to discuss all strong and modest classic intuitionists' ideas. So, I will just focus on Ross as an intuitionist who has attracted a lot of attention from moderate contemporary moral intuitionists. However, to prepare for the next chapter, I should say something about the new trend in the intuitionist tradition and the different kinds of intuitionism.

1.2 Emerging new moral intuitionism: Philosophical renaissance

From the latter half of the twentieth century to the present day, moral intuitionists have been enjoying a *philosophical renaissance*. Although classic intuitionism faded in the 1950s and 1960s, there have been some contemporary philosophers who defend and develop important aspects of moral intuitionism and work within the intuitionist tradition. As Philip Stratton-Lake mentions, it is with Rawls's 'reflective equilibrium' that we see a trend towards taking moral intuition and intuitionism seriously.[17]

Audi, for example, as one of the contemporary moral intuitionists whose classificatory works have contributed a lot to this renewal of interest, writes that moral intuitionism is the view that we can have, in the light of appropriate reflection on the content of moral judgments and moral principles, intuitive (hence non-inferential) justification for holding them. (1997a, 54)

Or, as he says elsewhere, we can understand moral intuitionism as

the thesis that basic moral judgments and basic moral principles are justified by non-inferential deliverances of a rational, intuitive faculty, a mental capacity that contrasts with sense perception, clairvoyance, and other possible routes to justification. (2004, 102)

However, one might get confused about how Audi can remain consistent while working with the non-inferentiality of intuition and with reflection. The very idea of a non-inferential but reflective intuition seems contradictory at first sight. In order to puzzle out this confusion, as I said before, I will put forward my account of reflection when I discuss Ross and Audi (*cf.* Chapters 4 and 5).

It is difficult to identify one central shared idea among these new intuitionists; however, most of them believe in forms of 'moderate intuitionism' which admit that some self-evident moral propositions are also *capable* of inferential justification.[18] The fact that some moral beliefs are basic in the sense that they are intuitively or non-inferentially justified is consistent with their being justifiably inferred from other beliefs.

Moreover, although moral intuitions are non-inferential, it does not follow from this that they are infallible. Rather, they are fallible in the sense that, in principle, via reflection and contemplation, we can come to believe that they are false, even though they are justified non-inferentially. In fact, error in moral intuitions that make them fallible is like some kind of illusion or hallucination.

Although moral intuitionists often share some ideas, it is hard to say that there is only one shared idea among these new contemporary moral intuitionists. It is plausible to think of different sorts of intuitionism, that is, 'intuitionisms'. Later, I will try to show how different kinds of intuitionism have been formed among those who label themselves intuitionists. However, following the Wittgensteinian idea of 'family resemblance', I will argue that even if we have many moral intuitionisms, we can meaningfully refer to moral intuitionism's markers as its definition.

1.3 The many 'intuitionisms' instead of one intuitionism

In his *Methods of Ethics*, Sidgwick talked about 'three phases of intuitionism . . . in the formal development of intuitive morality: Perceptional, Dogmatic and

Philosophical' (1967, 102).[19] Very briefly, Perceptional Intuitionism is the view that only particular moral judgements are self-evident. Perceptional Intuitionists, then, do not form a general system of our moral intuitions. Dogmatic Intuitionism is the view that the fundamental principles of morality are the ones endorsed by common moral consciousness. Philosophical Intuitionism identifies more general and abstract principles than Dogmatic Intuitionism.[20] Although it is not very clear what Sidgwick had in mind on the difference between Dogmatic and Philosophical Intuitionists, it seems that they can be distinguished by what they refer to in defending that there are certain basic principles. Dogmatic Intuitionists believe that certain moral principles are fundamental by referring to ordinary moral consciousness. Philosophical Intuitionists, however, believe that there are some abstract and general moral principles by reference to rational understanding.[21]

In addition to this classification, the tradition of moral intuitionism contains two types of theories: meta-ethical theories and a normative theory. Meta-ethical theories – which can be called 'meta-ethical intuitionism' – are about the nature of moral facts and moral epistemology, whereas a normative theory – which can be called 'deontological pluralism' – is about moral intuitionists' theory in normative ethics.

What exactly is the point of mixing up meta-ethical intuitionism with intuitionism as a normative moral theory? Indeed, surely clarity is served by recognizing that they are different. Bernard Williams and Isaiah Berlin are good examples of normative intuitionists (normative pluralists) who had contempt for meta-ethical intuitionism. Sidgwick and his student G. E. Moore are the prime examples of meta-ethical intuitionists who were not deontological pluralists.

Related to that point, Bernard Williams and John Rawls also distinguish two sorts of moral intuitionism: 'methodological intuitionism' and 'epistemological intuitionism'.[22] Methodological intuitionism holds that there is a plurality of first-order moral principles that can conflict, and there is no higher-order principle for resolving such conflicts. Methodological intuitionism is a subclass of pluralism theories, but not all pluralists are methodological intuitionists. S. Clarke, R. Price, H. A. Prichard, W. D. Ross, A. C. Ewing, C. D. Broad, Thomas Nagel, John McDowell, Susan Wolf, David McNaughton and Philip Stratton-Lake are the examples of proponents of methodological intuitionism. Epistemological intuitionism, however, is the view that some moral propositions are self-evident, that is, that these propositions can be known directly and non-inferentially by intuition.[23]

Even so, two things have to be considered at this stage: (I) first, epistemological intuitionists such as some ethical egoists need not be methodological intuitionists. Although many methodological intuitionists are also epistemological intuitionists, not all epistemological intuitionists are methodological intuitionists. Although W. D. Ross is a methodological and epistemological intuitionist, G. E. Moore and H. Sidgwick, for example, are two consequentialists who believed in epistemological intuitionism but not methodological intuitionism. They believed that the plurality of moral principles could be derived from a single consequentialist principle, yet this first principle is known non-inferentially.

Similarly, in contemporary moral philosophy, we can seek methodological and epistemological intuitionists in the same way. For example, McNaughton (2002) is a methodological and epistemological intuitionist, although he may have an intuitionist epistemology where what is intuited is what to do in particular cases. Stratton-Lake (2000) also is a moral intuitionist both in normative theory and epistemology. However, Scanlon (1998) is an epistemological intuitionist but a Contractualist in normative theory; Audi (2004) is an epistemological intuitionist but a Kantian–Rossian intuitionist in normative theory; Nagel (1970 and 1997) is an epistemological intuitionist, but he believes in Kantianism as a normative theory; Hooker (2000a) is an epistemological intuitionist but a Rule-Consequentialist in normative theory, and finally Parfit (2011) is an epistemological intuitionist, but he argues that three single-principle normative theories (Kantian Contractualism, Rule-Consequentialism, and Scanlonian Contractualism) converge on the same set of moral rules which then determine right and wrong in particular cases.

(II) Second, methodological intuitionists such as Bernard Williams and Jonathan Dancy need not be epistemological intuitionists. Dancy, for example, is a modern methodological intuitionist-particularist who does not believe in *general* non-inferential self-evident moral principles. Nevertheless, he might believe in *particular* self-evidence.[24] If this is the case, we can categorize him as a 'Perceptional Intuitionist' in the Sidgwickian sense.

Moral intuitionism might also be classified in terms of 'what moral intuitions are'. Following Bedke (2010) and Stratton-Lake (2016a), we could make a distinction between self-evidence intuitionism and seeming intuitionism. Seeming intuitionists treat moral intuition as a non-epistemic state. For example, as Huemer (2005) endorses, to have a moral intuition that p is to have a mental state whereby it seems that p. According to seeming intuitionists, seeming justifies us in believing in something in the absence of reason to doubt.

Self-evidence intuitionists, on the other hand, treat intuition as an epistemic state.[25] Most classic intuitionists, for example, Ross and Sidgwick, advocate such epistemology according to which the content of moral belief is justified in terms of its being a self-evident proposition.

The list of different forms of moral intuitionism can be extended. I do not claim to have offered all conceivable classifications. All I want to highlight here is that it is very hard to find one and only one particular kind of moral intuitionism. Nonetheless, this does not explain that we cannot sensibly employ and refer to moral intuitionism. Let me explain this by using the Wittgenstein idea of 'family resemblance' and the concept of 'game'.

In his *Philosophical Investigations*, Wittgenstein (1953, §65–71) explains the concept of 'game' by discussing the idea of family resemblances. He argues that there are resemblances between different examples of games similar to the resemblances among the members of a family (resemblances between the eyes, eyebrows or mouth of a mother and father with those of their children). Wittgenstein writes,

> What does it mean to know what a game is? What does it mean, to know it and not be able to say it? . . . Isn't my knowledge, my concept of a game, completely expressed in the explanations that I could give? That is, in my describing examples of various kinds of game; shewing how all sorts of other games can be constructed on the analogy of these. (1953, 35)

For example, consider these examples of games: basketball, football, chess and boxing. Although football and basketball share a property such as having ball, no ball is involved in chess and boxing. This implies that it is hard to find an attribute presented in all the above-mentioned games. That is to say, if someone wants to find a shared property that exists in all the above-mentioned games, it would appear that there is none. However, this does not entail that we cannot refer to the concept of game or we cannot understand the meaning of the game. Our linguistic intuition can help us to convey meaning in an entirely acceptable way. No one would doubt employing and applying the concept of 'game' to football, basketball, etc.[26] To arrive at the meaning of the concept 'game', for Wittgenstein, looking at similarities and dissimilarities plays an indispensable role.[27]

Isn't there at least one property all these games share – being rule-governed in some way? Like the concept of 'game', we can think of many moral intuitionisms. Yet this does not imply that we cannot sensibly refer to moral intuitionism. Even if there are many moral intuitionisms, we can think of some marks of moral intuitionism as defining properties of moral intuitionism. Later,

I will show that it is possible to think of common marks between different forms of moral intuitionism. These marks work in such a way that if x meets the conditions m1, m2, m3 . . . mn, x is a kind of moral intuitionism. I will argue that the application of Wittgenstein's concept of 'family resemblance' to understanding the relatedness of various moral intuitionisms provides as much insight into the problem of defining 'intuitionism'. I will specify a set of necessary and jointly sufficient conditions requisite for any theory to qualify as 'intuitionist'.

1.3.1 Marks of moral intuitionism

Different sorts of moral intuitionism have a list of things to share. For example, almost all classic moral intuitionists believe in self-evident propositions, and they are non-naturalists and realists. Since no other view endorses all these elements, I believe it is plausible to pick these marks out as the defining ones for classic intuitionism.[28]

The list of shared ideas can either be derived from the views of the great past intuitionists or by reflection on how intuitionism can be constructed similarly to theirs. I will provide a list of 'marks of moral intuitionism', which contains epistemological and non-epistemological commitments as follows. Not all moral intuitionists have to meet all these marks; rather, moral intuitionists just need to meet at least several of them.[29] These marks are therefore by no means necessary and sufficient. Here is an example of a flexible list:

> *Mark 1: pluralism about right*; moral intuitionists are suspicious of the idea of a Supreme Ethical Principle. They tend to believe in several moral principles which contribute to all-things-considered right and wrong.

Of course, as I showed before, there is no need for intuitionists to be pluralists about the right. Intuitionists such as Sidgwick and Moore are monists about the right.

> *Mark 2: realism*; moral intuitionists tend to believe that there are some real facts in ethics.
>
> *Mark 3: cognitivism*; moral intuitionists tend to believe that moral judgement is a cognitive state.

I know of no moral realist who is not also a moral cognitivist, and I suspect this is because moral realism entails moral cognitivism, although, while moral realists are moral cognitivists, not all cognitivists are realists. John Skorupski (1999) is the contemporary example of a cognitivist who is not a realist. 'Irrealist cognitivism' entails that moral propositions can be objectively true or false, even if there are no real entities 'out there' to make them true or false – 'their truth is not a matter of correspondence'. Even so, there is no need for intuitionists to be realists. For example, Bedke (2013) makes a connection between 'intuitions and quasi-realism'.

> *Mark 4: non-naturalism*; moral intuitionists tend to believe that the facts at issue are non-natural facts.

However, David Copp (2003 and 2007) and, to some extent, Audi (2004) believe that moral intuitionism is compatible with naturalism.[30] Roger Crisp also writes: 'it is unwise to saddle it [moral intuitionism] as an epistemological thesis with any metaphysical commitment to non-natural properties' (2002, 59).[31]

> *Mark 5: self-evidence*; moral intuitionists tend to believe that some normative facts are self-evident and known *a priori*.

There is no need for moral intuitionists to be cognitivists to believe in self-evident propositions. Bedke (2014 and 2013), for example, thinks that the notion of self-evidence does no epistemic work, but he can make sense of it, and he is a non-cognitivist.

> *Mark 6: foundationalism*; moral intuitionists tend to believe in some foundational beliefs (e.g. self-evident propositions) that cannot be justified by reference to other beliefs.[32]

However, some moral intuitionists, such as Dancy (2004a), believe in self-evident propositions but embrace coherentism in their epistemology. Furthermore, some moral intuitionists, for example, Audi (2004), believe that basic self-evident propositions can get extra justification.

> *Mark 7: independence of right*; moral intuitionists tend to believe that the theory of right is not dictated by the theory of good.

Nevertheless, some moral intuitionists might think that it is not true that the right is independent of the good if this is supposed to mean that the good has no influence on or relevance to the right. These intuitionists accept that the right is influenced by the good, in that, for example, a duty to benefit others is one duty, which is nearly always relevant to determining the right. Of course, very often, the duty to benefit others gets outweighed by some other duty. So, according to these moral intuitionists, all we can say is that the right is not 'wholly determined' by the good.

So far, so good. Following the Wittgensteinian idea of 'family resemblance', I argued that although it is hard to find one particular kind of moral intuitionism, we can think of different common markers of moral intuitionism to refer to them as the definition. Like the concept of 'game', we can think of many moral intuitionisms with common properties though we can meaningfully refer to them and employ them in different sensible contexts. I discussed many kinds of moral intuitionism to show that there is no one particular kind of moral intuitionism throughout history. However, I characterized different markers of moral intuitionism to be used as moral intuitionism's definition. This implies that moral intuitionism is definable, though we have many moral intuitionisms.

Some of the marks discussed earlier are related to the normative theory of intuitionism or methodological intuitionism, that is, deontological pluralism. Some other marks are related to the meta-ethics of intuitionism or epistemological intuitionism. W. D. Ross is a good example of having both these kinds of marks.

In the next section, I discuss the Rossian ethical framework as a representative of modest classic moral intuitionism. I start off by introducing – as far as it is necessary – Ross's normative theory. This helps us to have a better understanding of his moral epistemology, which will be covered next. In Chapter 7, I will return to Rossian normative ethics, especially with regard to conflicts of duties, while responding to the critics of epistemological intuitionism. In the end, I evaluate Ross's epistemological ideas to see whether it is appropriate for contemporary new intuitionists to adopt his ideas.

2 Rossian ethics as a representative of modest classic moral intuitionism

The Rossian version of intuitionism (1930 and 1939) has been accepted and developed by a number of contemporary moral philosophers. Some philosophers praise his normative theory, and some highlight his moral epistemology.[33] In what follows, I shall discuss some of the most important features of his ideas, such as principles of *prima facie* duties, pluralism, self-evidence, foundationalism and particularism. In order to do so, I discuss Ross's ethical framework under two main sections: the doctrine of *prima facie* duties and moral epistemology. Although Ross's moral epistemology is at the centre of my attention in this chapter, it seems necessary to start with a discussion of Ross's idea of *prima facie* duties in his normative ethics. This is because Ross's moral epistemology and doctrine of *prima facie* duties are interrelated. Since

Ross uses the terminology of *prima facie* duties in his epistemology, we need to have a clear mind about what a *prima facie* duty is before going on to discuss moral epistemology.

2.1 Ross on the doctrine of *prima facie* duties

Ross's ethical framework was first published in *The Right and the Good* (1930), which, according to C. D. Broad, is 'the most important contribution to ethical theory made in England for a generation' (1940, 228). I shall mostly outline Ross's theory of *prima facie* duties as follows. I then touch upon the issue of moral pluralism in *prima facie* duties, though the topic of pluralism can be discussed in Ross's epistemology as well.

2.1.1 Prima facie *duties versus actual duties*

Ross's contribution idea of *prima facie* duty has been admired by A. C. Ewing as 'one of the most important discoveries of the century in moral philosophy' (1959, 126). Ross argued that the rightness of actions is not totally determined by their good consequences.[34] In Ross's view, we have some duties other than producing good results and sometimes these duties override the duty of producing a good result.[35]

Ross believes that we should distinguish between *prima facie* duties and actual duties or a duty proper. He sometimes calls a duty proper a 'toti-resultant attribute' of an action and a *prima facie* duty a 'parti-resultant attribute' (1930, 2002, 28).[36] Whether an act is a *prima facie* duty depends on whether it has a morally relevant non-moral property. However, Ross believes that '[w]hether an act is a duty proper or an actual duty depends on all the morally significant kinds it is an instance of' (1930, 2002, 19–20). In the same pages, Ross tries to give a definition of '*prima facie* duty'.[37] Consider the following quote by him:

> I suggest '*prima facie* duty' or 'conditional duty' as a brief way of referring to the characteristic (quite distinct from that of being a duty proper) which an act has, in virtue of being of a certain kind (e.g. the keeping of a promise), of being an act which would be a duty proper if it were not at the same time of another kind which is morally significant. Whether an act is a duty proper or an actual duty depends on all the morally significant kinds it is an instance of . . . . There is nothing arbitrary about these *prima facie* duties. Each rests on a definite circumstance which cannot seriously be held to be without moral significance. (1930, 2002, 19–20)

We encounter two stages here. At the first stage, a right-making feature leads us to a *prima facie* duty if we disregard other morally relevant properties of the situation.[38] At the second stage, we should consider all right and wrong-making features of the action in question. If the right-making features outweigh the wrong-making features, we are led to an actual duty.[39]

Two things must be noted about the idea of *prima facie* duties. (1) First, Ross does not use the terminology of '*prima facie* duty' to refer to a duty that seems to be a duty *at first sight*, though it may turn out to be illusory on further reflection. Rather, the phrase '*prima facie* duty' is supposed to refer to a duty that comes from *part* of the nature of the moral situation. This duty that comes from *part* of the nature of the moral situation must be distinguished from overall duty that arises from the *whole* nature of the situation.[40]

To illustrate this, suppose I promise my wife that I will be out with her tonight; however, my mother is sick, and I should stay with her. I have then two *prima facie* duties of fidelity and beneficence. To find out which duty is my actual duty, we have to use our judgement or perception in an 'all things considered' way. We should consider the *whole* nature of the situation to reach our verdict. Of course, we may make a mistake in identifying something as a *prima facie* duty, but we may also make the same mistake in identifying something like an actual duty. Some of what we take to be actual duties may turn out to be illusory as well.

Moreover, it is not true that the contrast between *prima facie* and actual duties is a contrast between an *apparent* and a *real* duty. *Prima facie* duties are real moral considerations, not ones that seem to be duties at first sight.[41] This leads us to think that a *prima facie* duty, in fact, is *not a type of duty*. But it is *related to duty in a particular way*.[42] Ross explicitly writes in this regard that

> [The *prima facie* duties] suggest that what we are speaking of is a certain kind of duty, whereas it is in fact not a duty, but something related in a special way to duty. (1930, 2002, 20)

So Ross's distinction between *prima facie* and actual duties is not the distinction between apparent and real duties. I think the terminology '*pro tanto* duties' for *prima facie* duties and 'all-things-considered duties' for actual duties is less misleading.[43] Hooker, for instance, writes,

> [T]he term 'pro tanto' is less misleading than 'prima facie'. For the idea is that a duty or consideration is overridable, not that it can be seen at first glance but on closer inspection may prove to be an illusion. (1996, 534, fn. 6)[44]

The idea behind *pro tanto* duties is that certain properties or features of situations count morally in favour or against action. Of these properties, some are more important in some cases, but others are more important in other cases. For example, suppose that A borrows a gun from his friend B, promising to give it back as soon as B asks. After one week, B asks for his gun. But A knows that B wants his gun to kill someone. On the one hand, A should keep his promise and return the gun to B. On the other hand, A has a *pro tanto* duty of non-maleficence. So relevant here are A's two *pro tanto* duties of fidelity and non-maleficence. On reflection, we come to believe that, of course, A's all-things-considered duty is not to keep the promise.

(2) Second, we should be aware that the term *pro tanto* should not be employed as an adjective to refer to a certain kind of duty, but as a name for a *disposition* that we find in some kinds of acts to become an all-things-considered duty. A *pro tanto* duty would become an all-things-considered duty after all other morally relevant non-moral properties or opposing *pro tanto* duties are ruled out.[45] For example, if I promise someone to do something, this makes my doing the act in question my *pro tanto* duty. This act could turn into an all-things-considered duty if it does not come into conflict with a more important *pro tanto* duty, such as the *pro tanto* duty to prevent the death of an innocent person. However, if there is a more important *pro tanto* duty that conflicts with my keeping my promise, my *pro tanto* duty to keep my promise remains in existence. My situation is different from that of someone who had never made a promise.[46]

2.1.2 Ross on moral pluralism

Moral intuitionism, historically, is often identified as a pluralistic theory according to which there are irreducibly different grounds for moral properties of rightness and wrongness.[47] However, as I showed before, there is no logically necessary connection between moral intuitionism and pluralism. Although one might be an intuitionist about both right and wrong (epistemological intuitionism) and the plurality of moral principles (deontological pluralism), some philosophers are intuitionists about wrong and right but not intuitionists about the plurality of moral principles.[48]

Ross, as a moral intuitionist, is a pluralist about both good and right. However, he believes that we cannot understand moral properties such as good and right by deconstructing moral propositions and analysing moral notions. This is because, according to Ross, moral notions such as goodness and rightness are indefinable.[49]

Nonetheless, it is not the case that intuitionists must believe in the indefinability of moral concepts such as good and right. There is no necessary connection between intuitionism and the indefinability of basic moral concepts because one can be an intuitionist and hold that goodness and rightness are definable. For example, one can think that for X to be good is for X to have properties that give us reason to take on some favourable attitude towards X, and for action A to be right is for action A to have properties that give us convincing reason to do that action. So, such a view is completely compatible with the view that there is an irreducible plurality of moral principles that can be known by intuition.[50]

Unlike Ross, although Moore is a pluralist about the good, as I stated before, he is not a pluralist about the right.[51] Ross criticizes the Moorian monistic theory of the right and argues for pluralism about both goodness and rightness. Ross, following Prichard, argued for moral pluralism on the grounds that not all duties can be grounded in goodness. In order to do this, Ross rejects both Utilitarianism and Kantianism since both of them try to reduce different moral duties to a single duty, and they hold that moral judgements could be drawn from a single basic moral principle.[52]

To set up his pluralistic doctrine of *pro tanto* duties, Ross attacks the best views that try to ground right acts in a single principle: the agent's own good (ethical egoism), the impartial goodness of the consequences of the act (consequentialism), and the intrinsic goodness of the action itself ('good will view').[53] First, Ross rejects ethical egoism on the grounds that there are many moral duties that benefit others regardless of the cost to the agent. Second, Ross rejects consequentialism or 'ideal utilitarianism' because it 'ignores, or at least does not do full justice to, the highly personal character of duty' (1930, 2002, 22).[54] He actually says that consequentialism does not consider special relations of one person to another, such as the relation of being a member of the agent's family or being the agent's friend.[55] Third, Ross argues against the 'good will view', according to which the intrinsic goodness of the act itself explains why we ought to do it. Ross argues against this view by pointing out that actions can be intrinsically good only if we consider the motive from which actions are done. The reason is that any intrinsic value that actions have derives from the intrinsic value of the motive. So if our actions are explained by the intrinsic goodness, then we need not only to do certain acts but also do them from a good motive. However, in Ross's view, it is not true that we always ought to act from a good motive since motives are not under the control of the will. Therefore, since we cannot choose to act from a good motive, it is not the case that we ought to act from a good motive. It follows that the good will view is incompatible with the 'ought implies can' principle.[56]

According to Ross, these three views represent the best attempts to ground right acts in a single principle. If we can show that these views are false, then it is very likely to think that monism is false, he thinks. After examining these views, Ross concludes that since the right cannot be grounded in the good, all forms of monism are false, and our duties should be subsumed under a plurality of fundamental moral principles.[57]

Having argued that monist theories are wrong, Ross formulates five basic plural principles or duties in this way: promoting good (duties of beneficence, justice and self-improvement), fidelity, gratitude, reparation and non-maleficence (avoiding evil).[58] Ross appealed to commonsensical phrases such as 'direct reflection on what we really think' (1930, 2002, 23), 'what most plain men think' (1930, 2002, 28), 'it becomes harmonious with other opinions' (1939, 3) or 'test of reflection' (1930, 2002, 41) to justify that a pluralistic theory in ethics is more plausible than a monistic theory.[59] In Ross's view, there is a plurality of duties, which tend to conflict, and our judgement in the particular situation shows which duty is the all-things-considered one. Ross believes that the monistic theories discussed earlier cannot show the 'complexity' of morality.[60] He writes in the *Foundations of Ethics* that a monistic theory

> ignores the fact that in many situations there is more than one claim upon our action, that these claims often conflict, and that while we can see with certainty that the claims exist, it becomes a matter of individual and fallible judgment to say which claim is in the circumstances the overriding one. In many such situations, equally good men would form different judgments as to what their duty is. They cannot all be right, but it is often impossible to say which is right; each person must judge according to his own individual sense of the comparative strength of various claims. (1939, 189)

To conclude this section, although the Rossian ethics of *pro tanto* duties is a kind of deontology that holds it is our *pro tanto* duty to produce as much good as we can for ourselves and for other people, we also have other *pro tanto* duties such as the duty to keep our promises, etc. The doctrine of *pro tanto* duties clearly entails moral pluralism whereby there are many irreducible morally relevant non-moral properties of which each has an independent role in determining what we should do. That is to say, there are some basic moral principles that cannot be subsumed under one single fundamental principle.[61] However, although it is true that Rossian pluralism holds that there is no more basic principle that underlies and justifies/explains the *pro tanto* duties, it is not true that ethics of *pro tanto* duties must hold this. Suppose by 'plural pro tanto duties', one means simply 'duties that favour or disfavour actions but can be outweighed by other such duties'. In that case, it is not true that commitment to *pro tanto* duties entails that there is not some more basic principle that underlies and justifies/explains them.

2.2 Ross on moral epistemology in meta-ethics

Like many other intuitionists, Ross believes that there are self-evident basic moral principles or duties, that moral properties are real properties in the world (realism), that moral properties are not identical with natural properties (non-naturalism), and finally that moral statements express beliefs and that they are apt for truth and falsity (cognitivism).

Ross considers the nature of moral knowledge in different places in *The Right and the Good* and *Foundations of Ethics*. He believes that acquiring moral knowledge is comparable with acquiring mathematical knowledge since

> both in mathematics and in ethics we have certain crystal-clear intuitions from which we build up all that we can know about the nature of numbers and the nature of duty. (1939, 144)

Ross compares ethics with mathematics in the sense that both of them are synthetic *a priori*, intuitive or non-inferential and justified by intuition.[62] In both mathematics and ethics, Ross thinks, some particular truths will be found by direct intuition.[63] Ross writes that

> If we now turn to ask how we come to know these fundamental moral principles, the answer seems to be that it is in the same way in which we come to know the axioms of mathematics. Both alike seem to be both synthetic and *a priori*; that is to say, we see the predicate, though not included in the definition of the subject, to belong necessarily to anything which satisfies that definition. . . . We see first, for instance, that a particular imagined act, as being productive of pleasure to another, has a claim on us, and it is a very short and inevitable step from this to seeing that *any* act, as possessing the same constitutive character, must have the same resultant character of *prima facie* rightness. (1939, 320)

Although Ross compares ethics with mathematics, he does not support the idea that our moral intuition is infallible. In what follows, I will elaborate on the key elements of Rossian moral epistemology. I investigate the idea of self-evidence, fallibility, justification and their relation in detail. To clarify the notion of self-evidence, I shall discuss the relation between the justification of self-evident moral propositions and 'further reflection' in the Rossian framework. As many contemporary Rossian moral philosophers do, I believe that there is no necessary connection between self-evidence and obviousness. I will show that some beliefs about self-evident propositions require further justification by further reflection to be justified. Also, it does not follow from Ross's epistemology that beliefs about self-evident propositions are infallibly true. Rather, some beliefs about self-evident propositions (*pro tanto* principles) are fallible.[64] After that, I shall investigate Ross's theory of justification. In order to do so, I discuss the idea of 'modest foundationalism'. Finally, I shall discuss particularism in all-things-considered duties and generalism in *pro tanto* duties.

2.2.1 Belief about **pro tanto** *duties and all-things-considered duties*

There are two kinds of beliefs in Rossian epistemology. One kind consists of beliefs about *pro tanto* duties, which are basic, intuitive and self-evident. The other kind consists of beliefs about all-things-considered duties, which are not self-evident. Although Ross's *The Right and the Good* maintains that basic moral beliefs can be justified intuitively or non-inferentially, his earlier paper 'The Basis of Objective Judgments in Ethics' says that basic moral beliefs can be justified in both ways, that is, inferentially and non-inferentially.[65] In fact, Ross thinks there are some intuitively true beliefs about *pro tanto* duties that *can* be recognized directly. But this does not commit Ross to hold that *all* basic moral propositions *are* known directly.

Ross's moral intuitionism has many commonalities with earlier intuitionists; however, his idea about fallibility (infallibility) is different. He thought that beliefs about *pro tanto* duties could seem true at first sight, though further reflection shows that they are false. This entails that although beliefs about self-evident *pro tanto* duties can be justified non-inferentially, they are not infallible. Rather they might turn out to be false and can even be refuted. We can come to believe they are false, albeit inferentially. So, Ross thinks that our beliefs about *pro tanto* duties are fallible.[66]

Ross himself explicitly showed that beliefs about *pro tanto* duties are not unchangeable and can progress over time. For instance, Ross altered his idea about the list of *pro tanto* duties at one point. The list of *pro tanto* duties seems, at first sight, incomplete and open-ended. This is because Ross's initial list of seven duties can become shorter or longer.

Rossian Initial List: (1) Fidelity; (2) Reparation; (3) Gratitude; (4) Justice; (5) Beneficence; (6) Self-improvement; (7) Non-maleficence

However, Ross goes on to reduce these to five duties as (4), (5) and (6) can be seen as *pro tanto* duties to bring about good.[67] Ross thus holds there are five basic types of moral considerations and that all others can be derived from these. Ross thought that the list of five basic duties could explain all obligations. So, the final list would be

> *Rossian Final List*: (1) Fidelity; (2) Reparation; (3) Gratitude; (4) Promoting the good; (5) Avoiding evil

However, one might get confused about how fallibility works for *pro tanto* duties. For example, 'keep your promises' might be fallible in the sense of wrong in certain cases, but self-evident *pro tanto* duties such as 'it is a *pro tanto* duty to keep your promises', if intuitive, would be infallible. So what, exactly, is intuitive? In response, we should be careful not to confuse the fallible/infallible distinction with the distinction between propositions that are only sometimes correct and propositions that are always correct. Although there is an epistemological distinction in terms of fallibility/infallibility, we can make a distinction between propositions that are only sometimes correct (e.g. 'keeping your promise is morally right all-things-considered') and propositions that are always correct (e.g. 'keeping your promise is one of your *pro tanto* duties'). However, there is a further question of whether a proposition that is always true is one that we can know with certainty will always be true. I think the answer is that whether a proposition is always true is one thing, and whether we can have certain knowledge of a proposition's always holding true is another.

To explain how our beliefs about *pro tanto* and all-things-considered duties work, we can use the terminology of 'moral value' or deontic valence and 'moral weight'. The deontic valence of morally relevant non-moral properties and the way in which they contribute to the moral evaluation of different situations are constant and invariant. In other words, morally relevant non-moral properties are not contextual in the *direction of their valence*. On the other hand, the moral *weight* of the relevant non-moral properties may vary from case to case.

But how is it that their valence always remains fixed, yet their weight can change?[68] Let me show this with an example. Consider an analogy with mass and weight in physics. We learned in physics that the mass of a metal ball is an intrinsic property of the ball, that is, it is dependent on the ball's internal structure. However, the weight depends on the gravitational force, so it varies from place to place. Now, consider the physics equation: '$W=M*G$' (W=weight, M=mass and G=gravitational force). According to this equation, the weight of the ball would vary depending on the gravitational force in different places, though in all cases, the mass is invariant.[69] Similarly, in Ross's story, the moral valence is constant, but the moral weight would change from case to case.

If this analogy works, on Ross's view, which *pro tanto* duty is overriding in particular cases varies. A *pro tanto* duty with the greatest importance in one case may be less important in another case, though the *pro tanto* duty's valence remains invariant. For instance, the fact that an act would be an instance of promise-keeping is, everything being equal, a right-making feature with an invariable deontic valence. Its weight, however, which depends on what one has promised or whether the promise was made under threat, may vary from context to context. Although the value of promise-keeping remains unchanged, its weight may differ from case to case.[70]

Consequently, our beliefs about all-things-considered duties must be formed with respect to the detail of each case, but this does not entail that we cannot generalize the belief of one case to another similar case. Although we might not know what our all-things-considered duties would be in a different case, or as Audi points out, there is no pre-existing pattern for that, we do know that in relevantly similar circumstances, the same verdict would hold.[71] For example, on every occasion that at least one *pro tanto* duty favours one alternative and none speaks against that alternative, we know that that alternative is morally right, all-things-considered.[72]

2.2.2 Ross on moral self-evident propositions and 'Further Reflection'

Self-evident propositions are thought and supposed to be evidently true with no *need* of supporting evidence, Ross believes.[73] If one considers and understands self-evident propositions, supposedly one can see their truth without any need of proof. Ross writes,

> That an act *qua* fulfilling a promise, or *qua* effecting a just distribution of good ... is *prima facie* right, is self-evident; not in the sense that it is evident from the beginning of our lives, or as soon as we attend to the proposition for the first time, but in the sense that when we have reached sufficient mental maturity and have given sufficient attention to the proposition it is evident without any need of proof, or of evidence beyond itself. It is evident just as a mathematical axiom, or the validity of a form of inference, is evident. . . . In our confidence that these propositions are true there is involved the same confidence in our reason that is involved in our confidence in mathematics. . . . In both cases we are dealing with propositions that cannot be proved, but that just as certainly need no proof. (1939, 29–30)

Although Ross denies in this passage that self-evident propositions are provable, it is possible that one can identify some arguments in favour of them. This is actually what Ross himself seems to think when he writes in his separate article that

> And in any case, even if it could be inferred that love or aesthetic experience is good, I feel sure that our judgment that they are so is intuitive; that something can be inferred does not prove that it cannot be seen intuitively. (1927, 121)

So, self-evident propositions *can* receive an independent justification, and it is not true that they are unprovable. Although self-evident propositions can be known on the mere basis of an understanding of them, they can also be known in other ways, for example, proposing an argument or illustration in favour of them.[74] However, since such arguments are *not* necessary to be justified in believing a self-evident proposition, they are 'epistemically supererogatory'.[75]

However, one might object by asking how the intuitionist knows whether the inferential justification, which might be possible but is optional as far as justification is concerned, is not contaminating or influencing the judgement that a proposition is intuitive? In response, although an intuitive proposition might receive an extra-inferential justification, this does not influence the judgement that the proposition is non-inferential. In intuitionists' view, we have intuitions about some self-evident moral propositions. Since these self-evident propositions are justified on their own, that is, by mere adequate understanding, and do not need any other propositions to be justified, they are non-inferential. In fact, these propositions do not need any inference or argument to be justified. Thus, these self-evident propositions are intuitive without being contaminated by inferential justification. Furthermore, one might need to know *why* some intuitive and non-inferential propositions are self-evident. In that case, one needs to use some inference to do that, but again, this is not influencing the judgement that there are some non-inferential self-evident moral propositions.

When Ross writes that a self-evident proposition is 'evident without any need of proof, or of evidence beyond itself', this implies that sufficient understanding of a self-evident proposition is enough to be justified in believing that proposition. But this does not entail that other forms of justification for believing it cannot exist.[76] Again, it is a misunderstanding if we think that self-evident propositions can be justified in *only* one way, that is, by sufficiently understanding them. This misunderstanding arises from using the term 'self-evidence' and leads some philosophers to think that the term 'self-evidence' has often been misused and so needs to be changed. For example, Hooker writes that because the term 'self-evident' has so often been misused by popular moralists to express an unreasonable degree of certainty and to silence further dispute, I feel more comfortable using a wider term that does not have those associations. (2002, 163)[77]

Hooker prefers to say that moral intuitions are propositions that come with 'independent credibility'.[78] An independently credible proposition is attractive without reference to evidence beyond itself and yet might turn out to be mistaken.

To understand better what Ross had in mind when he wrote that self-evident propositions are not 'evident from the beginning of our lives', we need to explain his method of intuitive induction, which he borrowed from Aristotle. Ross did not believe in a special faculty of intuition for knowing universal principles in ethics. He thought that reflection on particular cases and intuitive induction could help us to gain knowledge of moral principles. To explain the idea of intuitive induction, let me begin with Aristotle's framework.

In his *Metaphysics*, Aristotle argues that all derivative knowledge is based on non-derivative knowledge. According to him, to know the conclusion of a demonstration, one must first know the premises of that demonstration. The premises, however, are not always based on other premises since we cannot justify an infinite series. So, there must be some premises that are known; however, they are not known on the basis of other premises. Demonstrative (non-basic or derivative) knowledge must eventually rest on a non-demonstrative and basic foundation, namely, one that is known but not inferred from other premises. Aristotle calls such basic propositions *Archai*, which means axioms or first principles. In Aristotle's view, these first principles or axioms are foundational in the sense that they are a basis from which we generate justified knowledge. These axioms, Aristotle believes, must be true, primitive, immediate, more familiar than what we derive from them, prior and explanatory of what we derive from them.[79]

However, how do we know these first principles, which cannot be known by other premises or arguments? Aristotle replies by 'intuitive induction' (epagoge). Aristotelian induction should not be conflated with induction in the modern sense, that is, 'empirical induction'. What Aristotle means by epagoge is extremely interesting from an intuitionist point of view, but not at all the same as the modern sense. Intuitive induction is not a prediction based on empirical evidence, namely empirical induction. Whereas empirical induction can generate only knowledge of empirical and contingent truths, intuitive induction purports to generate knowledge of necessary truth. For example, when we, as students in schools, understood an exceptionless universal truth (like six apples and six apples are twelve apples (6+6=12)), intuitive induction may help us to see straight off that whenever six things are added to six other things, there will be twelve things. On the other hand, if I see 1,000 black ravens, it would be a fairly safe bet for me to say that the 1,001st raven will also be black. And yet, that ravens are black is a contingent truth derived from an empirical induction. But is there anything more that can be said about intuitive induction other than what it is not (empirical induction)? Can we show how we use intuitive induction?

Intuitive induction is the exercise of our ability to leap from our knowledge of some particular facts to knowledge of some universal principle. For example, we move from the perception of a single particular truth – such as this particular set of six apples added to that particular set of six apples adds up to twelve apples – to grasping the universal truth that 6+6=12. Thus, the knowledge we gain by intuitive induction is a way in which we see a self-evident truth or axiom by reflection. When we encounter a proposition like 'The angles of all triangles always add up to 180 degrees', by intuitive induction from knowledge of a single particular example (this triangle's sum of angles is 180 degrees), we assert that the proposition is true. Our knowledge of particular instances of the universal is simply like a ladder that we use to ascend to reach the knowledge of universals. We can put the ladder away once we have climbed it up. Once we have a clear understanding of the axioms, we can know them simply on the basis of understanding them – that is, directly, non-inferentially, intuitively or self-evidently.[80]

Likewise, Ross thought that the principles of *pro tanto* duties are known via their self-evidence in the sense that we gain such moral knowledge through a reflective non-inferential procedure, for example, 'intuitive induction' (1939, 170). Since intuitive induction is not like Humean induction, it uses our ability to leap straight from the knowledge of particular moral cases to the knowledge of strictly universal principles as a necessary truth. So, by the method of intuitive induction, Ross thought, we reflect on particular moral cases to know universal moral principles. In this regard, he writes that

> The induction here is not proof of the principle, but the psychological preparation upon which the knowledge of the principle supervenes. The knowledge of the principle is not produced by reasoning but achieved by direct insight. (1939, 49)

Again, since the method of intuitive induction is not a logical process, we understand the universality of *pro tanto* moral truth when we reflect on some particular moral cases. But this is not inferential; it is intuitive. In other words, seeing many individual cases of keeping a promise is not important, for this method is not enumerative.[81]

However, one might still be confused that although epagoge looks like an abstraction of universal from particular, this does not tell us anything about how the particular is known. As a response, we know some particular moral cases because they are what we come across in our moral experiences in daily life. In fact, there are some particular moral experiences in which we can be struck by the seeming wrongness or rightness of some actual or contemplated action. So, moral intuitions that consist of seemings help us to form beliefs about particular cases, and through imagination and reflection, we abstract universal principles. For example, when I experience that Ben's keeping his promise seems right in situation A, I am able to form a general principle that keeping a promise, ceteris paribus, is right.

One of the common objections to the idea that some moral propositions are self-evident is that being self-evident necessarily entails obviousness.[82] However, self-evident propositions need not be obvious. Some propositions that are self-evident are not obvious to everyone. For example, propositions such as 'circles are figures bounded by a line that is equidistant from its centre' and some complex mathematical proofs or axioms such as 'when an equal amount is taken from equals, an equal amount results' are self-evident but not obvious to everyone, at least at first sight.[83] However, it seems that the objection is not all about obviousness or its lack. What can we say about disagreement and lack of consensus? This lack can and does also come despite and after reflection.

Critics emphasize disagreement among moral intuitions about basic self-evident moral principles. Although these critics believe that self-evident propositions are not obvious ones, they argue that even moral philosophers do not have a consensus and have different moral intuitions about moral self-evident principles or propositions and that there thus are no moral self-evident principles or propositions. One of the famous examples of this disagreement is between Moore and Ross. Both Moore and Ross had the same moral intuition that promoting good is a basic self-evident principle. However, they have different moral intuitions about whether this is the 'only' basic self-evident principle.[84]

Although I will not discuss here in detail which of Moore or Ross is right, I think it is very natural for two philosophers to have different ideas about self-evident duty. The important thing here is that we should examine their arguments or illustrations to determine which has given a more plausible account of a self-evident duty. We should ask ourselves why Ross thought promoting good is not the only basic duty and why Moore thought it is. The answer, I think, has to be that Moore simply failed to see the things that Ross saw. Thought experiments and careful reflection help Ross to see things Moore had not seen. So, a clash of intuitions (Moore and Ross) is to be resolved by what looks like an argument.[85]

Ross explicitly acknowledged that our moral intuitions about self-evident propositions could be questioned. Self-evident moral propositions or principles are not obvious 'from the beginning of our lives', and we need further reflection to understand them carefully. Ross followed Aristotle in supposing that 'sufficient mental maturity' is necessary (1930, 2002, 33). Some self-evident propositions are clearer than others – which propositions are clearer completely depends on each person's mental development. Or, as Huemer holds, some intuitive moral propositions are 'more intuitive' (2005, 104).

Ross did not talk about 'moral maturity'; rather, he prefers 'mental maturity', which comes with the development of the ability to think about general terms.[86] However, it does not follow from this that if one achieves the level of maturity, one can *necessarily* find the truth of these propositions at first sight. In some cases, their truth may not be evident at first sight, and one does need further reflection to know self-evident propositions. Ross writes in this respect that

> In fact it seems, on reflection, self-evident that a promise, simply as such, is something that *prima facie* ought to be kept, and it does not, on reflection, seem self-evident that production of maximum good is the only thing that makes an act obligatory. (1930, 2002, 40)

Ross considers various forms of reflection: considering particular situations, thought experiments and asking whether our moral convictions are consistent.[87] Thought experiments, which form an important part of Ross's reflection on moral conviction, help us understand something in a better way on the grounds that we can think about some individual concepts alone and in an isolated way. Although isolation does not work in some situations since some notions cannot be understood as existing in isolation, thought experiments can provide us with an argument to believe in something (*cf.* Chapter 1).[88] However, this idea is contentious among philosophers. So, a plausible question can come to mind: Is it possible to understand thought experiments in morality as arguments?

I think we can defend a plausible account that considers thought experiments as parts of good arguments, though some philosophers like Dancy think that using imaginary cases (thought experiments) in ethics is regularly futile.[89] One of the famous examples of moral thought experiments is Judith Thomson's case for the moral permissibility of abortion. In her paper, 'A Defence of Abortion', she imagines that in

> *The Violinist Case*: A violinist has a very unusual medical condition, and there is only one cure that you can do for the violinist. One night, a society of music lovers attaches to you an unknown 'innocent' thing for nine months for curing the violinist. Are you morally obliged to make a huge sacrifice for a violinist?[90]

The answer that may spring to mind is no. In this story, Thomson argues in favour of abortion by telling a story as an argument. The thought experiment, in fact, played a crucial part (as a premise) in an argument in favour of permitting abortion.[91]

Ross uses different methods of reflection, such as thought experiments to justify some self-evident propositions. He often uses the terminology of 'further reflection', generally referring to one of the three forms of reflection mentioned earlier. But the important thing is that, in Ross's view, these methods do not create inferences. So, one is still non-inferentially justified even if one uses methods of further reflection.

To better understand the idea of Rossian further reflection, take Wittgenstein's example of 'Duck-Rabbit'. In *Philosophical Investigations*, he borrowed a picture from Jastrow and then called it duck-rabbit since 'it can be seen as a rabbit's head or as a duck's' (1953, 194). He then distinguished between two kinds of seeing: 'continuous seeing of an aspect' and 'dawning of an aspect'. One looks at that picture and just finds a rabbit in it. However, by continuously seeing or noticing other aspects, one can find a duck as well. Wittgenstein's use of 'continuous seeing' seems similar to what I have been discussing about Rossian 'further reflection' here.[92] Now let us examine an example of further reflection in Ross's works.

One of the examples of further reflection found in both of Ross's books is about pleasure being intrinsically good. In *The Right and the Good*, he wrote that the proposition 'pleasure is intrinsically good' is self-evident. However, through further reflection and thought experiments, he changed his mind and held that the proposition 'pleasure is not intrinsically good' or 'pleasure is an extrinsic good' is self-evident.[93] One of his arguments, for example, is that

> While we call a man good, or at least admirable (for 'good' as applied to men tends to be limited to moral goodness) in respect of his actions and dispositions and in respect of his intellectual or artistic activities, any goodness that pleasure may be supposed to have is not in this way reflected on its enjoyer. A man is not good in respect of the mere fact of feeling pleasure. (1939, 271)

Thus, we can see that 'further reflection' might help philosophers argue in favour of or against propositions that they thought self-evident earlier. If further reflection can support or discredit propositions previously thought to be self-evident, then even basic moral intuitions or convictions about self-evident propositions can be altered as a result of 'further reflection'.[94]

Finally, although Ross discusses some points about self-evident propositions, it seems that he does not have a positive account of self-evidence, that is, what it means to say that moral principles are self-evident. Most of what he says is negative. For example, he maintains that a self-evident proposition is *not* necessarily one that is obviously true.[95] Ross thinks that we have direct knowledge about self-evident moral principles where this knowledge is often not derivable; however, in some cases, a self-evident moral proposition or principle might be derivable from other propositions.

2.2.3 Ross's theory of justification

The role of coherence and consistency in Rossian epistemology is controversial among Rossian intuitionists. Ross thinks that both incoherency and inconsistency among moral convictions can give us a negative reason or justification to discard at least some moral convictions. However, does coherence generate a positive reason to believe in something? Although Ross did not explicitly consider whether coherence gives us reason to believe in some propositions, it is possible to interpret his ethical theory as holding that coherence can generate a positive reason.[96]

However, one can ask whether coherence or consistency is compatible with intuitionistic foundationalism. In other words, can Ross think of coherence or consistency as providing justification for self-evident propositions? I think – as do some intuitionists – the answer is 'yes', coherence provides justification for self-evident propositions depending on what they are coherent with. In order for a proposition to be self-evident, it needs an epistemic justification of intuition; however, this does not rule out other ways of justification.[97] Bertrand Russell, for instance, famously said the same thing about the propositions of arithmetic. He maintains that although some propositions can be inferred from the general principles of logic,

> the simple propositions of arithmetic, such as 'two and two are four', are just as self-evident as the principles of logic. (1912, 112)

And yet, of course, they can also be inferred from other arithmetical propositions. So, a self-evident proposition can be (but need not be) inferred from other propositions. In the next part, I will investigate a kind of foundationalism dubbed 'modest foundationalism'. The central idea of it is that there is no problem with combining foundationalism with an element of coherentism.

2.2.3.1 Modest foundationalism: Reflective equilibrium

Ross believes that there is an important methodological difference between ethics and natural science. We start with the empirical data obtained by sense perception in natural sciences, while obviously, moral facts are not empirical facts. In ethics, according to Ross, we have to start with the opinions of wise people. While there are some dissimilarities to suppose, opinion partly plays the same role as observation does in natural science. In this view, we have to reflect on and think about these opinions critically, remove their ambiguities and eliminate their conflicts. Ross writes in *Foundations of Ethics*,

> The method of ethics is in this respect different from that of the physical sciences. In them it would be a great mistake to take as our starting-point either the opinions of the many or those of the wise. For in them we have a more direct avenue to truth; the appeal must always be from opinions to the facts of sense perception; and natural science entered on its secure path of progress only when in the days of Galileo men began to make careful observations and experiments instead of relying on *a priori* assumptions that had hitherto prevailed. In ethics we have no such direct appeal. We must start with the *opinions* that are crystallized in ordinary language and ordinary ways of thinking, and our attempt must be to make these thoughts, little by little, more definite and distinct, and by comparing one with another to discover at what points each opinion must be purged of excess and mis-statement till it becomes *harmonious* with other *opinions* which have been purified in the same way. (1939, 3, italic added)

I think that, in this passage, Ross can be interpreted as espousing 'modest foundationalism'.[98] In fact, if we take classic foundationalism to be the view that we can know some things by inference and other things non-inferentially and that inferential knowledge is based on non-inferential knowledge, then Ross's epistemology of intuitionism is a form of foundationalism-coherentism. This is because some of those opinions of the wise *may* be justified with reference to other beliefs in a coherent whole.[99] We may come to doubt some moral intuition by having reflection on other beliefs. Thus, it can be difficult to interpret Ross as a classic foundationalist, someone who believes in an asymmetrical relation between basic and non-basic beliefs.[100] It is not the case that non-basic beliefs can be arrived at from basic ones but not vice versa. Rather, the basic moral beliefs have symmetrical relations with non-basic moral beliefs.

What we are dealing with here is something like the method of 'reflective equilibrium' before the term was coined by John Rawls in his *A Theory of Justice*. As Gaut describes,

> reflective equilibrium is not a theory, but a method, of justification; it tells one how to justify one's moral beliefs, by attempting to render consistent one's moral principles with one's judgments about particular cases. (2002, 139–40)

We seek reflective equilibrium (roughly coherence) between our moral judgements at different levels of generality. So, our very general and abstract moral principles need to cohere with our less general moral principles and so on, down to our particular moral judgements. Rawls thought that we take nothing as a 'fixed point', that is, a belief incapable of being revised. However, following epistemological intuitionists, we can take the self-evident moral propositions as at least provisionally fixed, if not utterly fixed. These self-evident moral propositions are non-inferential, although one can use reflective equilibrium (coherence) to justify them inferentially. However, these propositions do not need any other propositions to be justified inferentially.

But if at least some of the *pro tanto* duties are self-evident, then – obviously – we do not need the method of seeking reflective equilibrium (i.e. coherentist reasoning) to discover them or justify them. However, as I argued earlier, propositions can be self-evident and yet also discoverable and justifiable via inference. We might think, for example, that the best explanation of a string of particular moral judgements we confidently make is that there is a *pro tanto* duty to Φ. That we can reach this *pro tanto* duty via inference does not entail that the *pro tanto* duty is not also self-evident. Indeed, different people might reach this *pro tanto* duty in different ways – for example, Jack might reach it via self-evidence, and Jill might reach it via trying to find the best explanation of a string of particular moral judgements she makes.

Beliefs in various *pro tanto* duties might be the result of moral intuition (construed as seeming) or might be the result of seeking reflective equilibrium. We can get their justification from reflective equilibrium even if we do not have the moral intuition that they are correct. This entails that the pursuit of reflective equilibrium sometimes reveals to us a *pro tanto* duty we had not previously intuited. For example, Jack might not have had a pre-theoretical belief about promise-keeping, but then is brought to see that there must be such a duty in order for his firm moral intuitions about various cases to make sense. Jill might not have seen that there is a moral duty of gratitude, but then she comes to see there must be such a duty in order for her firm moral intuitions about various particular cases to be correct.

On the other hand, although the pursuit of reflective equilibrium can reveal *pro tanto* duties we had not seen before, the pursuit of reflective equilibrium is often unhelpful to reveal all-things-considered duties in different cases. It seems to me often wrong to reserve reflective equilibrium for the discovery of all-things-considered wrongness in particular cases. Here is why.

Suppose someone tells me that it is always wrong to harm one innocent person in order to help others. Suppose that I reply by citing a case in which I can save a billion innocent people by stepping on some innocent person's toe hard enough to bruise it. Once we understand the proposition that it is not all-things-considered morally wrong to step on some innocent person's toe hard enough to bruise it if this is the only way to save billions of innocent people, we are struck with the moral intuition (construed as seeming), and form the belief, that this proposition is correct. Now that was a moral intuition and belief about all-things-considered moral wrongness, and not one arrived at via reflective equilibrium.

Now suppose I pose a different thought experiment. Is it always morally permissible to harm someone when this would produce a greater overall net benefit? Suppose Sarah could harm Jack in some way that would benefit Jill slightly more than it would harm Jack. Again, most of us would have the moral intuition (construed as seeming) that harming one innocent person for the sake of bringing some slightly larger benefit to someone else is morally wrong. Our belief about this does not seem to come via reflective equilibrium.

What inclines me to think that the pressure to achieve reflective equilibrium will not be much help in the case of all-things-considered duties is the idea that normally, the pressure to achieve reflective equilibrium comes into principles with judgements about particular cases. Comparing principles at different levels of generality might also come into play to achieve reflective equilibrium. In fact, one might think that the billion people/toe cases posed in the previous paragraphs involve a comparison of principles with different generality. Because one is about harm/benefit in general, the other is about micro-harm/mega-benefit. Furthermore, the billion people/toe cases seem to show that the 'negative' *pro tanto* duty not to harm the innocent does not always outweigh the 'positive' *pro tanto* duty to help others/prevent harm, and therefore that the principle that it is always all-things-considered wrong to harm an innocent person is false. Let me explain.

Suppose someone holds the very general principle that an act cannot be all-things-considered or even *pro tanto* wrong unless someone is harmed. Suppose this person also holds the less general principle that all acts of promise-breaking are *pro tanto* wrong. Unless this person has the ridiculous view that all acts of promise-breaking harm someone, this person has moral principles at different levels of generality that do not cohere. In the face of the conflict here, some people give up on the less general principle that all acts of promise-breaking are *pro tanto* wrong, and others instead give up on the more general principle that an act cannot be all-things-considered or even *pro tanto* wrong unless someone is harmed (I myself give up here on the more general principle). Examples of attempts to achieve reflective equilibrium between principles at different levels of generality could be multiplied ad infinitum.

Finally, I am not claiming that beliefs about all-things-considered duties *cannot* get their justification from the method of reflective equilibrium. All I claim is that moral intuition qua moral intuition (construed as seeming) can be enough to justify beliefs about all-things-considered duties. Moral intuition is enough, absent undermining defeaters. Otherwise, moral intuitions could not be sufficient to justify.

2.2.4 Particularism and generalism

In this section, I will show that Rossian ideas about *pro tanto* and all-things-considered duties can be classified into generalistic and particularistic views. I show that Ross is a generalist about *pro tanto* duties and a particularist with respect to some all-things-considered duties. The decision about appropriate all-things-considered duty is dependent on the situation of each particular case, whereas *pro tanto* duties are general, since the status of promise-keeping, for instance, in new cases, is clear in advance and always has positive moral valence.

To illustrate, consider that I have promised my kids that I will take them to the park at the weekend. Unfortunately, my wife becomes sick at the weekend and cannot find anybody else to stay with her. So she asks me to stay with her all weekend. Obviously, there is a conflict between my *pro tanto* duties here. On the one hand, I have a *pro tanto* duty of fidelity to keep my promise to my kids, and at the same time, I have a *pro tanto* duty of gratitude to my wife, which I owe her for the many favours she has done for me in the past, and she needs me to be with her. As I mentioned earlier, according to Ross, if I encounter such a situation, it is not clear at all in advance which duty is the all-things-considered duty.

In contrast, if I am confronted with just one *pro tanto* duty, I obviously have to do what it requires, so my all-things-considered duty would be clear. However, in the earlier case, to find out which *pro tanto* duty is my all-things-considered duty, I need to determine which one is more important, and clearly, I cannot do this by resorting to general principles. Ross clearly says that no pre-existing second-order principle can be used to resolve the conflict between different *pro tanto* duties in *every* particular case. The only way in which we arrive at a plausible account of an all-things-considered duty in cases of conflict between *pro tanto* duties, Ross believes, totally depends on our moral perception or rational judgement. As Ross, following Aristotle, put it: 'The decision rests with perception' (1930, 2002, 42n).

The idea behind generalism is that a moral feature can contribute to moral judgements about different cases in a similar way. According to this approach, the ultimate moral result is not clear in advance and may vary from case to case. The way in which a moral feature contributes to the moral judgement of various cases is invariant, though the ultimate result can vary depending on other moral features that contribute to the moral status of the act.

What, then, can be said about the particularity of all-things-considered duties? Particularists, in general, say that 'moral judgments are not or should not be based on general principles' (Sinnott-Armstrong, 1999, 2).[101] Ontological particularists claim that there are no general moral principles. Epistemological particularists, however, say we do not know a general moral principle because it is always possible that we will find a new moral feature that overrides what we now take to be an ultimate moral principle.[102] Yet, this does not, generally, imply scepticism; all it implies is that we cannot infer from the fact that C is a moral reason *here* that C will be a moral reason *anywhere else*.

It seems that one might be able to distinguish between two kinds of particularism with regard to Ross's all-things-considered duties: ontological particularism and epistemological particularism. Ross thought that there are no principles of all-things-considered duties. In addition to that, in his view, we do not know that there are not. Ross says that beliefs about all-things-considered moral duty are

> more or less probable opinions which are not logically justified conclusions from the general principles that are recognised as self-evident. (1939, 31)

Since, in the case of all-things-considered duties, we infer a probable opinion (or a fallible judgement) from more general and self-evident principles, our justified beliefs about all-things-considered duties are not non-inferential. It becomes clear that for all-things-considered duties, Ross does not use the kind of justification that he uses for *pro tanto* duties. Therefore, it seems that beliefs about all-things-considered duties are not *generalizable*, according to Ross.

However, there are some particular cases in which we have, at least, one all-things-considered duty, so it can be generalizable. And this could be a problem for Ross's idea that all-things-considered duties in particular cases are not generalizable. For example, consider a case where keeping my promise would produce 1,000 units of good and breaking it would produce 1,001 units of good. Assume we really do know that act-utilitarianism's verdict about all-things-considered duty in this particular case is mistaken, and this is why we are utterly justified in rejecting act-utilitarianism. This argument employs the premise that we really do know that act-utilitarianism's verdict about all-things-considered duty is mistaken in this particular case. But it seems that, of course, we can generalize this conclusion to any other case in which only promise-keeping and beneficence are relevant, and the amount of impersonal good produced by breaking the promise is just slightly greater.[103]

We can restate the Rossian view about generalism and particularism by considering the distinction between 'moral valence' and 'moral weight again'. Every *pro tanto* duty has an invariant and constant deontic valence, which does not vary from case to case; however, its weight may vary. Suppose we are considering a case in which just one pro tanto duty, like promise-keeping, is morally relevant. In that case, the weight of this moral consideration determines our all-things-considered duty. We are able to generalize this case to similar cases where other things are equal. But suppose we have more than one morally relevant property in play, and there is a conflict between the morally relevant properties. In that case, we have several invariant deontic valences and different moral weights, which can vary from case to case.

To conclude, Ross generally holds morality is grounded in a limited number of principles of *pro tanto* duties. He embraces the view that there is an irreducible plurality of moral principles, duties or fundamental moral considerations. In cases in which two or more *pro tanto* duties come into conflict, each *pro tanto* duty contributes to the deontic status of the act. The ultimate outcome or all-things-considered duty depends on the way in which these *pro tanto* duties, or more precisely, the features they pick out, are combined together. There is no higher-order principle that can enable us to find out what our all-things-considered duty is in such cases. In order to find this out, we have to use our rational judgement and decide for ourselves.

In the epistemology part, I elaborated that Ross can be interpreted as espousing a kind of modest foundationalism that holds that there are some self-evident moral propositions (basic propositions) and non-basic propositions with a symmetrical relation, and they can support each other mutually. These self-evident propositions are not necessarily obvious; rather, some of them need reflection to be seen. Finally, our beliefs about *pro tanto* principles are fallible, and it may be found after reflection that they are false.

Up to now, I have tried to outline different important elements of the Rossian intuitionist framework both in normative ethics and epistemology. I have also tried to qualify and elaborate on some smaller points within each section. This could help us to have a big picture of what Ross did for moral intuitionism. I shall now evaluate the Rossian intuitionists' epistemological claims after spelling out each in turn in the next section. In order to do that, I repeat some points discussed earlier as we need to have a clear picture of Ross's intuitionist framework before going on to discuss contemporary moral intuitionism in the next chapter.

3 Evaluating Rossian framework: Spelling out the problem of explanation

We can distinguish at least three claims in the Rossian ethical framework, that is, two metaphysical claims and one epistemological one.[104] According to the

> *first metaphysical claim*: There are several (five) *pro tanto* duties or principles which are general. These principles determine the moral status of actions and contribute to the moral evaluation of concrete ethical situations.

And according to the

> *second metaphysical claim*: There is no hierarchy for these *pro tanto* duties, i.e. it is not the case that some *pro tanto* duties automatically outweigh any other in cases where they conflict. *Pro tanto* duties combine together and contribute to the deontic evaluation of different cases in such a way that we cannot know what would constitute the ultimate outcome (all-things-considered duty) in advance or even afterwards.

The second claim is controversial and must be explained. The issue is whether there is some way of thinking of *pro tanto* duties as a flexible hierarchy. For example, as a commentator, Dancy believes that there is no structure to Ross's five basic *pro tanto* duties. Dancy thinks no sense can be given to the claim that promises are more important than, say, good production. So, in his view, it is not true that one duty is more important than another. This leads Dancy to hold that there is no hierarchical order between *pro tanto* duties. Instead, we have a formless list of duties. Dancy writes,

> There is no general ranking of the different types of *prima facie* duty.... There is just a shapeless list of them. (1991a, 221)

However, Dancy's interpretation might be wrong. In *The Right and the Good*, Ross lists five duties. He thought that these five basic duties or principles are the minimal number of such duties or principles.[105] Ross says that some *pro tanto* duties are more stringent than others, and in fact, he offers a flexible hierarchy for them. He states that the duties of non-maleficence, fidelity and reparation are weightier than beneficence.[106] Elsewhere, in the *Foundations of Ethics*, he says that the *pro tanto* duty to keep a promise can be cancelled under certain conditions, and in those circumstances, the fact that one has made a promise carries no deontic weight.[107] Yet, the duties of non-maleficence, fidelity and reparation do not *always* outweigh beneficence. All Ross can say is that reparation, for instance, can be overridden only by a significant amount of well-being for others. However, an account of 'significant' can vary from case to case.[108]

Thus, the bottom line is that, on the basis of Ross's position, we cannot produce a higher-order principle to establish which *pro tanto* duties are more important than others. In fact, 'the importance' or weight of each duty turns out differently in different contexts. So, we can restate the second claim this way. According to the

> *second metaphysical claim-revised*: There are no rigid hierarchies (such as a lexical ordering) between *pro tanto* duties, according to which one is always more important.[109] Although there is no such thing as a rigid hierarchy for *pro tanto* duties, there might be a flexible hierarchy for them.

In many cases, one can think of a sort of flexible hierarchy for pro tanto duties; for example, we can imagine that non-maleficence, fidelity and reparation *generally* outweigh beneficence. But it is not the case that we have a rigid hierarchy in that, for example, fidelity *always* outweighs beneficence. What is supposed to be the difference between the original version of the second metaphysical claim and the revised version is that although neither version accepts a rigid hierarchy, the second metaphysical claim states that there is no hierarchy for *pro tanto* duties, but the revised version states that there might be a flexible hierarchy for them.

Finally, according to the

> *epistemological claim*: The basic principles of *pro tanto* duties are self-evident in the sense that they *can* be known directly though sometimes they need reflection.[110] We *often* are justified in believing these moral principles non-

inferentially.¹¹¹ In order to arrive at a moral judgement about our all-things-considered duty in a concrete moral situation, we have to use our *rational judgement*; however, these judgements are not self-evident.¹¹²

Taking some principles as self-evident does not entail that they are obvious and that there is no debate about them.¹¹³ We conclude the ultimate outcome of the combination of principles of pro tanto duty by looking at the case and reflecting on it in more detail to arrive at a moral judgement. Note that this is not a matter of non-inferential knowledge. The reason is that there is no such thing as a higher set of moral rules that can guide us to arrive at moral judgements.¹¹⁴

However, based on these claims, critics such as John Searle (1987, 81–90) object that Ross's metaphysical and epistemological accounts of all-things-considered duties, and the way in which different *pro tanto* duties are combined together and contribute to the moral evaluation and judgement in *moral conflict* cases, are vague and unclear. Let us call this

> *The Problem of Explanation*: Ross did not give us any clear explanation of the combination of *pro tanto* duties, i.e. *how* principles of *pro tanto* duties can combine. Following from this, he did not explain *how* we could arrive at overall justified moral judgements.

This, however, needs to be qualified. As I have shown earlier, in the Rossian framework, we cannot determine in the abstract what would be the ultimate outcome of a case in which, for example, fidelity is combined with another *pro tanto* duty, say gratitude, because the ultimate outcome strongly depends on the details of the case. Yet, as there is no rigid hierarchy for these principles of *pro tanto* duty, we have to judge how they combine together and contribute to the moral evaluation of the case. In order to do that, we pick out the outcome of the combination of several principles of *pro tanto* duty when we look at the case carefully and through further reflection on more details. So, according to Ross, in order to arrive at an all-things-considered judgement in a concrete ethical situation, one has to consider all the principles of *pro tanto* duties and think about the whole case and its characteristics insofar as one can. Let me elaborate this with an example of

> The *Manager Case*: Suppose that a manager of a company arranges an appointment that is crucial for the company, financially speaking. However, just half an hour before the appointment, he learns that his mother has been hospitalised following a car accident.

What is his all-things-considered duty? Would he be justified in cancelling his appointment to go and see his mother in the hospital, or should he fulfil his promise, leave his mother on her own and ask somebody else to see her? According to Ross, the manager has two different *pro tanto* duties, fidelity and gratitude (or beneficence), which come into conflict in this case. On the one hand, fidelity, which rests on the previous action of the manager, requires him to fulfil his promise. On the other hand, gratitude, which rests on the previous actions of his mother, requires him to stay with her in such a critical situation. What would Ross say if the manager asked Ross how he could arrive at a justified moral judgement in this situation?

The manager has to use his judgement to determine the outcome of this conflict of *pro tanto* duties. He must look at the case, reflect on it in more detail, and consider everything that is morally relevant. So, one can understand how different *pro tanto* duties are combined and how we can arrive at a tenable moral judgement by looking at the case and reflecting on it in more detail. In fact, there is no other thing here to which we can appeal. Just exercise more reflection on the case, use your *judgement* and decide.

Critics, however, are not persuaded by the earlier Rossian story because they are confused about how 'reflection' or 'looking' is an explanation of anything. Consider again the manager case provided earlier. Later on, if the manager says that he still cannot see the point, what should he do to grasp the more weighty principles of *pro tanto* duties? According to the earlier story, the manager has to look at the case again, look again and use his judgement. That is all. He cannot say anything else. So, the manager has to look at the case over time to arrive at a justified moral judgement. Nevertheless, the manager can say, 'I am still perplexed, and I do not know straight off what to do.'

Critics believe that the manager is not, in effect, offered an account that tells him which is the most important of the conflicting *pro tanto* duties. Although the Rossian metaphysical account of the combination of principles of *pro tanto* duties in moral conflict cases and their contribution to the moral evaluation of different cases is understandable, the epistemological Rossian account is obscure. Thus, it seems that the Rossian account of *how* we could arrive at justified moral judgements in moral conflict cases has to be revised.

The problem of explanation is not, I think, compelling. First of all, it is based on the classical account of *pro tanto* duties, that is, the *first metaphysical claim*.[115] Principles of *pro tanto* duties can be understood in another way, that is, in terms of reasons that might help to respond to the critics.[116] Furthermore, critics fail to see some evidence in Ross about how we can arrive at moral judgements. Let me explain.

In his *Second Thoughts in Moral Philosophy*, Ewing talks about *pro tanto* duties and all-things-considered duties with reference to reason. He distinguishes between a good and a conclusive reason for action.[117] Having a *pro tanto* duty to do an action provides a good reason to do (or not to do) it. To have an all-things-considered duty for doing an action provides a conclusive reason for doing or not doing that. Of course, it is not the case that wherever there is a good reason to do X, there is also a *pro tanto* duty to do X. That is, it is not the case that if one has good reasons to do things, then one has a real duty of any kind to do them. For instance, I have a good reason to take a painkiller right now but no duty to do so. Although one can think that duties (or obligations) provide reasons, it is not plausible to say that reasons provide duties (or obligations), and hence we cannot accept that there are duties if there are reasons. As another example, imagine that I have been very generous to Oxfam. I nevertheless have a reason to spend even more money on that charity, the reason being that even more will do even more good. However, if I have already made very big contributions at a large cost to my own good, I have no duty to make further contributions.[118]

Following Ewing, Urmson and Stratton-Lake, I believe that understanding *pro tanto* duties in terms of reasons, that is, providing moral reasons to do acts, is more persuasive than the classic understanding.[119] Principles of *pro tanto* duties specify facts that provide moral reasons for certain actions and explain why certain acts ought or ought not to be done. This is a kind of reply that Ross can give with regard to how *pro tanto* duties are combined.

However, one might object that it is not helpful to convert talk of *pro tanto* duties into talk of reasons. This conversion makes us pay a theoretical cost. All *pro tanto* duties are universal, although they can be outweighed. They are defined in terms of their force and have an element of *insistence* in them.[120] But reasons purely as such do not have such an element. As a response, to be sure, *some* reasons explain and justify but do not insist, and others do insist.[121] The morally important reasons are mainly the ones that insist. For the sake of argument, by 'moral reasons' here, I mean the insisting ones. Again, talking about insistence lends some credence to the point I made earlier about duties providing reasons and not *vice versa*.

Principles of *pro tanto* duties specify moral reason-giving facts. These principles state which facts provide reasons. I am not claiming that duties themselves are facts that provide reasons. The duty might be 'to meet you at 1:30'. The fact that provides the reason is 'that I promised to meet you at 1:30'. Hence, the *pro tanto* duty of fidelity entails that the fact that I have promised to Φ gives me a moral reason to Φ.

This understanding of *pro tanto* duties in terms of reasons allows us to think of the conflict of *pro tanto* duties as a conflict of *moral reasons*. Therefore, to put my understanding of principles of *pro tanto* duties in a general form: if F is the feature that is *pro tanto* right and contributes to making Φ your all-things-considered duty, then

> If F explains why you ought to Φ, then F gives you a reason to Φ. (Stratton-Lake, 2011a, 369)

So fidelity, for instance, is a right-making feature. In other words, there are facts that provide reasons arising from fidelity; fidelity has an invariant deontic valence, and it contributes to the moral evaluation of different cases in the same way.[122] But has the explanation problem been solved?

It is true that Ross said that looking at a moral case and reflecting on it gives us an account according to which we can arrive at a tenable judgement. This is how Ross expresses the point:

> When I am in a situation . . . in which more than one of these *prima facie* duties is incumbent on me, what I have to do is to study the situation as fully as I can until I form the considered opinion (it is never more) that in the circumstances one of them is more incumbent than any other; then I am bound to think that to do this *prima facie* duty is my duty *sans phrase* in the situation. (1930, 2002, 19)

However, this is not the whole story. In some complicated cases, Ross would suggest that where relevant, we should aim to get further information, which might (for example) involve asking people what they are up to. He said that reflecting upon other cases might help us. Consider the following quote from Ross:

> The general principles of duty are obviously not self-evident from the beginning of our lives. How do they come to be so? . . . we see the *prima facie* rightness of an act which would be the fulfilment of a particular promise, and of another which would be the fulfilment of another promise, and when we have reached sufficient maturity to think in general terms, we apprehend *prima facie* rightness to belong to the nature of any fulfilment of promise. What comes first in time is the apprehension of the self-evident *prima facie* rightness of an individual act of a particular type. From this we come by reflection to apprehend the self-evident general principle of *prima facie* duty. (1930, 2002, 32–3)

In my view, we can develop the Rossian account by using the notion of 'seeing other similarities' and seeing things as *similar*. Although Ross did not use these terminologies, I believe they already have a place in the Rossian framework. So, we can say that in the Rossian framework, *looking away* at other similar cases is an indispensable ingredient to understanding. Sometimes, just *looking at* one case and *reflecting* on it might not help us to reach a justified moral judgement. I believe *looking away* is important because one of the most significant and familiar forms of moral thinking involves thinking about cases *like* the one at hand but with the crucial difference that the roles are reversed – for example, we have to think of ourselves as being on the receiving end of what we are considering doing to someone else. Let me explain my view with the following example.

> *The Robbery Case*: Consider the case of a man chatting to his friend that one day when he was in a rush to his meeting, he saw two boys hitting an old woman to steal her money. Having seen this scene, he decided to stop them, but he also wanted to be punctual at his job. When he tells the story, his friend responds that the man should have helped the woman even if he was in a rush. The man tells his friend that he was trying to keep his promise to be on time. However, his friend gives the man more details by citing examples of what he would do if he saw his mother or sister getting robbed. His friend also gives some more examples to illustrate that helping people in danger is more important than punctuality.

In fact, the man's friend tries to convince him that he would not do the same in the case of his mother's robbery. His friend also tries to convince him by referring to other *similar* cases that helping people in danger is more important than being on time. His friend does not appeal to common properties and intrinsic features of stealing to improve his argument. So, instead of just looking at this case, the man has to *look away* at similar and dissimilar cases and ask other people to arrive at the judgement.[123]

According to Ross, different *pro tanto* duties are combined together and contribute to the moral evaluation of cases in different ways. But, on the basis of the element that I highlighted in the Rossian framework, we can give an account to resolve the problem of explanation: *looking away* at similar combinations of *pro tanto* duties in different cases and getting opinions from other people can help.

We now have an account of how we behave reasonably in different ethical contexts grounded in how we are engaged in *looking away* at *similar* cases. In doing so, our behaviour in different contexts makes sense. One can understand how different principles of *pro tanto* duties are combined and how we can arrive at tenable moral judgements by looking at other *similar* cases, asking other people and *reflecting* on the different comparable reasons in more detail.

The more the man looks away at similar cases in the robbery case, the more he can see whether he should have helped the woman. Similarly, in the *manager case*, he will arrive at the justified moral judgement to the extent that he is engaged in seeing *similar* cases. There is no theoretical account available that can be used to crank out the justified moral judgement. Rather, he has to *look away* at *similar* cases to see what has to be done in the case. For example, if the manager sees other similar cases, it is very likely that he comes to the conclusion that he should abandon his promise under the new condition.

However, there is one possible objection here. One might ask: Does not 'looking away', 'reflecting on other cases' or 'getting opinions from others' just generate a regress? If our object is the judgements of others or merely other similar factual situations, the same problem arises. As a response, although there are some complex situations where our reaching a final judgement is difficult, and we might need to ask others' opinions, Rossians would believe that this does not necessarily create a regress. Almost all pluralists and at least some monists (e.g. Kantian Contractualists and Rule-Utilitarians) might do the same in reaching the final judgement. So, this is not a special problem – if it is at all – for intuitionists. They all need to think about difficult cases and consult with other people. In the cases where the judgements of others or similar situations are at stake, the only plausible answer which Rossians can advise is to practise more and more. All we have, in these cases, is to practise reflection, comparing cases and getting opinions from others. But looking away at some other cases (such as cases in which you are in my shoes and I in yours) and getting other people's opinions might be enough to stop an infinite regress as they give us plausible reasons to reach a judgement. Although there is no such thing as a valid principle for resolving all regresses in different moral cases, it does not follow from this that nothing can be said to explain how to deal with such regresses.

3.1 Practice brings you mastery

We have seen how we can address the problem of the explanation of *how* different principles of *pro tanto* duty are combined. The same approach can be assumed with regard to the way in which we become competent with the principles of *pro tanto* duties. We can see that promise-keeping is right with practice and through seeing the similarities and dissimilarities, for example, seeing that that is a promise, that this is a promise, that that is not a promise and so on.[124] The more we are engaged in seeing moral cases, the more we see how the principles of *pro tanto* duties work. For instance, if we are wondering whether or not the new situation we are dealing with can be regarded as an example of gratitude, we have to *look away* at other cases of gratitude and compare the case at hand with them.

According to Ross, we arrive at moral principles about *pro tanto* duties by seeing what features of actions count either morally for or morally against actions in different instances. Perhaps, when Ross is talking about *sufficient mental maturity* and its vital role in grasping a *pro tanto* duty, he has something similar in mind. Consider the following quote:

> when I reflect on my own attitude towards particular acts, I seem to find that it is not by deduction but by direct insight that I see them to be right, or wrong. I never seem to be in the position of not seeing directly the rightness of a particular act of kindness, for instance. (1939, 171)

For Ross, seeing a number of examples helps us see the *rightness* or *wrongness* of promise-keeping (or seeing the fact that states the *reasonableness* of promise-keeping). One could arrive at the general principle that promise-keeping is a *pro tanto* duty by seeing different cases. The more we see different promise-keeping cases, the more we see what promise-keeping is. In effect, in Ross's ideas, we come to know the *rightness* or *wrongness* of moral duties or principles by knowing particular instances. For instance, we come to know that promise-breaking is *pro tanto* wrong by becoming acquainted with some particular cases of promise-breaking.[125]

The whole point is that the procedure of grasping a moral principle is open-ended. It does not follow from this that there is no such thing as a principle. What does follow is that the more we are engaged in seeing different cases, the more we see what the principle is. In other words, the more we are engaged in seeing different *reasons*, the more we acquire mastery of how the *reasons* can contribute in different moral cases.[126]

4 Conclusion

This chapter was about the epistemological constituents of classic moral intuitionism. Although I argued for different 'moral intuitionisms', I particularly highlighted and outlined the Rossian intuitionist framework epistemologically. However, the Rossian ethical framework, critics have argued, has a problem concerning explanation. According to the problem, how different principles of *pro tanto* duties are combined and make all-things-considered duties, both metaphysically and epistemologically, is vague and unclear. In order to tackle the problem, I introduced the reason-giving account of *pro tanto* duties and suggested that by bringing in the notion of 'looking away' and 'seeing other similarities', which already exist in the Rossian framework, we can give an account of how we arrive at a justified moral judgement in a concrete situation. The Rossian notion of principles of *pro tanto* duties can be better understood in the light of such illumination.

In the next chapter, I deal with the contemporary moral intuitionist epistemology. I investigate how much they are influenced by classic moral intuitionists (e.g. Ross) and how they contribute to a more tenable intuitionist epistemology.

5

Towards the new moderate intuitionism
Recent revivals of contemporary moral intuitionism

1 Introduction

Having seen the central ideas of classic intuitionists, we now turn our discussion to moral intuitionism among contemporary philosophers. There are numerous analytic philosophers who have done a lot for the renewal of moral intuitionism. For example, some contemporary moderate moral intuitionists such as Robert Audi, Jonathan Dancy, Brad Hooker, John McDowell, David McNaughton, Thomas Nagel, Derek Parfit, Joseph Raz, Tim Scanlon, Philip Stratton-Lake and David Wiggins have developed and defended moral intuitionism from common criticisms.[1] Most of them focus on the epistemology of moral intuitionism, and some of them consider the normative theory of intuitionism as well. They try to show that a moderate form of intuitionism is a plausible moral theory.[2] In order to do so, they redeploy the ideas of non-inferentiality, fallibility and classic foundationalism in a more tenable way. I do not have enough space here to elaborate on the works of all these intuitionists. Going forward, Audi's epistemology of moral intuitionism will be the centre of my attention.

In the previous chapter, I contended that the important feature of modest classic moral intuitionism is the idea that self-evident moral propositions are justified not only by moral intuition but also in other ways. Moreover, some moral intuitions and basic moral beliefs are defeasible and thus subject to revision and even rejection.

In moderate moral intuitionists' view, and that of some classic moral intuitionists, some basic moral beliefs are capable of more than one kind of inference. That is to say, basic and non-basic moral beliefs have mutual relations in the sense that they can be nourished and inferred from each other. As Audi puts it, moderate epistemic foundationalism 'is committed to unmoved movers; it is not committed to unmovable movers' (1998b, 208). So, moderate moral intuitionists are not committed to classic foundationalism; rather, they believe in epistemic foundationalism along with the reflective equilibrium method.

Moderate moral intuitionists have tried to propose a theory for moral intuition and self-evidence. They also tried to explain the relationship between these two central concepts in intuitionist epistemology. I have already sketched Audi's theory of moral intuition in terms of belief-like states (*cf.* Chapter 2). In this chapter, I will spell out his theory of self-evident proposition and its application to his intuitionist framework. At the end of this chapter, based upon the seeming account of intuition (*cf.* Chapters 1 and 2), I propose an alternative theory of self-evident proposition in terms of the seeming account.

Audi has developed Rossian intuitionism along with Kantianism as a normative moral theory, but here I am more interested in his development and refinement of the epistemology of moral intuitionism. In this chapter, I will not talk about Audi's normative theory.[3] In what follows, I shall discuss the central moral intuitionists' epistemic idea of intuitive justification first. Then, I will examine the concept of self-evidence. I elaborate on the idea that even self-evident propositions might have inferential justification though they do not need it. Finally, I elaborate on the Audian version of moral intuitionism, which he calls 'ethical reflectionism'. I also address some common criticisms of epistemological intuitionism.

2 Intuitive justification

Audi's version of moral intuitionism adopts a Rossian style of intuitionism. Audi follows Ross in many ways; however, he does not take up Ross's account of self-evidence and intuitive justification. Audi reads Ross as denying that a self-evident proposition can be known inferentially and non-inferentially at the same time because, in Audi's view, Ross holds that principles of *pro tanto* duties do not admit of proof. However, as I have shown before, Ross endorsed in a separate article, three years before *The Right and the Good*, the idea that although self-evident propositions are known and justified non-inferentially, this does not entail that they *cannot* be justified inferentially.[4] That is, a self-evident proposition, which can be known non-inferentially, can be justified inferentially as well.

Nevertheless, Audi himself believes that although the intuitive justification of some moral beliefs is non-inferential, it does not entail that those moral beliefs *must* be justified non-inferentially. Rather, those beliefs *can* be justified by inference as well. Therefore, it is possible to have inferential justification for moral beliefs that are also intuitively justified. Audi writes,

> There can be a moral theory that both explains and provides inferential grounds for moral propositions which, given sufficient reflection, can also be seen, non-inferentially, to be true. What is, at one time, only a conclusion of reflection – and in that way a candidate to be an intuition – can become a conclusion of inference. It can still derive support simultaneously from both the newly found premises and any remaining intuitive sense of its truth – an appropriately non-inferential, pre-theoretical sense of its truth may survive one's inferring it from premises: seeing a thing in a new light need not prevent one's still seeing it in its own light. (1993, 305)[5]

In his epistemology of moral beliefs, Audi distinguishes two different kinds of inferential justification: *justification from below* and *justification from above*. Justification from below is a justification that derives intuitively justified moral principles such as the Rossian *pro tanto* duties from a more fundamental principle such as the Categorical Imperative. Audi writes, for example, that 'from . . . categorical imperative . . . one might try to derive the Rossian duties'.[6]

On the other hand, the justification from above, which is the central element of the intuitionist epistemology for Audi, is a kind of justification compatible with the method of reflective equilibrium. In this kind of justification, according to Audi, although we have some intuitively justified moral principles, we can evaluate them in such a way that if they have intuitively plausible and attractive consequences, this gives us further justification for believing them. We reflect on them and consider whether they are still 'intuitively appealing'. As Audi puts it,

> We might, for instance, contemplate a life in which we recognize duties of beneficence versus one in which we do not, and consider whether, in the light of what we really think about those lives and about the beneficent social practices they would imply, the relevant duties still seem to be *prima facie* duties, as opposed to, say, mere charities or even meddling with others. (1996, 119)

Audi goes on and says that if the consequences are intuitively appealing, then we have additional evidence for those principles.[7]

Intuitive justification, according to Audi, is defeasible, and intuitive beliefs are fallible. Intuitive beliefs can be revised, modified and even rejected. 'Further reflection' on some of our intuitions or intuitive propositions can help us to understand that some of them are false. For instance, suppose we have an intuitive belief that God exists. But further reflection might give us reason to believe that this is false. The concept of falsity has a sense in which the falsity of P = there being a reason not to believe P. In fact if P is false, there is not only a reason not to believe P but also a conclusive reason not to believe P. When further reflection helps us to understand that P is false, there is a reason that P is false.[8] For example, suppose someone asserts that the first human to live more than 200 years will have brown eyes. Suppose further that reflection reveals that this assertion is actually false. Thus, there is a reason now that the assertion is false.

Nevertheless, the fallibility of moral intuitions does not imply that their justification is only inferential and that they depend on other beliefs even for their *prima facie* justification. Rather, they still can have some initial non-inferential justification.[9]

But how can revision of an intuition in virtue of further reflection be at all reliable? Why should one trust the new intuition? Further reflection might reveal that we have at least a reason against some of our intuitions. After we revise our intuitions in virtue of reflection, we might have a reason to believe them unless we find another reason against them. Suppose I have a moral intuition that P. Then I reflect and find that I have some reasons to reject P – for example, P does not fit well with my other moral beliefs. So, although I have a reason to believe that P, namely that P *seems* true, I have a reason not to believe that P, namely that P does not fit well with my other beliefs. So, reflection makes our intuitions reliable because it gives us plausible justification to believe them unless we find a reason to abandon them.

Audi advocates modest foundationalism in his epistemology. As stated in the previous chapter, modest foundationalism is a form of foundationalism that is compatible with the method of reflective equilibrium. The kind of justification that is acquired by moral intuition, in modest foundationalism, is non-inferential, initial and defeasible and, at the same time, intuitively justified beliefs are capable of inferential justification. Hence, moral beliefs *can* gain their justification from the method of reflective equilibrium.[10] Derek Parfit, for example, supports this sort of epistemology when he writes that

> Though it is intuitively clear that certain acts are wrong, most of our moral beliefs cannot depend only on such separate intuitions. We must also assess the strength of various conflicting reasons, and the plausibility of various principles and arguments, trying to reach what Rawls calls *reflective equilibrium*. The kind of intuitively-based reflective thinking is not only, as Scanlon writes, the best way of making up one's mind about moral matters . . . it is the only defensible method. (2011, Vol. 2, 544)

One might, however, object that this sort of epistemology needs to be explained, as it seems to be inconsistent with other elements of moral intuitionism, say, the idea of self-evidence. Moral intuitionists like Audi need to explain how they combine the notion of inferentiality with self-evidence. The method of reflective equilibrium obviously focuses on inferential justification, which seems far from intuitionists' focus. But as I clarified earlier, so long as there is intuitive justification, inferential justification is optional, that is, unnecessary but permissible. Although this response is initially compelling, in the next section, I investigate Audi's notion of self-evidence to see how he can manage to marry inferentiality and non-inferentiality. Furthermore, Audi needs to be clear about how one can employ various things to reflect on self-evident propositions, albeit without drawing any inferences.

3 The concept of self-evidence: Changing the cliché

Audi tries to refine and categorize the idea of self-evidence, as he wants to shape his own view of moral intuitionism, which he has dubbed 'ethical reflectionism'. Moral intuitionists like Audi believe that some propositions are self-evident if, and only if, an understanding of them is sufficient justification for believing them and is sufficient to know the proposition, provided one believes them on the basis of one's understanding of them. He characterizes self-evident propositions such that

(1) if one can sufficiently understand them, then in the light of that understanding, one is justified in believing them, and
(2) if one believes them on the basis of that understanding, then one can know them.[11]

Of course, one might know that p even if one does not know that p is self-evident. In other words, '[w]e do not need to know that p is self-evident to know that p on the basis of an understanding of it' (Stratton-Lake, 2002b, 20).[12] Thus, for the sake of clarity, we can distinguish between

(a) knowing a self-evident proposition
    and
(b) knowing that this proposition is self-evident.

Apprehending the *truth* of a self-evident proposition is one thing, but apprehending its *self-evidence* is another thing. It is the understanding of the truth of a self-evident proposition that is all a moral intuitionist needs to claim.[13] Because one might know some self-evident propositions but might not know that they are self-evident. However, it is not true that (a) and (b) are not connected at all, for to know that a proposition is self-evident, one needs at least to know the self-evident proposition in question based on adequate understanding.

To illustrate, consider young children who know certain simple, self-evident mathematical propositions but do not even have the concept of self-evidence at all. Similarly, we can have rational and reasonable beliefs even if we do not have any beliefs about reasons. Parfit, for example, observes that

> Young children respond rationally to certain reasons or apparent reasons, though they do not yet have the concept of a reason. (2011, 118)

When we refer to an adequate understanding of a self-evident proposition, provided one believes that proposition, this does not entail that one *necessarily must* believe it. Self-evident propositions are knowable on the basis of a sufficient understanding of them. But understanding does not necessarily cause one to believe them. To understand a proposition entails 'being able to apply it to (and withhold its application from) an apparently wide range of cases, and being able to see some of its logical implications' (Audi, 1998a, 22). If one does not have the ability to draw at least one inference *from* the proposition in question, one probably does not really understand the proposition.

In Audi's view, since self-evident propositions are those propositions one can justifiably believe on the basis of adequately understanding them alone, Audi's view makes it sound like self-evident propositions must be all *a priori* truths.[14] This is because, on the one hand, we merely need adequate understanding for justifiably believing in self-evident propositions. On the other hand, this condition is what we need for justifiably believing *a priori* truths. Audi, for example, notes that this proposition is self-evident: 'The mother-in-law of my father's son-in-law is my mother.' If one has an adequate grasp of this proposition, one can know it to be *true*, provided that one believes it on the basis of this understanding. For self-evident moral propositions are such that we can know them to be *true* on the basis of understanding them adequately and need not be known on the basis of any other things beyond a grasp of the proposition itself. Audi claims that such moral knowledge is *non-inferential*.

According to Audi, we can distinguish the notion of self-evidence into two types, from two aspects in terms of understanding. First, we have 'hard' self-evident and 'soft' self-evident propositions.[15] Second, we have 'immediately' self-evident and 'mediately' self-evident ones.[16] A hard self-evident proposition is

(1) strongly axiomatic, in the sense that there is no other proposition which is better justified than it, (2) immediately understandable, in the sense that it does not need reflection to be understood, (3) indefeasibly justified and (4) cognitively compelling, in the sense that if one understands it one cannot resist believing it.[17]

However, Audi believes that a soft self-evident proposition has none of these features. Soft self-evidence, Audi thinks, can hold for all Rossian *pro tanto* duties.[18] Nevertheless, it is hard to believe that Audi is committed to an exhaustive dichotomy between hard and soft self-evidence. Perhaps there is a continuum from completely soft (none of (1)–(4)) to completely hard (all of (1)–(4)). If so, then a proposition that has some but not all of (1)–(4) can still be a hardish proposition.

Audi believes that hard self-evident propositions are often found in logic and mathematics. So, comparing self-evident moral propositions such as *pro tanto* principles to mathematical propositions is an epistemological mistake, which some classic moral intuitionists, for example, Ross, committed. Audi thinks that 'moderate intuitionism' does not commit this mistake. He writes, for example, 'I believe that the kind of self-evidence to which a moderate intuitionism is committed lies quite far at the soft end' (1998a, 24).

Furthermore, an immediately self-evident proposition is, Audi says, 'readily understood by normal adults', in the sense that its truth is immediately obvious or clear upon the understanding. Mediately self-evident propositions, however, are endorsed or accepted 'only through reflection on them' (1998a, 22). For example, a proposition like 'a bachelor is an unmarried man' is an immediately self-evident proposition. Audi himself uses the phrase 'luminously self-evident' when he talks about very clear propositions that do not need reflection to accept them.[19] However, consider, for instance, the self-evident proposition introduced by Audi as a self-evident proposition that is not obvious and needs further reflection to find its truth or falsity: 'if there have never been any siblings, there have never been any first cousins' (1996, 114). Whenever propositions are self-evidently true (no matter whether the self-evidence is immediate and hard, or soft and mediate), they are knowable non-inferentially, or, as Audi says, '[i]f they are even mediately self-evident, they may be taken to be knowable non-inferentially' (2004, 23).

Nevertheless, one might be sceptical of how Audi's discussion of reflection generally is supposed to work. Although there are some self-evident moral propositions mediated through reflection, we need to be clear about the consequence of this claim. How is it possible that one reflects on a self-evident proposition but still remains non-inferentially justified?

This question leads us to the idea that this section started with earlier, that is, the relation between inferentiality and self-evidence. In order to explain how self-evident moral propositions mediated through reflections work, we should discuss what it means when we say that self-evident moral propositions might have both inferential and non-inferential justification. Although Audi does not use this terminology, in the next section, I introduce a distinction between two concepts, that is, 'self-evident truth' and 'self-evident justification', to give a plausible explanation of how reflection might work in Audi's framework. This distinction, I believe, helps us better understand contemporary moral intuitionist epistemology.

However, before going to the next section, I want to consider the two following points about hard and soft self-evident propositions.

(1) Although most 'hard' self-evident propositions such as many mathematical and logical propositions are justified non-inferentially, there are at least some hard self-evident propositions, for example, 'every integer greater than one, either is prime itself or is the product of prime numbers', that *can* be justified inferentially. Likewise, 'soft' self-evident propositions *can* be justified inferentially. 'Hard' self-evident propositions are often accepted at first sight, but 'soft' self-evident propositions need reflection in order to be persuasive.[20] Of course, reflection and mental maturity are matters of degree, but this does not entail that the justification that emerges after further reflection *must* be inferential.[21]

(2) Recall that being a self-evident proposition does not entail that it is obvious to everyone. Some self-evident propositions may need lots of reflection to believe. However, there are some self-evident propositions that can be accepted easily without any effort. Of course, people might not believe a self-evident proposition if they do not understand it. And some people cannot know a self-evident proposition because they believe it on the basis of inadequate understanding.[22]

3.1 Self-evidently justified versus self-evidently true

Immediately self-evident propositions like 'all vixens are female' do not need a high level of understanding for justification, according to Audi's version of self-evidence. We easily and immediately accept and believe the proposition 'all vixens are female' (if we know the meaning of vixen). Immediately, self-evident propositions, which we can instantly realize the truth, are 'self-evidently true' to us. These self-evident propositions are presented to us as true, and we do not need any further reflection to believe them.

On the other hand, although some immediately self-evident propositions are self-evidently true and everybody can understand and accept their truth, at first sight, there are also some mediately self-evident propositions that might not be known easily and need further reflection to be understood adequately. Such further reflection might involve drawing inferences from the proposition so as to understand it better. But this does not entail that they *cannot* be non-inferentially justified because one might know some self-evident propositions non-inferentially but might know that they are self-evident inferentially.

Mediately self-evident propositions do need further reflection. Reflection is needed to have an adequate understanding of the proposition. The truth or falsity of this sort of proposition is not known before reflection and at first sight. It is possible that a proposition that one considers to be self-evidently true may turn out not to be true, as we see after more and more reflection.[23]

Nevertheless, to reject a proposition based on reflection does not imply that the proposition was not initially intuitive or non-inferential. For example, in Copernican physics, some axioms or postulates were thought to be self-evident. The scientific community then saw the emergence of Newtonian or Einsteinian physics, which has some parallel self-evident axioms.[24] This illustrates the possibility that an *apparently* self-evident proposition may be shown to be incorrect after further reflection by other scholars in one scientific society. Similarly, this could happen in the area of morality when we discover that some *apparently* self-evident moral propositions are not true.[25]

Since it is hard to accept mediately self-evident propositions, at first sight, one can think that these propositions are not self-evident. We might need further reflection to understand them adequately as self-evident. The more we reflect on a proposition, the better we find out whether it is self-evident or not. However, some further inferences might be needed to know (justify) that some mediately self-evident propositions are actually self-evident. Thus, since some inferences might be needed to know that some mediately self-evident propositions are actually self-evident, it is better to call mediately self-evident propositions 'self-evidently justified'.

The elements which have been discussed so far in Audi's epistemology, such as intuitive justification and different classifications of self-evidence, will gather together to establish his framework in the epistemology of moral intuitionism as the method of 'ethical reflectionism'.

4 Reflectionism as a method

To make moral intuitionism more tenable, Audi outlines a method he calls 'ethical reflectionism'. To explain the method of reflectionism, Audi appeals to what philosophers of science label 'context of discovery' and 'context of justification'.[26] The standard formulation of the context of discovery and the context of justification is that they are distinct in the sense that we discover something through processes and justify or test it later by different methods.[27] In Audi's view, although we have some non-inferential moral intuitions (context of discovery), we *can*, but do not necessarily, use further evidence to justify them (context of justification). What Audi must mean here is that although there is some non-inferential moral intuition with the content that P, we *can* use further evidence to justify P. Although Audi's reflectionism involves inferential justification at some points, this does not entail that reflection is necessarily about coming to see P as inferentially justified. Because, in Audi's view, we do not necessarily need to use inferential justification on every occasion. After all, reflection is supposed to come into play *after* we already have intuitions.

However, my favoured account of intuition is different from Audi's doxastic account of intuition. According to my account of moral intuitions as seemings, moral intuitions as mental states cannot be justified. But these seemings can justify beliefs with the same contents as the seemings. And these beliefs can get additional justification by fitting coherently with other things we believe (*cf.* Chapters 2 and 4). Furthermore, my account of reflection is different from what Audi appeals to as reflection. Although Audi is right about using reflection, I believe he is not clear on how reflection provides non-inferential justification. We need to explain what reflectionism maintains to see if it is not the case that P is inferentially justified. At the end of the chapter, I will return again to the idea of reflection, raise my criticism and propose my understanding of reflection.

Audi noted not only that there is no contradiction between foundationalism in Rossian intuitionism and the method of reflective equilibrium but also that he is happy to say that his method of reflectionism is compatible with the method of reflective equilibrium.[28] He thinks that he builds up 'the most credible form of ethical intuitionism' by this combination.[29] This credible form of moral intuitionism is a

> fallibilist, intuitionist moral rationalism that uses reflection as a justificatory method... encompassing both intuitions as *prima facie* justified inputs to ethical theorizing and reflective equilibrium as a means of extending and systematizing those inputs. (1993, 311)

In Audi's view, the method of reflectionism 'is and deserves to be our basic method for justifying ethical judgments' (1993, 308). This method helps us in 'justifying, refining, or discovering general moral principles' (1993, 311).[30] Audi thinks that the common attack on moral intuitionism that it postulates a strange faculty that can recognize moral truths is rejected when we enter the method of reflectionism. For this method, in Audi's view, understands moral intuition as an ability or capacity by which reflection might be improved. So reflection plays an important role in the new moral intuitionism.[31] Audi states that some moral believers are justified since they have beliefs based on reflection. But is having reflection or adequate understanding sufficient for justification?[32]

What makes the content of moral intuitions justified is controversial among moral intuitionists. For example, Russ Shafer-Landau holds that the justification comes from a reliable process. Tolhurst states that the justification of moral intuitions comes from experience and appearances. Finally, Mark Timmons believes that justification comes from social contexts.[33] Sinnott-Armstrong calls these intuitionists 'reliabilists', 'experientialists', and 'contextualists', respectively.[34] I do not have space to discuss these philosophers' accounts in more depth. However, at the end of the chapter, I will come back to the issue of whether reflection or mere sufficient understanding can justify us in believing self-evident propositions. While I argue that Audi's account is not persuasive and we need to seek an alternative, I present the seeming account of self-evident propositions.

But, before doing that, we need to consider other objections to Audi's version of moral intuitionism. Audi himself has replied to many of these common criticisms. Some of these replies can be found in his seminal work, *The Good in the Right*.[35] In the next section, I shall briefly address some important criticisms, along with replies.

5 Moral intuitionist epistemology and common criticisms

In this short section, based upon what I have discussed as Audi's epistemological intuitionist framework, I try to offer responses to some common objections against moral intuitionism. Although at some point, this might be repetitive, I try to respond to them in the way in which Audi responds.

The first common objection is related to the claim that intuitionism is dogmatic.[36] Korsgaard, for example, says that if someone asks an intuitionist whether one ought to do some particular act, all an intuitionist can say is, 'Yes, it is true that you ought to do this because it is self-evident.' But if one says that he does not see the truth of self-evident propositions, all that intuitionists can do is assert that they are true dogmatically. This implies that intuitionists are committed to dogmatism since they believe that our intuitions about self-evident propositions are supposed to have indefeasible justification. Audi's epistemology, however, does not say that intuitions have indefeasible justification. His version of intuitionism provides a place for *reflection* and *inference*, and he admits only defeasible justification of moral beliefs.[37]

Another criticism is related to being arbitrary. Critics often say that moral intuitionism is arbitrary because using intuitions to make judgements can be arbitrary. However, in Audi's view, we are not entitled to use *all* intuitions to make judgements. Since Audi's version of moral intuitionism distinguishes between *reliable* and *unreliable* moral intuitions, this objection fails (*cf.* Chapter 2). As I explained earlier, in Audi's account, only reliable moral intuitions that are derived from 'the exercise of reason', sufficient understanding or the method of reflective equilibrium can be used to make judgements. A sufficient understanding of moral judgements often requires further reflection, and this may lead us to appeal to the method of reflective equilibrium.[38]

But critics again object with the following argument: how can intuitions be intrinsically reliable if it takes reflective equilibrium to establish their reliability? It seems that the reflective equilibrium is doing all the work. As I said before, intuitionists, including Audi, believe that there are some self-evident moral propositions that we have intuitive beliefs about. They are intrinsically reliable as they are justified on their own unless we find at least a reason against them. We can also justify that they are reliable by doing further reflection or using reflective equilibrium. However, this is not necessary since one might be justified based on intrinsically reliable intuitions without using reflective equilibrium. So, the reflective equilibrium is not doing all the work, as it is optional.[39]

The last objection to moral intuitionism relates to disagreement about moral intuitions. Critics think that disagreement shows that appealing to intuition is not a reliable means for the justification of moral beliefs. They say that if we have intuitions about basic self-evident moral principles, then why do we still have many controversial debates in ethics? However, in Audi's view, some basic moral principles are self-evident but mediately self-evident. They are not obvious and need reflection and discussion. Audi says, 'we should not expect ready consensus on them, or even a high degree of consensus after some discussion or reflection' (1998a, 28–9).[40]

Given that what Audi says about disagreement is generally plausible, disagreement is not a special problem for intuitionists. Almost all ethical theories, for example, Kantians, Utilitarians and Virtue Ethicists, might have disagreements among their scholars. Although intuitionists, for example, Audi, believe that moral intuitions are carrying some non-inferential self-justificatory weight, they do not believe that there is no disagreement about these non-inferential intuitions. Disagreements might even help intuitionists to modify their intuitions. Nonetheless, we should bear in mind that although there are some disagreements among intuitionists, there are many agreements among them about some moral intuitions.

Keeping the big picture of Audi's epistemology of the moral intuitionist framework in mind, we are now able to focus on his claims and evaluate (or develop) them within the moral intuitionist tradition.

6 Evaluating and developing Audi's epistemological intuitionism

Sidgwick tried to establish a systematic account of self-evidence, that is, to elaborate what it is for a proposition to be self-evident. He mentioned at least three conditions for self-evident propositions: (1) the proposition must be clear and precise; (2) reflection needs to ascertain the proposition's self-evidence; (3) self-evident propositions must be consistent. Sidgwick believes that these conditions are for 'a significant proposition, apparently self-evident, in the highest degree of certainty attainable' (Sidgwick, 1967, 211–12, 342–88).[41] Parfit clarifies Sidgwick's view about self-evidence in this way:

> When Sidgwick calls our knowledge of some normative truths *intuitive*, he is not referring to any special faculty. Sidgwick means that we can recognize the truth of some normative beliefs by considering only the content of these beliefs, or *what* we are believing. These beliefs do not need to be inferred from other beliefs. Sidgwick also calls some of these beliefs *self-evident*. In using this word, Sidgwick does not mean that such beliefs are infallible. These beliefs, he claims, may need careful reflection, and they may be false. Such beliefs may merely seem to be self-evident. These beliefs may also be *indubitable*, or *intrinsically credible*. Such credibility is a matter of degree. (2011, Vol. 2, 490)

Now recall Audi's account of self-evident propositions. In almost the same way, he believes that self-evident propositions are propositions, a *sufficient understanding* of which provides *sufficient justification* for believing and knowing them. Thus, a proposition is self-evident when it is a *truth*, such that a sufficient understanding of it satisfies the two conditions as follows.[42] Audi's description of self-evidence, then, becomes

> *Audian Self-evidence*: A self-evident proposition is a truth such that
> (a) In virtue of having an adequate understanding of the proposition, one is justified in believing it.
> (b) If one believes the proposition on the basis of an adequate understanding of it, then one knows it.

Some critics, such as Tropman (2009), believe that Audi's account of self-evidence does not explicitly make room for particular self-evident propositions. This is because Audi himself admits that his view rules out the self-evident particular moral truths.[43] Audi grants that moral intuitionists need only claim the *general* self-evident moral principles or 'generic intuitionism'.[44] In Tropman's view, while Audi's notion of self-evidence helps us to see how *general* moral truths such as Rossian principles of *pro tanto* duty are evident to us in themselves, his account does not care about the self-evidence of *particular* moral truths, such as those moral truths in *concrete* cases. Yet, in what sense are particular propositions self-evident if not in Audi's sense?

Tropman would argue that we could still have particular self-evident propositions like general ones in Audi's sense, although his account does not explicitly entail that. In her view, we can develop Audi's account to cover a non-inferential real-world-particular knowledge of moral facts. For example, consider a particular propositional belief such as 'the lie my brother told yesterday was *pro tanto* wrong'. Tropman believes that we can learn substantive moral facts about the action in question solely by reflecting on the conceptual meaning of 'my brother's action'. A particular act of lying is self-evidently wrong because knowledge of self-evident truths depends totally on the conceptual meaning of the constituents. So, the proposition can be qualified as self-evidently true.

Furthermore, we can argue that if the general principle, say, lying is wrong, is self-evident, then it will be self-evident that any particular act of lying would be wrong. If the general proposition is self-evident, why cannot the particular instance be? For example, if it is self-evident that the fact that an act counts as a lie is a *pro tanto* reason not to do the act, then how could it not also be self-evident that the fact that this particular act counts as a lie is a *pro tanto* reason not to do the act? Hence, once again, Tropman would maintain that Audian self-evidence should consider a non-inferential real-world-particular knowledge of moral facts.

However, one might object that this kind of arguing can be problematic in some cases. It is true that in some moral cases, if there can be self-evident general propositions, then there can be self-evident particular ones too. For instance, if it is *pro tanto* wrong to rape someone for pleasure, it is also self-evidently wrong that Jack rapes Jill. However, this cannot be true in any case of, say, mathematics or geometry. For example, if it is self-evident that any triangle's angles sum up to 180 degrees, then it is not self-evident that this triangle's angles sum up to 180 degrees. The reason for this is that it is not self-evident that 'this is a triangle'; rather, it is something we establish by looking at the object, not by *a priori* reflection. Nonetheless, one can respond to this objection that, as far as conditional propositions can be self-evident, a proposition such as 'if this is a triangle, its angles sum to 180', looks like an intuition about a particular self-evident in geometry. In fact, by having established that this is a triangle, we can know straight off that this triangle has 180 degrees.

Whether or not my argument or Tropman's argument for particular self-evident moral knowledge can work, we certainly can think of different moral particular self-evident propositions in our daily life. It seems obvious that a particular truth may be adequately understood, so it may be known on the basis of that sufficient understanding. For example, in the case of my brother's lie or a proposition such as 'my friend killed her husband for fun', we can have a morally relevant particular self-evident proposition by reflecting on the nature of a lie or killing. Following some classic intuitionists who consider particular self-evidence, we can take a broad view of particular self-evident propositions in terms of adequate understanding.

For example, Clarke and Prichard, as two classic intuitionists, tended to seek self-evident propositions more often in concrete and particular cases.[45] They thought that individuals just see some specific (obligatory) actions. In fact, although these philosophers discussed the idea of self-evidence, they suggested that we can think of something like the *intuitive perception* of moral facts when we are faced with particular concrete moral cases.

Ross also seemed to believe that *pro tanto* duties in concrete situations could be self-evident. He thought that the first thing that came to mind was the particular *pro tanto* self-evident duties in concrete cases.[46] Consider, for example, this passage from Ross:

> [W]e see the *prima facie* rightness of an act which would be the fulfillment of a *particular* promise, and of another which would be the fulfillment of another promise . . . What comes first in time is the apprehension of the self-evident *prima facie* rightness of an *individual* act of a *particular* type. From this we come

by reflection to apprehend the self-evident *general* principle of *prima facie* duty. (1939, 170, emphasis added)

Ross thought that the self-evidence of *pro tanto* rightness or wrongness of a *particular* action comes to our apprehension, even if we do not recognize the relevant *general* moral principle.[47] However, by reflecting on different similar and dissimilar particular actions, we can form self-evident general principles. For Ross, these particular moral facts come to our cognition non-inferentially in the sense that some particular moral beliefs are credible independently of their inferential relations to general moral principles.

Although Audi calls his intuitionism 'Rossian style intuitionism', his version of intuitionism does not say explicitly much about particular moral facts as he defines self-evidence in terms of generality. However, following Ross, we can say something plausible about independently credible moral judgements about particular situations.

Related to that point, although Audi follows Rossian intuitionism, it seems that Audi's account of self-evidence does not make room for the psychological element of presentationality (*cf.* Chapters 1 and 2). By the psychological element of presentationality, I mean something like what Ross thought about the self-evident proposition as 'spontaneously or immediately evident in itself'. This implies that our moral intuitions about self-evident propositions might *present* themselves to us involuntarily. However, Audi's notion of self-evidence focuses on an epistemic element, that is, 'understanding', when he says that a self-evident proposition 'could be known on the basis of an adequate understanding of the proposition'. Although Audi's account could have a presentational element, since the belief could be based on a presentation, he does not mention that it presents itself as true once we understand a self-evident proposition.

On the other hand, Audi rules out the psychological element of presentationality from his theory of moral intuition. Let me remind the reader that Audi's definition of 'moral intuition' is typically to believe the truth of self-evident moral propositions non-inferentially (*cf.* Chapter 2).[48] He actually defines intuitive moral knowledge in terms of self-evident propositions and describes moral intuition with reference to a doxastic element, that is, *belief.* Although a doxastic account of moral intuition might have a psychological element, Audi's account does not have one. Since Audi defines moral intuition with reference to self-evident proposition and his account of moral intuition is doxastic, Audi's theory of self-evidence does not make room for the psychological element of presentationality.

One might object that it is not plausible to have a psychological account of self-evidence – because, strictly speaking, the term 'self-evident' can only apply to a proposition or statement. Self-evidence is not a mental state. A belief thought of as a proposition or propositional content can be self-evident, but a belief thought of as a psychological state cannot be self-evident.

Yet, I am not saying that we can have a psychological account of self-evidence. What I want to defend here is the existence of a psychological element (presentationality) in moral intuition. If we understand moral intuition in terms of something other than belief, that is, a seeming state, we can have a psychological element of presentationality in moral intuition. Audi, I think, confines his theory of moral intuition to belief-like states (i.e. the doxastic view).[49] If he wants to have a comprehensive theory of moral intuition and self-evidence, he must make room for the psychological element of moral intuition. In the next section, I will come to this point to give my alternative account of self-evidence based on a non-doxastic account of moral intuition, that is, seemings, which introduces a psychological element. However, before that, let me complete my discussion of Audi's account of self-evidence about particular propositions.

Although Audian self-evidence does not clearly say anything about particular moral self-evident propositions, I want to highlight one element in Audi's epistemological framework, which one might think of as something similar to particular self-evidence, albeit he does not say this directly. It seems that Audi has something similar to particular intuitions about self-evident propositions in mind when he talks about 'conclusion of reflection'.[50] As I stated before, since intuition can be yielded by reflection, Audi thinks we are able to distinguish between two categories of conclusion, that is, 'conclusion of inference' and 'conclusion of reflection'. An intuitive self-evident proposition can be the conclusion of an inference. Likewise, it can be the conclusion of reflection (*cf.* Chapter 2).

Audi gives two examples to make clear what exactly this distinction is. Suppose someone reads a letter of recommendation that refers to itself as 'strong'. It is possible to infer that the recommender means 'strong' in another way, that is, actually means weak, as the recommender never directly praises the applicant. The reader forms the judgement that the recommendation letter is not really strong by picking points that show the recommender does not directly praise the applicant. Since this judgement is based on an inference from evidence, Audi calls this a 'conclusion of inference'.

On the other hand, as an example for 'conclusion of reflection', one might see a subtle commitment and indirect praise in the letter. It is possible that one simply *feels* elements of 'strength'. In this case, Audi believes, since the judgement is made by global intuitive sense and reflection, unlike the conclusion of inference, the conclusion of reflection is supposed to be non-inferential. In fact, the conclusion of reflection is a result of reflecting upon the *overall nature of some phenomenon* as a *whole*.

However, it might be objected that although Audi did not directly connect the idea of conclusion of reflection to the particular intuition, it seems that 'conclusion of reflection' cannot be a good example of non-inferential (self-evident) propositions about *particular* facts or *pro tanto* duties. This is because a conclusion of reflection is drawn by considering *all aspects* of its phenomenon and necessitates considering the phenomenon as a *whole*. Yet, a belief about a *pro tanto* duty necessitates considering just one of an act's aspects. We need not consider all of the action's features in order to gain knowledge of *particular* instances of *pro tanto* duties. So, Audi's conclusion of reflection cannot explain our non-inferential beliefs about particular concrete *pro tanto* duties.[51]

This objection is not persuasive, though. One can reflect on all aspects of a particular situation as a whole, including different self-evident facts about the situation. Also, although one could reflect on all aspects of something, there is nothing about the notion of reflection which means one must reflect on all elements. So, reflection on some parts of the situation could be sufficient.

Nonetheless, it is unclear how Audi can match the distinction between the conclusion of reflection and the conclusion of inference to his Rossian-style intuitionism. On the one hand, it seems that the idea of the conclusion of reflection is closer to Ross's *pro tanto* duties than all-things-considered duties. We come to beliefs about our *pro tanto* duties by reflection, not by inference. However, Audi thinks that our beliefs about *pro tanto* duties *can* be inferential. For example, recall his distinction between 'justification from below' and 'justification from above' (*cf.* Chapter 4). The justification from below, in his view, aims to derive intuitively justified moral principles, such as Rossian *pro tanto* duties, from a more fundamental principle, such as the Categorical Imperative.[52]

What sounds puzzling in Audi when he introduces the conclusion of reflection is that Audi does not clearly explain what reflection amounts to when he says that we can remain non-inferentially justified in reflecting on a self-evident proposition. Suppose someone reflects on a particular self-evident proposition. It seems that one needs to take account of various properties in that particular situation to believe in the proposition. However, in Audi's framework, it is supposed that taking different properties does not require someone to form a belief inferentially. How is it possible that, in reflection on something such as a situation, we are supposed to take in various properties of the thing and then, without drawing any inferences, reach a self-evident truth about the thing?

The objection, in fact, is that it just does not seem plausible that reflection does not involve drawing inferences. To understand Rossian principles adequately or reflect on self-evident propositions, we sometimes need to consider and form judgements involving drawing inferences from hypothetical scenarios. This leads us to think that inferences drawn play a role as premises for the overall conclusion. For example, consider the self-evident proposition such as 'when an equal amount is taken from equals, an equal amount results'. When one reflects on this proposition, one might need to draw some inferences to adequately understand it.

Audi tries to provide an answer to sceptics such as Sinnott-Armstrong (2007), who raise this issue (*cf.* Chapter 2). Audi believes that forming a belief by attaining an adequate understanding (or reflection) does not necessarily involve inferences. In his view,

> the perception of a property can ground a judgment without doing so by yielding beliefs that supply premises for that judgment. Consider, for instance, facial recognition regarding someone you have not seen for many years. If the judgment that the person is, say, an old friend from high school, arises from thoughtfully contemplating facial properties, but is not based on beliefs of supporting propositions, we may call it a conclusion of reflection even if the person could formulate 'corresponding premises'. The judgment may, then, be both non-inferential and intuitive. (2007, 204)

However, Audi's example of facial recognition is not illuminating, in large part because facial recognition is very unlike recognizing the truth of a self-evident proposition. Even in contemplating facial properties, it is not clear whether there is a dependency on a proposition in a way that is, in fact, *not* inferential. So, it is not obvious that Audi's move can avoid the objection about inference.

Nonetheless, it is not true that reflections (or adequate understanding), at all times, necessarily involve inferential justification.[53] Although there are some difficult cases in which reflections explicitly work as an inference, I believe there are still some cases where reflection does not work as an inference. In my view, to attain reflection (or have an adequate understanding) about a proposition, one needs (1) to have at least the capacity to tease out the meaning of the constituents; (2) to be able to use the terms correctly and apply them reliably and (3) to draw some inferences *from* the proposition in question. In fact, these three conditions together make our understanding adequate or reflection sufficient. But none of these conditions makes us form an explicit argument or inferential reasoning.

Hence, although for having a sufficient reflection, one needs to be *able* to draw some inferences, this does not entail that one *must* actually go through drawing inferences when one considers a proposition. Furthermore, even if one draws some inferences in order to reflect on a proposition's meaning, this need not involve forming an explicit argument or inferential reasoning. This account of reflection makes our beliefs non-inferential. Drawing inferences to form an explicit argument or reasoning makes us inferentially justified. But merely having the capacity to draw inferences does not cross the line into inferential justification.

There are clear cases where we have a non-inferential belief based on a reflection about a proposition. For example, by having reflection on the meanings of the constituent words in the proposition 'all squares are rectangles', we are non-inferentially justified in believing the proposition. Reflection on the meanings of the words in the proposition is not an argument. On the other hand, for the proposition 'helium is twice as heavy as hydrogen', we need some proof, inferential reasoning or argument to show that it is true. There are some clear cases of reflection *without* explicit argument. There are some clear cases of reflection *with* explicit arguments. I do not deny that, in some cases, it is unclear whether we need an explicit argument. For example, in the proposition 'God probably necessarily exists', it is not clear whether we need an explicit argument or just the ability to understand the meanings of the constituent words in order to be justified based on reflection.

This account of reflection and adequate understanding allows us to have direct content when we consider a self-evident proposition. So, it seems more likely that we are non-inferentially justified when we form our beliefs on the basis of adequate understanding or reflecting on self-evident propositions. Thus, if one believes a self-evident proposition on the basis of reflection or adequate understanding, one can non-inferentially know it.

7 An alternative account to Audian self-evidence

Moral intuition and self-evidence are two important aspects of intuitionist moral epistemology. Most moral intuitionists talked about each of them separately. For example, as we have seen, Audi treated intuitions as something like belief and defines a self-evident proposition in terms of understanding and non-inferential justification. Although moral intuition is a type of mental state and self-evidence is a property of propositions, we need to discover how they are related. Let us start with self-evidence.

Almost all epistemological intuitionists maintain that there are some moral propositions that are self-evident. For example, Locke says that a self-evident proposition is one that 'carries its own light and evidence with it, and needs no other proof: he that understands the terms, assents to it for its own sake' (1969, 139). Or Richard Price believes that a self-evident proposition is immediate and needs no further proof.[54]

However, contemporary moral intuitionists such as Audi and Shafer-Landau never include the element of obviousness in their account, and yet they define a self-evident proposition in terms of understanding. This definition of self-evidence is currently the standard understanding of self-evidence among moral intuitionists. For example, Shafer-Landau writes,

> Beliefs are self-evident if they have as their content self-evident propositions. A proposition p is self-evident=df. p is such that adequately understanding and attentively considering just p is sufficient to justify believing that p. It is possible that agents who adequately understand and attentively consider just p may yet fail to believe it; for instance, other beliefs of theirs may stand in the way. If I have a standing practice of believing whatever my guru tells me, then his say-so in a given case may be sufficient to prevent me from believing a self-evident proposition that I understand and have attentively considered. Still, if I do get all the way to believing a self-evident proposition, my belief is justified. (2003, 247)[55]

In Shafer-Landau's view, one's adequate understanding of self-evident propositions is sufficient to justify believing them. On that view, if one adequately understands a self-evident moral proposition, such as 'it is *pro tanto* wrong to rape anyone', one's mere understanding can justify one to believe the proposition. But I believe it is not plausible that a mere adequate understanding can be evidence to justify our belief. Let me explain.

We can doubt whether an adequate understanding of a self-evident moral proposition is evidence and can justify our belief in the proposition.[56] This is because the evidence for p must be something that can give us reason to believe that p and provide justification for us. For example, the introspective experience of p provides justification to believe that p or to remember that p is the sort of evidence that can provide such reasons to believe that p. But our mere understanding of a moral proposition is not evidence and cannot provide justification for us. Although an adequate understanding of a self-evident moral proposition is needed for us to believe in something, it does not look as though that adequate understanding is evidence to provide the justification for that belief.

But this argument depends on what we mean by evidence. One might object that understanding a self-evident proposition counts as evidence for its truth, in which case my argument is wrong. Or one might object that understanding a self-evident proposition does not count as evidence for its truth since self-evident propositions can be known true without evidence, in which case, once more, my argument is wrong.

However, such objections are not convincing if we consider my account of evidence elucidated earlier (*cf.* Chapter 3). Evidence (e) for (p), in my view, is a mental state or proposition that raises the (epistemic) probability of p being true. It is true that evidence is indeed the existence of a mental state – for example, that I am in pain or that such-and-such seemed to me to be true. But of course, not all evidence consists of mental states. So I do not deny that evidence can be a fact – for example, that there is blood on the carpet. Nevertheless, I am not using 'evidence' to mean merely 'whatever justifies belief' because it follows trivially that if understanding justifies, then it is evidence.[57] On my account of evidence, a mere understanding of a self-evident proposition is not evidence because a mere understanding of a proposition cannot raise the probability of that proposition's being true. So, on my account of evidence, a mere understanding of a proposition cannot be evidence of its truth and thus cannot justify our belief in the proposition.

If evidence is whatever raises the (epistemic) probability of p, self-evident propositions are facts (true propositions) that are inherently evidence. For example, the propositions 'all cows are female' and 'a finite whole is greater than, or equal to, any of its parts' are facts that do not need any other propositions to justify their truth. They are evidence in themselves. In other words, self-evident propositions are credible on their own independently of any other propositions. Indeed, self-evident propositions are self-justified in the sense that they are justified on the basis of their conceptual meaning.

But if self-evident propositions are facts, can we say that they are all analytic propositions? All analytic propositions such as 'all triangles have three sides' are self-evident. Analytic propositions are propositions whose truth is knowable by knowing the meanings of the constituent words and their relation. In fact, in an analytic proposition, the predicate concept is contained in its subject concept.[58]

But not all self-evident propositions are analytic. Suppose that it is self-evident that there is a *pro tanto* duty not to harm others, or at least innocent others. In other words, the fact that an act would harm an innocent person imposes on any agent a defeasible requirement not to do the act. Is the very meaning of '*pro tanto* duty' such that there *must* be a *pro tanto* duty not to harm the innocent? No. Is the very meaning of 'harm the innocent' such that there *must* be a *pro tanto* duty not to harm the innocent? No. Is the very meaning of, for example, 'justice' such that every agent *must* have a *pro tanto* duty to promote it? No. Is the very meaning of '*pro tanto* duty' such that there must be a *pro tanto* duty to promote justice? No, and the same applies to each of Ross's other *pro tanto* duties. Although self-evident moral propositions must be *a priori* truths and must be necessary truths, they manifestly are not analytic truths. However, depending on how we understand 'moral', there are some self-evident moral propositions that can be analytic as well. For example, insofar as the concept of murder is the concept of wrongful killing, the proposition 'murder is wrong' is analytic.[59]

In addition to that, all self-evident propositions such as 'all bachelors are unmarried' are *a priori*. *A priori* propositions are propositions that one can reasonably believe without empirical evidence. *A priori* propositions are justified independently of sensory experience. We can believe an *a priori* proposition on the basis of pure thought and by simple reflection on its content.

But are all *a priori* propositions self-evident? Self-evident propositions are the foundation for the *a priori*. That is, although most *a priori* propositions are self-evident, there are some *a priori* propositions that are not self-evident. For example, consider a proposition like 'all bachelors are unmarried, or Obama's eyes are blue'. The proposition is *a priori*, but it is not self-evident in itself. The proposition 'all bachelors are unmarried' is self-evident, and this can be put in a disjunction with any other proposition. The result, however, will be true *a priori* because a disjunction is true as long as one of the disjuncts is true. The disjunctive propositions with one true disjunct need not be self-evident, since one needs to know the logic in order to know that they are true, and indeed needs to make the inference: this is a disjunction with at least one true disjunct, and disjunctions with at least one true disjunct must be true. As another example, although it is *a priori* that '0.9 recurring equals to 1', it might be debated whether it is self-evident.[60] Also, for some moral philosophers, it is *a priori* that 'Happiness is an intrinsic good', but it is controversial whether it is self-evident. So, it is not true that all *a priori* truths, no matter how complex, would come out as self-evident.[61]

Thus far, I have elaborated on whether self-evident propositions are analytic and *a priori*. I have also criticized the standard Audian understanding of self-evident propositions in terms of my account of evidence. I believe it is not plausible that an adequate understanding of a self-evident moral proposition is evidence to justify belief in the proposition. If the adequate understanding of a self-evident moral proposition does not provide justification for believing it, the Audian self-evidence account is not the whole story about self-evident moral propositions. Although having adequate understanding is a necessary condition for the self-evidence account, mere adequate understanding is not a sufficient condition for that.

I believe that *intuition* is the part that can provide justification. However, this idea depends on how intuition is understood. Our theory of moral intuition can help us to distinguish intuition from certain similar mental states, such as guesses, gut reactions, hunches and commonsense beliefs. In Chapters 1 and 2, I already argued that moral intuitions are not belief-like states, and we should not understand intuitions in terms of doxastic accounts. Rather, the seeming account of intuition is better. So I propose a self-evidence theory based upon an account of intuitions as seeming states rather than mere beliefs. This theory is an alternative to the Audian self-evidence account.[62]

7.1 The seeming account of self-evident propositions

The doxastic account of intuition does not allow for cases where an intuition that p (non-inferentially) justifies a belief that p. As I argued before, on the doxastic account, the intuition that p is either the belief that p or an inclination or disposition-to-believe that p. Neither of these justifies the belief that p. The belief that p cannot justify the belief that p. The inclination or disposition-to-believe that p does not by itself justify the belief that p. It might be the case that I know that it is not true that 'I am inclined to believe that p' but this does not prevent its seeming to me to be true. Furthermore, as I said before, the inclination or disposition-to-believe account is not informative about why we should believe that p. Even if one argues that 'I am inclined to think that p and things that I am inclined to think are very often true. So in the absence of reason to think not-p, I am justified in thinking p', we are entitled to ask why one is inclined to think that p.

However, the non-doxastic or seeming account of intuition can do this. For example, a belief can be based on an intellectual seeming with the same content. So, if we regard intuition as defeasible evidence for its content, having an intuition that p can justify us in believing that p. Even if the disposition or inclination accounts of intuition can work in some cases, seemings can do this job better (*cf.* Chapter 1).

Having said that, then, we need to have a new account of self-evident propositions consistent with the seeming account of intuition. I now revise the Audian account of self-evidence. In this new account, since intuitions (construed as seemings) have the upper hand, the self-evidence account is based on intuition but not vice versa.[63] I call this account

The Seeming Account of Self-evidence: A self-evident proposition (P) is a truth such that
(a) Attaining an adequate understanding of P gives one an intuition (construed as seeming) about P.
(b) The intuition (construed as seeming) about P, on the basis of an adequate understanding of P, is what provides a justification for believing P.
(c) If one forms a belief about P on the basis of an intuition (construed as seeming) about P, then one knows P.

But how is it possible that forming a belief on the basis of both an adequate understanding and intuition can be regarded as non-inferential? This certainly depends on how we formulate our accounts of adequate understanding and intuition. As I explained before, my preferred account of intuition is non-doxastic, and the non-doxastic account of intuition does not make our beliefs inferential. I also explained how adequate understanding could lead us to be non-inferentially justified if we construe adequate understanding in terms of extracting the meaning of the constituents, being able to use the terms correctly and having the ability to draw inferences. For example, if I am considering a self-evident proposition, for example, 'All Xs are Ys', I need to adequately understand it, of course. However, understanding it requires at least knowing the meaning of 'all', 'Xs', 'are' and 'Ys'. To know the meaning of a concept involves knowing how to use it to make inferences. So to test whether I adequately understand the elements of the self-evident proposition, I might need to see if I can use each of the terms to draw inferences. The propositions in which I try to use the terms will probably be other than the self-evident proposition whose meaning I am trying to adequately understand. This exercise of testing my adequate understanding of the concepts in the self-evident proposition I am trying to adequately understand is a kind of thinking. But such thinking is not a matter of inferring 'All Xs are Ys' from other propositions. So, while it is true that I might have to test my ability to draw inferences using the concepts in the target self-evident proposition, it is not true that these inferences are being offered in support of, or as arguments to, the target self-evident proposition.

So, even if we form a belief based on an intuition that is presented (given) by attaining an adequate understanding (or reflection), there is no need to involve inferences in order to be inferentially justified. Therefore, we can believe a self-evident proposition on the basis of intuition and adequate understanding while being non-inferentially justified. If we have an adequate understanding of conceptual meaning, that is, mere semantic understanding, this gives us an intuition (construed as seeming), and we take this to be grounds for believing the self-evident propositions. Thus, we have the justification of self-evident propositions on the basis of the seeming, which comes from the proposition's conceptual semantic meaning.

However, we should bear in mind that the seeming account of self-evidence does not entail that all intuitive propositions are self-evident, as this is obviously wrong. For example, when I say 'I hate this weather' or 'It is my duty to help my mother when she is in need' or 'abortion is wrong', they are intuitive for me but for sure not self-evident. Without this qualification, we cannot have a tenable account of self-evidence. Not all intuitive propositions are self-evident; only the propositions whose seeming true are based on adequate understanding or reflection *can be* self-evident. Nevertheless, there are some basic explanatory intuitive moral propositions that normative ethicists consider self-evident but vary from one normative moral theory to another. Hence, determining which intuitive propositions are self-evident depends on our normative moral theory. But how?

Many moral intuitionists assumed that belief about *pro tanto* duties were both epistemologically and metaphysically/explanatorily foundational. However, there are some moral philosophers such as Tim Scanlon, Robert Audi, Brad Hooker and Derek Parfit who think that moral intuitionists do not have a knockdown argument that all *pro tanto* duties have these statuses. They think that *pro tanto* duties might or might not be epistemologically or metaphysically/explanatorily foundational. These philosophers think that *pro tanto* duties are not metaphysically/explanatorily foundational because they derive their moral justification from the Categorical Imperative, or a Contractualist first principle, or a Rule-Consequentialist first principle. For such philosophers, the first principles are all the most basic propositions.[64]

The seeming account of self-evidence, unlike Audi's, is not truth-entailing. Rather, it is justification-entailing. This is because the seeming account of self-evident propositions is based on seemings and moral intuitions in terms of the seeming account cannot be justified but instead can be explained. Having a moral intuition justifies our belief in the proposition's content, but having a moral intuition cannot be justified. However, one can explain why a certain proposition seems to be true but cannot justify its seeming so (*cf.* Chapters 1 and 2).

According to the seeming account of self-evidence, beliefs in self-evident propositions that are based on moral intuition can be justified. We do not need anything other than moral intuitions of such propositions, presented by sufficient understanding, to justify our belief in them. However, when we say that self-evident propositions can be justified by moral intuition, this does not entail that some other ways of justification, for example, argument, are ruled out.

The seeming account of self-evident propositions thus provides salvation for my favoured moral intuition theory. The seeming account of self-evident propositions is grounded in moral intuitions as seemings, which I think is the right account of moral intuitions, in contrast to Audi's account. Nevertheless, we can adopt some elements of Audi's account to explain why sufficient understanding is necessary for having self-evident propositions. Although it is the intellectual seeming that justifies belief in self-evident propositions, the seeming must be based upon sufficient understanding. Having sufficient understanding means that we should at least be able to extract the conceptual constituents and have the ability to make inferences *from* the proposition in question.

Seeming must be based upon sufficient understanding because some things may seem true to us just because we do not have an adequate understanding of them. For example, suppose someone tells a kid: 'if all As are Bs, and no Cs are Bs, then no Cs are A'. Anyone who adequately understands the proposition can be presented by a seeming that the proposition is true. But how can a kid be presented by a seeming when the kid does not understand it adequately?

As another example, suppose that I tell someone that 'rape is absolutely wrong' in Persian. If one does not understand any Persian words, how can one be presented by a seeming that the proposition is true? Seemings are presented to us based on our adequate understanding, although this does not make our beliefs based on seeming inferential. If by adequate understanding we mean something that is not engaged with argument, seemings and beliefs based on them might be non-inferential.

The seeming account of self-evident propositions can provide us with a new explanation of what Ross might have in mind about intuition and self-evident proposition by putting words into his mouth. Ross did not use the word 'intuition'. He often used the word 'conviction' instead of intuition.[65] When Ross writes that self-evident propositions are 'propositions that cannot be proved, but that just as certainly need no proof', he might want to say that the intuitions about self-evident *pro tanto* principles are basic and non-inferentially justified. While having intuitions can justify belief in self-evident propositions, the having of the intuitions – having the seemings – cannot be justified. Saying that self-evident propositions can, but need not, be justified by means of argument is one thing. But to say that intuition about those self-evident propositions cannot be justified is another thing. Intuitions only give us the explanation of justifiably believing in self-evident propositions. We can have intuitions about self-evident *pro tanto* principles when we gain enough mental maturity. In the same vein, Ross believes it is not the task of moral philosophy to *justify* beliefs about *pro tanto* duties. Rather, the task of moral philosophy is to *explain* how knowledge and justification are possible in ethics.[66]

Let me conclude this section. I have discussed some concerns about the account of self-evident propositions endorsed by contemporary moral intuitionists (e.g. Audi and Shafer-Landau). However, I have provided an alternative account of self-evident propositions, which I call the seeming account of self-evident propositions. Although classic and some contemporary moral intuitionists believe that self-evidence is more important than that of intuition, I think intuition is more basic if intuitions are construed as intellectual seemings.

8 What is left: A modest new moral intuitionism

This is the end of Part II. In Chapters 4 and 5, I have reviewed and evaluated the classic and moderate moral intuitionist epistemology. I focused on Ross's (and to some extent Prichard's) main epistemic ideas such as intuitive justification, non-inferentiality, self-evidence and foundationalism. I also criticized some of Ross's ideas and tried to develop his account of *pro tanto* duties in terms of reason. I then examined Audi's moral intuitionist epistemology, especially his ideas of self-evidence and reflectionism. I criticized his account of self-evidence and tried to propose an alternative account of self-evident propositions.

If I am on the right track and my criticisms and developments of Rossian and Audian epistemological intuitionism work, we need to deal with two pertinent questions. Which classic and moderate intuitionism elements can be adapted to build up a new version of epistemological intuitionism? Furthermore, how can this new account of epistemological intuitionism work against various criticisms arising especially from empirical psychology?

In the remaining chapters, I will test my new form of epistemological intuitionism against what is called 'neuroethics'. But before doing so, let me bundle up the elements of my new account of epistemological intuitionism that I have already discussed. It is right to think that since this new form of epistemological intuitionism rests on seemings, it is a kind of seeming-based epistemological intuitionism. Based on what I have discussed so far, my favoured account of epistemological intuitionism – which I call the modest epistemological intuitionism – will consist of three parts:

8.1 Ontology

(1) My favoured account of philosophical and moral intuition defines intuitions in terms of intellectual seemings, similar to perceptual experiences (*cf.* Chapters 1 and 2).

(2) There are some philosophical and moral intuitions (construed as intellectual seemings) that can be treated as evidence (*cf.* Chapter 3).

8.2 Epistemology

(3) For engaging in further reflection to reach a moral judgement, it is not enough to look at the case in question more and more. We should look away at different similar and dissimilar cases and ask someone else to reach a plausible judgement (*cf.* Chapter 4).

(4) Reflective equilibrium can be easily combined with epistemological intuitionism. Our moral intuitions are fallible and sometimes turn out to be false after reflection. Modest foundationalism, that is, the combination of foundationalism and the method of reflective equilibrium, is the theory of justification with which moral intuitionism works best (*cf.* Chapter 4).

(5) There is no necessary connection between the epistemology of moral intuitionism and taking just general moral intuitions into account. Particular moral intuitions about particular situations can be considered as well. General and particular moral intuitions together make moral intuitionism more tenable (*cf.* Chapter 4).

(6) Following Ross and Audi, I think that, although our belief in self-evident propositions is justified non-inferentially, these propositions might also be justified inferentially (*cf.* Chapters 4 and 5).

(7) Adequate understanding of a self-evident moral proposition is necessary for justification as some propositions might seem true to us while we do not have an adequate understanding. Yet where adequate understanding of a self-evident proposition gives us the moral intuition (construed as seeming) that the proposition is true, we then have justification for believing the proposition in question (*cf.* Chapter 5).

(8) My account of adequate understanding and reflection is one that should explicitly be contrasted with having an argument or inferential reasoning.

All I mean by attaining an adequate understanding or reflection is to have at least the capacity to tease out the meaning of the constituents, to be able to use the terms correctly and apply them reliably and to draw some inferences from the proposition in question while we are still non-inferentially justified (*cf.* Chapter 5). I will come back to the issue of non-inferentiality in the next part of the book (*cf.* Chapter 7).

(9) Unlike Audi's, my account of moral intuition is not defined in terms of self-evident propositions; instead, my account of self-evident propositions is defined in terms of moral intuition (*cf.* Chapter 5).

(10) According to the seeming account of self-evident propositions: attaining an adequate understanding of a self-evident proposition (P) gives one an intuition (construed as seeming) about P, and the intuition about P is what provides a justification for believing P. If one forms a belief about P, on the basis of an intuition about P, then one knows P (*cf.* Chapter 5).

(11) Following Audi, I think, to be justified in believing some self-evident propositions, one should at least be able to draw some inferences *from* them. This is the minimum condition for having sufficient understanding. If someone lacks the ability to draw at least some inferences *from* the proposition that p, then that person does not adequately understand the proposition that p (*cf.* Chapter 5).

8.3 Psychology

(12) Having emotions in our seeming account of moral intuition can explain why particular moral intuitions about particular situations do matter. This helps us to respond to empirical moral psychologists properly. I will discuss this issue in the next part of the book (*cf.* Chapter 6).

(13) Defining moral intuitions in terms of seemings has some other advantages. Since seemings can be constituted by phenomenological features, such as a feeling, mental states such as emotions can be associated with moral intuitions without causing any threats. I will discuss emotional experiences in Part III of the book (*cf.* Chapter 6).

(14) The quasi-perceptualist account of emotion can explain how emotional experiences, like moral intuitions, are similar to perceptual experiences. Both emotional experiences and moral intuition can provide non-inferential justification for beliefs. I will address this issue in Part III (*cf.* Chapters 6 and 7).

The modest seeming-based epistemological intuitionism provides an attractive, explanatory picture of how and why moral intuitions work in the epistemological intuitionist framework. Having equipped ourselves with the modest epistemological intuitionism, we are well placed to address objections raised by philosophers and empirical psychologists against the epistemology of moral intuitionism. The works of Peter Singer and Walter Sinnott-Armstrong will be my centre of attention in Part III of the book.

Part III

Neuroethics

6

Scepticism about moral intuition

How my favoured account of intuition rebuts the neuroethicists' position

1 Introduction

Intuition sceptics believe that some of our intuitions do not have any epistemic value as they fail to provide moral knowledge (D. Sosa, 2006, 633 and E. Sosa, 1998).[1] There are at least two different sorts of scepticism about intuition: conceptual and empirical.[2] The most prominent form of conceptual scepticism is raised by Benacerraf (1973), who doubts the possibility of having successful intuition and intuitive knowledge since it is not clear what we can say about a *causal* relation between intuitions and what is intuited. The most prominent version of empirical scepticism comes from empirical studies that seem to suggest that intuitions are systematically and fundamentally biased. Although these two versions are different, they reach the same conclusion. Both claim that although we can think of conditions under which intuition has a positive epistemic status, those conditions are not, or *cannot* be, fulfilled.

My purpose, however, in this chapter will be to elaborate and critically examine empirical scepticism about intuition, not philosophical scepticism. Recent empirical studies in cognitive science and neuroscience mostly have been thought to suggest numerous worrying conclusions about philosophical and moral intuitions. For instance, they claim that intuitions about knowledge are culturally dependent (relativistic), that intuitions about intentional action have a biased source, and that moral intuitions are vulnerable to emotions, ordering and wording 'frame effects'.[3] These experimental works show that different kinds of intuitions that different philosophers work with in ethics, epistemology, philosophy of action, philosophy of language, etc. are systematically biased and epistemologically unsound. Swain, Alexander and Weinberg, for example, write,

> We take the growing body of empirical data impugning various intuitions to present a real challenge for philosophers who wish to rely on intuitions as evidence. (2008, 153)

However, among these experimental works about different subjects of intuition, I focus my discussion on issues raised in cognitive science, brain science and experimental psychology about intuitions used in ethics (henceforth neuroethics). I argue that the 'growing body of empirical data' does not create a problem for moral intuitionists, and empirical data does not necessarily create a threat to the epistemic status of moral intuition. In order to do that, I will show, first, there are other empirical findings that contradict the empirical findings cited by critics such as Singer and actually support rather than undermine moral intuition's epistemic status. Second, I will offer a new non-doxastic model for the epistemology and psychology of moral intuition that presents a theory of emotion suited to moral intuition. This will show that emotions do not *always* cloud moral intuitions' epistemic status.

The plan for this chapter is as follows. In the next section, I will introduce a famous empirical challenge to moral intuition – which greatly influences the literature – raised by Singer. I then reason that Singer's evolutionary debunking argument is not justified. In the section after that, I will discuss three empirical responses in support of moral intuitions. These responses are derived from moral cognitive science and social psychology.

The plan for this chapter is as follows. In the next section, I introduce a famous empirical evolutionary debunking argument against moral intuition raised by Singer. I argue that Singer's argument is not justified. After that, I discuss three empirical projects arguing that emotions *support*, rather than distort, the epistemic standing of moral intuitions. In this way, we can appreciate that the distinction between reason and emotion is less clear-cut than many have supposed. Then, I use my theory of moral intuition, the *non-doxastic seeming* account of intuition, advocated before to build up an integrated psychological-epistemological model that accounts for the role of emotion. This model, I show, can rebut the empirical psychologists' position against moral intuition and make room for intuition and emotion to be partners rather than contestants.

2 Singer's evolutionary debunking argument for radical anti-intuition ethics

In the last decade, empirical social and moral psychologists have developed an interest in expressions of (dis)approval which are called 'moral intuitions'.

They mostly believe that moral intuitions are, in fact, nothing but 'social intuitions', and social intuitions are, for example, first impressions or *immediate responses*.[4]

Peter Singer has long argued that we should be suspicious of our intuitive moral judgements. He defines moral intuitions as relatively *unreflective* moral judgements about *particular* cases.[5] Singer reasons that much of the opposition to our daily utilitarian judgements has come from counter-utilitarian moral intuitions. To justify his radical account, Singer has given a new argument to this effect, based heavily on empirical work in empirical moral and social psychology done by Joshua Greene and Jonathan Haidt (Singer, 2005). Singer claims that this new work shows moral intuition to be methodologically and epistemologically unsound.

In this section, I try to develop a counterargument to Singer's argument. In order to do that, I start by outlining the psychological research, the discussion of Greene's moral psychology and Haidt's social psychology about moral intuitions. I do this because their empirical works are the basis of Singer's central argument. Meanwhile, I shall raise some critical points about Greene's and Haidt's arguments, although I will keep my points to a minimum as it is not the duty of this chapter to discuss Greene and Haidt in detail. The discussion of Greene and Haidt will be somewhat cursory, as my main target is Singer's substantive ethical argument. All I want to knock down is Singer's argument. At the end of the section, I come back again to Singer's main argument to see whether it is tenable.

2.1 Joshua Greene's *Moral Tribes*

Joshua Greene and his colleagues have written numerous empirical works on the psychology of moral judgements (Greene et al., 2001; Greene et al., 2004; Greene, Paxton, and Ungar, 2011; Greene, Paxton, and Bruni, 2013). Greene's most famous research programme involves using functional Magnetic Resonance Imaging (fMRI) to study certain kinds of moral judgements. Subjects are placed in fMRI machines and asked to react to various moral and non-moral dilemmas. fMRI technology shows which parts of the brain are more active during this task and, presumably, which parts of the brain are more responsible for producing the relevant judgements.

In a series of works, Greene gives a philosophical account of such experiments (Greene, 2008; 2013, Chs. 4–5; 2014; 2015). He distinguishes between 'philosophical deontology' and 'philosophical consequentialism'. Philosophical deontology emphasizes moral rules, most often articulated in terms of rights and duties. Philosophical consequentialism states that moral decision-makers should always aim to produce the best overall consequences for all concerned, if not directly then indirectly.[6] In Greene's favoured terminology, deontology refers to judgements in favour of characteristically deontological conclusions, for example, 'It is wrong despite the benefits'. However, consequentialism refers to judgements in favour of characteristically consequentialist conclusions, for example, 'Better to save more lives'.

Greene posits that if it turns out that characteristically deontological judgements are driven by emotion, then that raises the possibility that deontological philosophy is also driven by emotion. To say that our deontological philosophy is driven by emotion, in Greene's view, means that we judge an action permissible because we feel good about it or have positive emotion towards it. Greene's account, which assumes a contentious Humean theory of motivation, posits that cognitive representations are inherently neutral representations in the sense that they do not automatically trigger particular behavioural responses or dispositions. In contrast, *emotions* have automatic effects and are behaviourally valenced.[7]

Greene found that answering moral dilemmas in a consequentialist manner takes longer and that fMRI shows greater frontal lobe activity (associated with cognitive processing) correlated to these judgements. In fact, Greene found that such responses revealed greater activity in *some* areas of the frontal lobe, particularly the Dorsolateral Prefrontal Cortex (DLPFC). By contrast, answering moral dilemmas in a deontological manner happens more quickly, and fMRI also shows that there is a correlation between the brain activity in the frontal lobe but a different part associated with emotional processing in the amygdala, Ventromedial Prefrontal Cortex (VMPFC), Default Mode Network (DMN), Temporoparietal Junction (TPJ), and these judgements (Greene, 2015).

Greene's empirical research suggests that, although intuitions largely influence morality (especially non-utilitarian moralities), individuals are still capable of fair moral reasoning. In their most well-known example, Greene and his colleagues try to explain the typical pattern of responses to the 'trolley dilemma'. In particular, they explain why many people judge one way in cases like 'the switch scenario' but another way in cases like 'the footbridge scenario'.[8]

The question, in both scenarios, is this: Is it morally permissible to choose the relevant action, that is, divert the trolley or push the stranger? In both cases, the comparison is between five deaths and one. But, as experiments show, people's judgements about these structurally similar cases are very different. They judge that it is morally permissible to divert the trolley but morally wrong to push the stranger.

It is characteristically deontological to judge that an agent may not push an innocent person to his death as a means of saving five others (the footbridge scenario). It is characteristically consequentialist to judge that an agent *may* divert a threatening vehicle from a track containing five innocents to a track containing one innocent (the switch scenario).[9]

> *The Switch Scenario*: A runaway trolley is headed for five people who will be killed if it proceeds on its present course. The only way to save these people is to hit a switch that will turn the trolley onto a side track, where it will run over and kill one person instead of five. Is it okay to turn the trolley in order to save five people at the expense of one?

The consensus among philosophers, as well as people who have been tested experimentally, is that it is morally acceptable to save five lives at the expense of one in the switch scenario.[10]

> *The Footbridge Scenario*: A runaway trolley threatens to kill five people, but this time you are standing next to a heavy stranger on a footbridge spanning the tracks, in between the oncoming trolley and the five people. The only way to save the five people is to push this stranger off the bridge and onto the tracks below. He will die as a result, but his body will stop the trolley from reaching the others. Is it okay to save the five people by pushing this stranger to his death?

When the footbridge scenario is presented to both philosophers and laypeople, the general consensus is that although it is acceptable to save the lives of five at the expense of one, it is not morally acceptable in the footbridge scenario.[11]

Greene takes the psychological evidence to suggest that the thought of pushing someone to his death in an 'up close and personal' manner (as in the footbridge scenario) is more emotionally *salient* than the thought of bringing about similar consequences in a more impersonal way (e.g. by hitting a switch, as in the switch scenario). Greene's rationale for distinguishing between *personal* and *impersonal* forms of harm is largely evolutionary: he says that 'up close and personal' violence has been around for a very long time, reaching far back into our primate lineage (Wrangham and Peterson, 1996). In contrast, when harm is impersonal, it fails to trigger this alarm-like emotional response, allowing people to respond in a more 'cognitive' way – perhaps because it involves a cognitive mechanism not present in our evolutionary past.

Crucially, Greene and his colleagues argue that the difference between these responses lies in our *moral emotions*. In personal dilemmas, the harm is *obvious*, *physical* and the harmed victim is *salient* in the sense that the harm done to them is *obviously* relevant. However, in non-personal dilemmas, the harm is more *abstract*, and the harm to the victim is *not salient*. Based on this distinction, they hypothesized that often, personal moral dilemmas trigger negative morally emotional responses and that these emotional responses cause moral judgements. They also hypothesized that non-personal dilemmas do not trigger emotional responses. Moreover, subjects who gave an unusually consequentialist response to personal dilemmas (e.g. judging it is permissible to push the stranger) took longer to respond than subjects giving the typical response (Greene et al., 2008). This suggests that the unusual respondents experienced some *cognitive* conflict when they were thinking it through (Greene, 2008, 63).

Greene and his colleagues argue that deontological patterns of moral judgement are driven by emotional responses, while consequentialist judgements are driven by cognitive processes. But why should deontology and emotion go together? Here are some clues to their explanation:

1. Moral emotion provides a natural solution to certain problems created by social life. The emotions most relevant to morality exist because they motivate behaviours that help individuals spread their genes *within a social context*.
2. It seems that when nature needs to get a behavioural job done, it does so with intuition and emotion wherever it can. This means that, from an evolutionary point of view, there is no surprise that moral dispositions evolved and that these dispositions are combinations of behavioural and emotional elements. Our moral judgements are driven by a hodgepodge of emotional dispositions, which themselves were shaped by a hodgepodge of evolutionary forces, both biological and cultural.
3. Deontological philosophy provides a natural 'cognitive' interpretation of moral emotion. It is a well-documented fact that humans are, in general, irrepressible explainers and justifiers of their own behaviour. Psychologists have repeatedly found that when people do not know why they are doing what they are doing, they just make up a plausible-sounding story.[12] In fact, there is a well-documented tendency for people to rationalize their intuitive behaviour as much human behaviour appears to be intuitive in the sense that people often do not act according to their reason.[13] Rationalist deontological theories are rationalizations for these emotional responses.
4. Greene suggests that deontology is a kind of 'moral confabulation'. We have strong feelings that tell us in clear and uncertain terms that some things *simply cannot be done* and that other things *simply must be done*.

But it is not obvious how to make sense of these feelings, and so we, with the help of some especially creative philosophers, make up a rationally appealing story. The story is there are these things called 'rights' which people have, and when someone has a right, you cannot do anything that would take it away or violate it (Greene, 2008, 64). However, almost certainly nobody can claim to have such an overarching moral theory accommodating our moral intuitions, or even part of one.

In contrast, in Greene's view, consequentialism is more 'cognitive' in the sense that it is systematic and aggregative by nature. All consequentialist decision-making is a matter of balancing competing concerns, taking into account as much information as is practically feasible. The advantage of having cognitive neutral representations is that they can be mixed and matched in a particular situation without pulling the agent in multiple behavioural directions at once. Thus, the cognitive representations enable us to have highly flexible behaviour (in contrast to emotional deontology-driven response).[14]

Greene has introduced additional features in more recent statements of his view. But we need not concern ourselves with these here since Singer's argument (my main target) relies on Greene's early work.[15] Before getting to that argument, let us briefly consider Haidt's social-psychological research.

2.2 Resisting Greene's conclusion

It is not the duty of this chapter to give a complete critique of Greene's position in empirical moral psychology. However, since I believe Greene's argument is wrong, I will mention some critical worries about Greene's argument before going further. It seems there are at least two main strategies we can adopt to resist Greene's conclusion.

On the one hand, we can deny that Greene's empirical findings, in *particular*, bear on our moral philosophies. For example, cognitive psychologists and philosophers might reject Greene's methodology.[16] I believe, following Kahane et al. (2010), Greene fails to explain what he suggested as his explanandum. Assuming that Greene's (2001) explanandum is: the different pattern in moral judgements exhibited by a large majority of people in response to the Footbridge dilemma as opposed to the Switch dilemma; one might argue that it is unclear what type of moral judgement is being made by a subject in different cases. Are the subjects in the experiments judging that it is bad that someone was hurt? Are they judging that the person who, for example, pushes the stranger off is cruel, or they are judging that the person's behaviour is wrong? It might be something else. The point here is that we should not leave these questions open in our methodological research, as this does not help us answer why subjects' reactions are different in different cases.[17]

If I am right, one can cast doubt on Greene's reported findings because it remains open to the proponent of moral intuition to suggest that there are some cases where moral intuitions are not produced by 'alarm-like' responses or unreliable responses. All Greene's findings can show is that there is a correlation between emotions and moral judgements. It is still unclear whether our emotions cause moral judgements or vice versa.[18]

On the other hand, we can accept that Greene's empirical findings might have a bearing on commonsense deontological thinking but deny that this attaches doubt to the possibility of developing a coherent moral deontological theory. In other words, Greene's argument tries to knock down 'rationalist deontology', as he defined it, by saying that emotion explains judgements on morally irrelevant grounds. However, he does not consider the possibility of another form of deontological moral theory that might be compatible with Greene's empirical findings.[19]

So far, so good. Having examined Greene's experiment and his argument against the epistemic value of moral intuition as an element of Singer's main argument, we should now consider Haidt's social-psychological worries against moral intuitions since these form another element of Singer's argument.

2.3 Jonathan Haidt's *Righteous Mind*

Singer interestingly anticipates a possible objection. The objection is that one can hardly accept Greene's limited scope of research, for Greene's experiments are only about physical harm cases and cannot explain anything about non-physical harm. What can be said about cases that do not involve physical harm, such as promises and lying? Here Singer proposes another line of argument to cover non-harm cases by appealing to Haidt's 'Social Intuitionism'.

As a social psychologist, Jonathan Haidt directs attention to psychological studies of the relationship between moral reasoning and intuition.[20] Haidt, among other psychologists, distinguishes between two cognitive states or processes: the *unconscious* intuitive process and the *conscious* rational one.[21] He says, in this vein, that moral intuition is

> the sudden appearance in consciousness of a moral judgment, including an affective valence (good-bad, like-dislike), without any conscious awareness

of having gone through steps of search, weighing evidence, or inferring a conclusion. Moral intuition is therefore the psychological process that the Scottish philosophers talked about, a process akin to aesthetic judgment. One sees or hears about an event and one instantly feels approval or disapproval. (2001, 818)

In Haidt's view, intuitions, in fact, control our daily moral judgements in a *rapid* and *immediate* way. For instance, when one is asked whether rape is permissible, she would respond very *quickly* that it is obviously wrong. Indeed Haidt, like Greene, states that if you ask people to *try* reasoning, they apparently just *confabulate* plausible-sounding rationalizations, which in fact bear no fixed relationship to their actual response. Hence, claims Haidt, this shows that reasoning was *unnecessary* to the process that produced the intuition. Although I believe that intuition, construed as seeming, has nothing to do with reasoning, I try to hash out Haidt's argument as follows.[22]

In *The Righteous Mind* and his famous paper, 'The Emotional Dog and Its Rational Tail: A Social Intuitionist Approach to Moral Judgment', Haidt tries to give an account of a descriptive theory of moral judgements based on the findings of neuroscience to have a better explanation of a role for the emotions in our moral judgements.

Haidt uses subjects' responses to thought experiments concerning societal taboos (e.g. incest and bestiality) to demonstrate a phenomenon he dubs 'moral dumbfounding'. In many moral situations, when we do not have any further arguments and have run out of reasons, we say 'intuitively' that the action is simply wrong. For example, imagine that a brother and sister start having sex, and they both feel it brings them closer as siblings. Most people have a very strong negative reaction to this scenario. Their intuitions say that this is morally wrong yet cannot explain why. Haidt writes that

> Intuitionist approaches in moral psychology, by extension, say that moral intuitions (including moral emotions) come first and directly cause moral judgments . . . moral intuition is a kind of cognition, but it is not a kind of reasoning. (2001, 814)

Haidt maintains that the majority of our moral reasoning is a kind of *post hoc* reasoning. Although people often have an intuition that incest is wrong, they do not have a reason for that. Rather, they seek to rationalize their intuition after it occurs to them. In order to explain this, Haidt refers to the findings of neuroscience to show that the *ventromedial* area of the prefrontal cortex of the brain (associated with automatic heuristics, which are often emotional) effectively houses these moral intuitions.[23] This suggests that moral intuitions are produced by our emotions.

Haidt believes that our moral intuitions have been evolutionarily grown through a critical period of mental development. He writes that morality is 'an evolutionary adaptation for an intensely social species ... that is better described as emergent than as learned' (2001, 826). He also uses the 'dog-tail' metaphor to show that human beings are intrinsically like emotional dogs that can only communicate 'rationally' via tails; however, it is the emotional body that causes the tail to wag.

In a nutshell, according to Haidt, most of our daily moral judgements are intuitive in the sense that reasoning and conscious deliberation do not directly make any contribution to our moral judgements.[24] In Haidt's view, *unconscious emotional* processing is responsible for most of our ordinary moral judgement, including not just judgements about harm but also judgements about other moral domains such as fairness. Haidt holds that each moral judgement stems from something *associated with* a particular *moral emotion*.

2.4 Commentary on Haidt's argument

Once again, since this chapter is devoted to Singer's argument, I will not evaluate Haidt's account in detail. However, since I believe Haidt's argument is wrong, let me consider some general worries before getting into Singer's main argument.

First of all, Haidt fails to address the possibility that even intuitions – based on his interpretation – can store some lessons that are previously experienced. For example, in the case of 'learning a language', one's linguistic knowledge sometimes passes from short-term memory or working memory to long-term memory. So, one's linguistic knowledge gradually becomes internalized. In much the same way, we can think of some stored lessons that can be internalized in our moral intuitions by experience. In fact, one might be having the moral intuition that 'promise-breaking is *pro tanto* wrong' because one might have some stored lessons that were previously internalized by experience.

Second, the examples of moral dumbfounding he presents can be explained differently. Societal taboos can be dictated to us by prior social thought – for example, that something is wrong, and this subsequently becomes like a code.

Third, Haidt sometimes says that what appears to be reasoning is really *post hoc* reasoning. He seems to conflate reasoning and rationalizing. Rationalizing might be what he calls *post hoc* reasoning, not reasoning.

Fourth, Haidt claims that reasoning is unnecessary to the process that produces intuition. He raised this claim as a criticism, but who would disagree with Haidt on this? Those of us who think that intuitions are seeming states do not have a problem with this claim. We simply say that this claim must be true; otherwise, they would not be intuitions.

Finally, I believe what Haidt argues about moral cases can be applicable to a large portion of our non-moral judgements as well. This implies that we have little room for rational deliberation as Haidt's theory engages in a 'wholesale rejection of reason'. However, following Pizarro and Bloom (2003), we can insist that there are many people who actively engage in reasoning, from morality to mathematics, in the real world.

Having discussed the Greene and Haidt research that Singer relies upon,[25] I now focus on Singer's main debunking argument. I argue that his argument is not justified.

2.5 Singer's attack: Evolutionary biology and the debunking of moral intuitions

Singer employs Greene's results in empirical moral psychology and Haidt's social psychology to support his argument against the epistemic status of moral intuition. However, Singer adds to the psychological work just described by invoking general principles of evolutionary psychology, which he builds towards an *evolutionary debunking* of moral intuition. Singer writes,

> Our biology does not prescribe the specific forms our morality takes. . . . Nevertheless, it seems likely that all these different forms are the outgrowth of behavior that exists in social animals, and is the result of the usual evolutionary processes of natural selection. Morality is a natural phenomenon. No myths are required to explain its existence. (2005, 337)

Per Greene and Haidt, our moral intuitions are produced by *emotional* processes. And this mechanism probably evolved in response to the selection pressures faced by our ancestors who lived in small societies. Singer writes,

> This becomes clearer when we consider how well Greene's findings fit into the broader evolutionary view of the origins of morality . . . . For most of our evolutionary history, human beings have lived in small groups, and the same is almost certainly true of our pre-human primate and social mammal ancestors. (2005, 347)

In Singer's view, evolutionary processes of selection shaped the moral psychology we have today, including the moral–social psychology that produces intuitions that are not reliable. In fact, our moral intuitions and convictions are pervasively shaped by evolutionary processes. So, moral–social psychology and evolution together can give us an explanation of how we *have* access to some of our moral intuitions. According to this explanation, we have intuitions because we have a certain psychological-mental mechanism that produces them, and we have that mechanism because of our evolutionary history. Singer then concludes that

> while I have claimed that evolutionary theory explains much of common morality, including the central role of duties to our kin, and of duties related to reciprocity, I do not claim that this justifies these elements of common morality. I am a supporter of an evolutionary approach to human behavior, and I am interested in ethics, but I am not an advocate of an 'evolutionary ethic' . . . Advances in our understanding of ethics do not themselves directly imply any normative conclusions, but they undermine some conceptions of doing ethics which themselves have normative conclusions. Those conceptions of ethics tend to be too respectful of our intuitions. Our better understanding of ethics gives us grounds for being less respectful of them. (2005, 343 and 349)

Singer's main debunking argument against moral intuition can be articulated as follows:

> (P1) The content of certain human systems of morality, that is, commonsense deontological morality, including the content of moral intuitions and moral beliefs, for example, egoistic intuitions and intuitions favouring kinship or altruism towards family and ones requiring reciprocity – except act-utilitarian intuitions – is shaped by evolutionary processes.[26]

> (P2) If the content of such moral intuitions and moral beliefs is shaped by evolutionary processes that have nothing to do with moral truth, we have no reason to believe that our moral intuitions reflect any rational and universal moral truth.

> (C) Therefore, moral intuitions – except act-utilitarian intuitions – are epistemologically (and methodologically) unsound and should be discarded.

I wrote 'commonsense deontological morality – except act-utilitarian intuitions' because Singer excludes act-utilitarian intuitions from his debunking argument. In *The Point of View of the Universe* (2014), de Lazari-Radek and Singer extensively argue that evolution cannot explain act-utilitarian intuitions. In fact, they think there is no evolutionary explanation to debunk act-utilitarian intuitions.[27]

Instead, they believe evolution can explain moral intuitions favouring altruism towards family and ones requiring reciprocity. They write,

> Evolution explains altruism towards kin by seeing it as promoting the survival of the genes we carry. We can do this in many ways, but in normal circumstances, we will do it best by living a long life, finding a mate or mates, having children, and acquiring the resources, status, or power that will improve the prospects of our children and other close kin surviving, reproducing, and in turn promoting the survival of their children. (2014, 194)

Thus, based on Singer's debunking argument, since moral intuitions (except act-utilitarian intuitions) are the product of the specific sort of evolutionary processes responsible for these moral intuitions, they had better be explained away.

However, Singer's argument, I believe, is not justified. The reason is that if we can have access to moral facts through, for example, our intuition, then evolutionary influence may not be strong enough to distort our systems of morality. But if this is so, the objection only works if we assume that commonsense deontological morality – except act-utilitarian intuitions – including moral intuitions, for example, egoistic principles, principles about giving preference to family and about reciprocating kindness or forbearance on the part of others, as well as being shaped by evolutionary forces, do not (more or less) reliably track moral facts. However, the premises of the argument simply assume that commonsense deontological morality – except act-utilitarian intuitions – do not reliably track moral facts, and so they cannot establish this as a conclusion.

But Singer might object that we cannot legitimately assume the reliability of especially deontological moral intuitions because the earlier trolley case is supposed to illustrate the unreliability caused by emotion. Singer, for example, writes,

> If, however, Greene is right to suggest that our intuitive responses are due to differences in the emotional pull of situations that involve bringing about someone's death in a close-up, personal way, and bringing about the same person's death in a way that is at a distance, and less personal, why should we believe that there is anything that justifies these responses? . . . In the light of the best scientific understanding of ethics, we face a choice. We can take the view that our moral intuitions and judgments are and always will be emotionally based intuitive responses, and reason can do no more than build the best possible case for a decision already made on nonrational grounds. (2005, 347 and 351)

However, all that trolley scenarios can do is create doubts about a reaction to, or a moral intuition about, a *kind* of case. Since Singer's main argument is based upon Greene's trolley scenarios, all his argument can prove is that the epistemic status of *some* general moral intuitions can be undermined. However, general moral intuitions such as 'it is *pro tanto* morally wrong to harm someone for one's amusement' can hardly be undermined by Singer's argument. The reason for this is that trolley scenarios do not ask about such general moral intuitions. Instead, subjects are asked about what is morally right action in a kind of situation, for example, whether it is right to push that stranger off the bridge in that situation. Hence, Singer's main argument is not justified if we take into account the reliable *general* moral intuitions. Singer cannot conclude that *all* general moral intuitions are unreliable from the premise that *this or that kind* of moral intuitions are unreliable. If Singer wants to save his argument, he needs to consider the general moral intuition into his account and grant that there are some reliable general moral intuitions. But if Singer enters some reliable general moral intuitions into his account, he hardly can justify his main argument.

Even if my earlier epistemological criticism does not work, there are some doubts about Singer's empirical premises that emotions always undermine moral intuition's reliability.[28] In the next section, I respond to him empirically to undermine his empirical premises and save the epistemic status of moral intuition. I present three empirical cases to bridge the gap between the psychology and epistemology of moral intuitions and show that emotions can be parcelled with moral intuitions without creating any threats to their reliability. However, this can happen only if *some* emotions have a cognitive element. Of course, I am not saying that *all* emotions have a cognitive element.[29]

2.5.1 Emotion as the lynchpin of Singer's argument

A natural response to Singer is to insist that deontological moral principles may be right *even if* their support comes from intuitions that are shaped by evolutionary forces. Suppose that Singer is right, and so our deontological intuitions are caused by evolutionary forces. Suppose as well that there's no *positive* reason to believe that evolutionary forces have much to do with the moral truth. All this shows is that we are unable to provide a *positive* reason for believing that the causal process behind deontological intuitions is hooked up to moral truth. This *does not* show that deontological intuitions are false. They *may* very well be true; it is just that we cannot demonstrate grounds for trusting their reliability.[30]

Singer's position would be more convincing if we had evidence that deontological intuitions are caused not by a process of uncertain reliability but by a process of demonstrated proneness to error. The difference here is between relying upon an untested telescope that was made by a process that has nothing to do with making a good telescope and relying upon a telescope that we *know* has produced bad measurements in the past. So far, Singer has only shown that our moral intuitions are an untested telescope. But he wishes to go farther: he wishes to show that our intuitions are demonstrably prone to errors.

This is the point of introducing the Haidt and Greene research. Singer wants to claim that this research shows that our intuitions are caused by *emotional* psychological processes. And emotion, he supposes, is known to be a distorting factor. Evolution is simply disconnected from truth, but emotion is thought to be an active barrier to truthful perception. Singer writes,

> If, however, Greene is right to suggest that our intuitive responses are due to differences in the emotional pull of situations that involve bringing about someone's death in a close-up, personal way, and bringing about the same person's death in a way that is at a distance, and less personal, why should we believe that there is anything that justifies these responses? (2005, 347)

Of course, not everyone agrees with Singer that emotions as such are distorting (Mason, 2011; Lenman, 2015).[31] The rest of this chapter will argue that we can have reason to trust our moral intuitions *even if* they are caused by emotion-linked brain processes. In the next section, I introduce three empirical cases to bridge the gap between the psychology and epistemology of moral intuitions.

3 Emotion and intuition: Empirical evidence

Given what Singer argues, let us grant that all of our moral intuitions are the product of mechanisms that evolved and that they are mediated through emotional processes, as suggested by the research of Greene and Haidt. However, there is a gap between the psychology of moral intuitions that Singer endorses and the epistemological-methodological consequences he wants to infer. Although Singer supposes that moral intuitions are the product of emotional processes with a certain kind of evolutionary history, he is not clear why that should make them unfitting as a legitimate basis for moral judgements. For example, Singer holds that Greene's and Haidt's researches cast light on the role of emotions in producing intuitive moral judgements. Singer writes,

> Haidt's behavioural research and Greene's brain imaging studies suggest the possibility of distinguishing between our immediate emotionally based responses, and our more reasoned conclusions. (2005, 349–50)

Singer here seems to presuppose a familiar sort of pure rationalistic picture about moral intuitions according to which the presence of any degree or type of emotion distorts intuitive judgements. Such a pure rationalistic account of moral intuitions might be attractive to ethicists who thought that our moral judgements should derive from pure reason (e.g. Kant or Sidgwick, on some interpretations). If emotion is generally a distorting factor in moral thinking or for our intuitive moral judgement, then it is better not to attend to those moral judgements that are mediated through emotional processes. In other words, since we are emotional people, it is better not to pay much attention to our moral intuitions, or at least those affected by emotional influences.

However, there are some problems with this pure rationalistic account of moral intuition that distinguishes between 'immediate emotionally-based responses' and 'more reasoned and reflected ones'. I will now raise three empirically based objections to this picture:

(1) The first objection is that the distinction between emotional and reasoned responses itself is not as clear-cut as it appeared in Singer's, Greene's and Haidt's works. In fact, dividing up intuitive moral judgements into 'emotionally-based ones' and 'more reasoned ones' might not be possible. Defending a grey-area account of moral intuitions between emotion and reason seems more tenable.[32] For example, many researchers in cognitive science claim that at least *some* emotion *necessarily* has a *cognitive* component.[33] That cognitive component is, indeed, presumed to be an evaluative judgement. The view usually says that emotions are a species of evaluative judgement, not that all evaluative judgements are emotions. For instance, 'shame' might comprise the judgement that there has been damage to one's well-being together with a distinctive feeling or motivational state. So, if this is the case for shame, then having some emotions with cognitive elements can be a helpful rather than a distorting factor for our intuitions. This, however, does not entail that *all* emotions have a cognitive element.[34]

Of course, this view of the relationship between emotion and cognition is also contentious. But that is the point. Singer seems to assume that cognitive scientists have readily to hand a reliable distinction between emotion and cognition. But cognitive scientists are far from agreeing upon how to draw such a distinction or whether one is tenable at all. For example, Haidt himself dropped talk of emotion from his social intuitionist account, mainly for this reason (Haidt, 2013, Ch. 1). Greene also backed away from his earlier account, acknowledging that emotion plays some role in consequentialist intuition as well (Greene, 2014).

(2) The second problem with the pure rationalistic account of moral intuition is that even if we can divide our moral judgements into emotional intuitions

and reasoned intuitions, there is very little reason to think that, as a general psychological law, that emotion *always* distorts our intuitive judgements. It seems likely, on the contrary, that the relationship between emotion and intuitive judgements will be different from case to case. In some cases, we may indeed do worse when our judgements are influenced by emotion. But in others, emotion may, in fact, be *necessary* for *good* intuitive judgement.

Some of the works of Antonio Damasio and the famous case of Phineas Gage suggest just that (Damasio, 1994, 3–10).[35] Gage and Damasio's patients suffered from the attenuation of 'somatic markers' and injuries in some of the emotional regions of their brains (i.e. VMPFC).[36] As a result, although these people are normal in intelligence and semantic knowledge, they show weaknesses in what we might consider practical rationality, for example, taking what seem to be risks and doing poorly in gambling tasks. Damasio takes these patients to show that emotions sometimes carry important information about the environment and have a vital role in our reasoning.

For example, in a rigged game experiment (the Iowa Gambling Task), players were shown four decks of cards. They turned over cards from the decks in any order they wanted. Some cards paid money ($50 or $100), though some were penalties instead. Two decks were 'good', producing lower benefits but a higher total pay-out and two decks were 'bad', producing large earnings but greater total costs. Players were not given any explicit information about the existence of 'good' and 'bad' decks.

The study involved two groups of players – subjects without brain damage and patients with damage to the *ventromedial* prefrontal cortex. Normal players implicitly understood the distribution after turning about fifty cards; most of them concluded that 'Two decks are good, and two are bad'. The patients with brain damage, however, never understood. While people played, researchers measured skin conductance responses during the gambling task, and they recognized that 'the frontally damaged subjects did not have the feelings necessary for rational action' (Damasio, 1994, 212–17). They also found that these people showed no emotional response during the game. Damasio believes that after their brain injury, the brain-damaged patients tended to make poor financial and personal decisions and have difficulty with moral judgements.[37]

Here we have a case where emotions, far from being a distorting factor, are actually *essential* to having a good judgement. If this is the case for practical rationality in the way claimed by Damasio, then it might also be the case for the moral domain. That requires a tendentious assumption, but the point is that we just do not know enough about the relationship between emotional processes and good intuitive judgement to decide one way or the other. The pure rationalistic picture, although perhaps appealing, is not well supported by the psychological facts. So the fact that moral intuitions are produced by emotional processes is not enough to have doubts about them.

(3) The third empirical response to Singer can be derived from social psychology. Some social psychologists believe that moral intuitions, like other intuitions which come naturally in social situations, are more reliable than conscious deliberative judgements under certain conditions. The idea is that 'unconscious judgements' (or conclusions that do constitute moral intuitions) can be more reliable than 'conscious judgements' in some situations. To explain this, these psychologists mostly appeal to what is called 'social cognition' as a topic in social psychology that focuses on the ability to process, store and apply information about other people in social interactions. In fact, social cognition focuses on the role our cognitive processes play in social interactions. The development of social cognitions, these psychologists believe, is tightly connected with the development of 'social emotions'. It is widely accepted that social emotions are communicated to other people and generally shape our social processes.[38] Theorists often remark emotions such as shame, embarrassment and jealousy as social emotions. These emotions are social emotions because they depend upon other people's thoughts, feelings or actions in consideration of social norms, and they depend upon the awareness of other people's mental states. In contrast, basic emotions such as happiness and sadness need only the awareness of one's own mental state.

Since most psychologists think of moral intuition as something like social cognition and social emotion, they believe that moral intuitions help us in navigating our social world. In fact, social cognition, social emotion and moral intuition have overlapping subject matters, overlapping emotional effects and overlapping roles (namely, helping us navigate our social world), and thus are not so different. This implies that we can legitimately draw some conclusions about moral intuition from the observation that moral intuition has a subject matter, emotional effect and role that is shared with social cognition and emotion. For example, according to the philosopher Woodward and the psychologist Allman (2007), one of the roles of social emotions or moral intuitions is to help people circumvent the limits of analytical, rule-based or reason-based decision-making procedures such as cost-benefit analysis. They hold that the number of different dimensions or different kinds of considerations that human beings can fully take into account in explicit conscious rule or reason-guided decision-making is fairly *small*. In order to prove their claim, Woodward and Allman, in their joint paper, refer to studies by the psychologist Ap Dijksterhuis and his colleagues as evidence for this claim.[39] Let me first explain Dijksterhuis's experiment relating to social intuition, and then I shall come back to Woodward's and Allman's argument.

Dijksterhuis and colleagues differentiate between *mode* of thought or deliberation (conscious vs. unconscious), the *complexity* and *quality* of choice. Complexity is defined as the amount of information a choice is based on. A choice between objects for which one or two attributes are important is *simple*, whereas a choice between objects for which many attributes are important is *complex*. They hypothesized that conscious thought leads to good quality choices in simple matters because of its precision. However, conscious thought leads to worse quality choices with more complex issues because of its low capacity. On the other hand, unconscious thought, because of its relative lack of precision, that is, 'deliberation-without-attention', is expected to lead to choices of lower quality. However, since the quality of unconscious thought does not worsen with increased complexity, in complex circumstances, unconscious thought can actually lead to better quality choices than conscious thought.

Dijksterhuis and his colleagues investigated the earlier hypothesis in different experiments, and they compared the quality of choices between alternatives under different conditions. In these experiments, some participants were not given the opportunity to think at all before choosing between alternatives. Others were able to consciously think for a short time before choosing, and others were distracted for a brief period before choosing, during which they could engage in what Dijksterhuis and his colleagues called 'unconscious thought'.

For example, in one of Dijksterhuis's rigged experiments (2004), participants were given information about four hypothetical apartments in their home city, Amsterdam. Each apartment had twelve different features, for a total of forty-eight pieces of information, presented in random order. One of these four apartments was unambiguously more desirable than the others, whereas the second one was unattractive. The two remaining apartments were neutral. After the participants read the huge amount of information, they were asked to choose which one was better. Interestingly, only the 'unconscious thinkers' reported the appropriate preference for the desirable apartment. The participants who engaged in conscious thinking could not specify a preference for the appropriate apartment over the less undesirable ones because, as Dijksterhuis explains, their job was too difficult.[40]

Based on Dijksterhuis's findings, Woodward and Allman claim that unconscious processing – which social emotion can be part of – can sometimes lead to better judgements than conscious deliberation, such as in reason-based decisions. They also argue that there is a similarity between social intuitions and moral intuitions because social cognition, social emotion and moral intuition have overlapping subject matters and roles (namely, helping us navigate our social world). Hence, it is possible to draw a conclusion about the reliability of moral intuitions from studies on the reliability of social intuitions. If Woodward and Allman are right, we can assume that emotional, moral intuitions will at least sometimes lead to judgements or decisions that are superior to those arrived at on the basis of more deliberative, rule and reason-based decision-making strategies (Woodward and Allman, 2007, 185). However, much hinges on whether Woodward and Allman are right in suggesting that there is sufficient *similarity* between social and moral intuitions.

Again, even if one believes that Woodward's, Allman's and Dijksterhuis's claims are empirically wrong, this does not ruin my epistemological point. All I wanted to show is that social or moral intuitions can probably work even better in conjunction with emotional experiences.

If I were on the right track, I could manage to knock down some empirical arguments against moral intuition raised by Singer, Greene and Haidt. They appeal to neuroscience and brain science to cast doubt on emotion-linked moral intuitions and reject the epistemic reliability of our moral intuitions. But I have just surveyed three distinct psychological programmes suggesting that such an inference is too hasty. I argued that some cases in neuroethics show that their accounts are not powerful enough to systematically reject the epistemology of moral intuition. Emotions sometimes do not work as a distorting factor and thus cannot ruin moral intuition's epistemic status. But that is not enough for philosophers, I believe. We need a philosophical theory rather than empirical evidence to support the idea that emotion and moral intuition can sit comfortably beside each other without epistemic threat.

Before going on to the next chapter to discuss the empirical psychologists' account against the epistemology of moral intuitionism, we need clarity about whether moral intuitions in the epistemological intuitionists' tradition can tolerate emotions at all. Here is the question we need to address: What is the relationship between emotion and moral intuition based on my favoured seeming account of intuition advocated in Chapters 1 and 2? In the following, I will give an explanation of how our moral intuition's mental ontology can help us construct a theory of emotion. Having a theory of emotion together with a theory of moral intuition can also help us to provide a response to moral psychologists' skepticism about epistemological intuitionism, which will be covered in Chapter 7.

4 Integrating the psychology and epistemology of moral intuition: Can emotional experiences take part in the seeming theory of moral intuition?

Although the empirical arguments I have presented earlier can weaken Singer's, Greene's and Haidt's position against moral intuition, there is still one thing that is *lost* and has to be considered at this stage. These experiments only show that emotions *can* play a positive role in our intuitive moral judgements. But it seems that the role of emotion in our intuitive moral judgements has not yet been articulated well philosophically. We have to explain, by proposing a comprehensive theory, what this positive *role* is. Overlooking this important point is not plausible, especially for philosophers.

Recall that I empirically undermined the old taboo conception of the pure 'reason-emotion' distinction and introduced a hybrid account of them. I showed that it is not the case that intuitive judgements in practical rationality must be kept away from emotion in order for intuitive judgements to be reliable. Now, I try to do the same regarding the psychology and epistemology of moral intuition by proposing a theory of emotion that suits moral intuition. We can have a hybrid account of moral intuition and emotion to the extent that emotion does not necessarily undermine the epistemic reliability of moral intuition. Let me explain.

In the discussion of intuition, philosophers often distinguish two issues from each other: issues regarding the epistemology of intuition, which deals with questions such as 'does intuition justify?', and issues regarding the psychology of intuition, which deals with questions such as 'what is intuition?' and 'how can intuition be related to emotions?' Some of these philosophers, such as Sinnott-Armstrong, believe that the psychology of intuition should be differentiated from the epistemology of intuition because the epistemology of intuition is normative and is related to *when* beliefs are justified. This is a different question than the psychological question of *how* beliefs are formed, though it may be possible to use the answer to the psychological question to inform the answer to the epistemological question (Sinnott-Armstrong, 2008a, 50). In that case, the psychology and epistemology of intuition should be regarded as independent positions. However, this view, which is based on an understanding of intuition as a mere belief, is wrong.[41] By changing our theory of intuition, we can aim at an integrated perspective on the psychology and epistemology of intuition.

In order to integrate the psychology and epistemology of moral intuition, I describe moral intuitions as a kind of intellectual seeming of which the seemingness could be constituted by phenomenological features such as a feeling, appropriateness, familiarity, or confidence (*cf.* Chapter 2).[42] I argue that seeming theories of moral intuition combine the psychology and epistemology of moral intuition. However, in addition to the theory of moral intuition, we also need a theory of emotion. Based upon the seeming account of moral intuition, I try to introduce a theory of emotion that can be parcelled with seeming states. This gives us a clue as to explain how moral intuition and emotion can be combined. Let us start with the discussion of moral intuition first.

Recall what I have discussed before about seeming states. We can divide moral intuition's accounts into those that are doxastic, a kind of belief, and seemings that are not doxastic but *express* a non-inferential impression of truth.[43] As we have seen earlier, on the doxastic view, moral intuitions are regarded as non-inferred beliefs about self-evident propositions based on adequate understanding. An adequate understanding of self-evident propositions is sufficient for their justification.[44] Alternatively, on the non-doxastic view, I defended earlier, moral intuitions can be explained as seeming states, namely initial intellectual seemings (*cf.* Chapters 1 and 2).

Although I argued in Chapter 1 about the superiority of seeming states to the doxastic view, I now want to discuss a pragmatic advantage of the seeming account of moral intuition. The seeming account can easily integrate the epistemology and psychology of moral intuition.[45] The seeming view can answer both the epistemological question of 'does moral intuition justify?' and the psychological question of 'what is moral intuition?'

Consider the seeming account of moral intuition that I defended in this book. This account of moral intuition makes an analogy between moral intuition and perceptual experience.[46] This analogy can answer the psychological question that moral intuitions are like perceptual experiences, although they have differences. Moreover, there is a general epistemological question about whether moral intuitions justify, and if they do, what they justify. There is a further question of whether they justify directly or only inferentially. By saying that moral intuitions are like perpetual experience in being 'translucent presentations', we can answer the earlier epistemological questions about whether moral intuitions justify, and if they do, what they justify (*cf.* Chapters 1 and 2). In effect, translucent presentations confer non-inferential *prima facie* justification upon beliefs that are formed on the basis of the presentations. Calling moral intuitions translucent is a way of saying that intuitions are direct (or non-inferred).

Based on what I have explained earlier, the seeming account can give us a clue as to how the epistemology and psychology of moral intuition can be integrated. Seeming states can answer both the questions about 'what are moral intuitions' and 'how they justify'. However, we do not yet have any idea where emotion could stand. How does emotion relate to the seeming account of moral intuition?

Following Tolhurst (1998) and Pryor (2000), I believe that seemings have some connection with 'feeling' in the sense that when it seems to us that p, we are in a mental state which has a property of 'feel as if', 'feel of truth', 'felt givenness' or 'feel of veridicality'. These 'feelings' are markers of particular phenomenological states. This aspect of perceptual phenomenology has 'phenomenal force', and it is a justification-making feature of mental states (Huemer, 2001).[47] The distinctive characters of particular emotions are also features of phenomenological states, such as the 'feeling of sadness' or 'feeling of joy'. Since epistemologists are willing to credit 'felt veridicality', why not 'felt joyfulness' or 'felt relief' as indicators of some feature of the environment? Thus, the perceptual phenomenology of 'feelings' gives us an explanation of how particular emotions' phenomenological features can relate to the seeming account.

In other words, when we feel that the content of a seeming is true, we have the feeling of veridicality. Therefore, if we regard seemings as connected to feelings, given that emotional experiences, by virtue of being conscious experiences, are feelings, the seeming view might give us a clue as to where emotional experiences can stand in our theory of moral intuition.[48] For example, here is one way to put the seeming theorists' position in a lucid way. Jennifer Wright writes,

> [. . .] moral intuition (insofar as it is intuition) is . . . a 'seeming' of the rightness/wrongness (goodness/badness, kindness/cruelty, etc.) of a particular act, object, event, person, or situation. It is tightly (if not, in at least some cases, necessarily) connected to moral emotions: *seemings* are usually accompanied by (or accompany) *feelings*. (2006, 53–4)[49]

If I can show that some emotional experiences are like perceptual experiences (similar to moral intuition), we then have a case that moral intuition and emotion can go hand in hand. The similarity between some emotions and moral intuitions probably leads us to think that they do not create problems for each other. In this way, we can explain how moral intuition (seeming) is related to emotion. I can show that emotional experiences can be a potential cause for non-inferential moral belief (Tolhurst, 1990). Moral agents can have some non-inferential moral beliefs on the basis of emotional experiences. This will provide us with a philosophical theory to support the idea that moral intuition and emotion can sit comfortably beside each other without creating an epistemic threat and that the epistemology of moral intuitions is compatible with admitting a role for emotion. Moral intuitions and emotions are not contestants if we construe moral intuition as non-doxastic intellectual seeming and emotion as a non-doxastic perceptual-like state. This shows that emotions support, rather than distort, the epistemic standing of moral intuitions.

Note that although I will say that emotions are like perceptual experience and moral intuition is like perceptual experience, this does not entail that these two perception-like states are connected in *every* respect, and *all* emotions are connected to intuition. All I want to show is that there is a *possibility* that some emotions that are similar to perceptual experiences might be connected to moral intuitions in a way that both of them can form non-inferential beliefs. There is no doubt that there might be some other emotions that do not have any connection with moral intuitions. In such a theory of emotion, the irrational feelings that can render the epistemic value of moral intuition unreliable are not at stake. Instead, there are some emotional experiences that should be regarded seriously in the sense that they have a role in having non-inferentially justified moral beliefs.

4.1 Quasi-perceptualist theory of emotion

In recent years, attention has been paid to the development of neo-judgementalist and perceptual theories of emotions. For example, people like Brady (2009), Doring (2003), Prinz (2006) and Roberts (2003) hold that emotional experiences (e.g. guilt and indignation) can be similar to *affective construals*, *appearances* and *perceptions of value* in that they can represent the world of value. The view is that emotions *perceptually* represent value.[50] Jesse Prinz, for instance, argues that sentimentalism can vindicate intuitionism. He writes,

> intuitionists believe that moral judgments are self-justifying ... they seem to base this assertion on the phenomenology of moral judgments: moral judgments seem self-evident ... far from opposing intuitionism, sentimentalism offers one of the most promising lines of defense ... sentimentalism explains the phenomenology driving intuitionism, and it shows how intuitionism might be true. (2006, 37)[51]

Prinz believes that sentimentalism can offer a defence of intuitionism because sentimentalism can explain the phenomenology of intuition. Moral intuitions do not need further justification, and in this respect, they are similar to certain perceptual experiences. Likewise, emotionally grounded judgements are like perceptual experiences that do not need independent support. For example, one can feel that rape is wrong. In effect, if moral judgements are sentimental, then the judgement that 'promise-keeping is right' is self-justifying because promise-keeping generates the positive sentiment expressed by that judgement. The power to generate such positive sentiments is constitutive of being right.

Perceptual theorists generally believe that occurrent emotions are intentional and representational with a certain phenomenal character. It is natural to think that construals, appearances and perceptions are non-doxastic states. So, it is possible to draw an analogy between emotional experiences and perceptual-like states. Following Kauppinen (2013), I call this the quasi-perceptualist account of emotion. According to

> *The Quasi-Perceptualist Account of Emotion*: Some emotional experiences can be similar to non-doxastic states, such as perceptual-like states.[52]

Emotions, like perceptions, can come into conflict with our beliefs and judgements. Just like in the Müller-Lyer visual illusion, we might have a 'conflict' between our 'recalcitrant emotion' and belief (Doring, 2008). Recalcitrant emotions are emotions that are in tension with the subjects' settled judgement. For example, suppose I judge that my brother's action is justified, but I envy him at the same time, or I fear something while knowing that it is harmless (D'Arms and Jacobson, 2003).[53] The conflict between emotion and judgement provides us with good reason to construe emotional experiences as non-doxastic states. Importantly, this sort of conflict is rational without contradiction. As Doring (2003) points out, it is coherent to be afraid of the snake that we know is not dangerous.[54]

Although the account of emotion that I defend here is non-doxastic, this does not entail that emotions are essentially non-cognitive (Prinz, 2008). It is true that emotions have non-cognitive components, but it is not the case that these non-cognitive elements must have a constant association with the emotion in question. For example, in the case of imagining some emotion, for example, fear of something, non-cognitive components such as bodily states are not necessarily involved. As we shall see, emotions (e.g. compassion and shame) can involve evaluative thoughts, perception and judgement. Acknowledging this point does not require fully endorsing judgementalist theories of the emotions according to which evaluative judgements are identical to, or are necessary constituents of, emotions (Nussbaum, 2001, Ch. 1; Solomon, 1977).

But if the quasi-perceptualist account of emotion is true, our moral beliefs *can* be based on emotional experience. Emotional experiences can be treated as evidence for epistemic and rational beliefs. However, the rationality of the emotions is contentious. For example, Sinnott-Armstrong endorses the irrationality of emotions (Sinnott-Armstrong, 2006a). He believes that emotions are an epistemologically distorting factor that threatens the possibility of a non-inferential justification in ethics. Even Huemer, as a proponent of epistemological intuitionism, believes that emotion distorts moral judgement. He writes,

> [E]motions are known to impair judgment with respect to (other) factual questions, so, assuming the truth of moral realism, it is *prima facie* reasonable to assume that emotions impair our moral judgment as well. (2008a, 378)

However, as I argued earlier, cognitive sciences show us that seeing all emotions in this excessively pessimistic way is not plausible. To think about emotional experience as always being a source of epistemic distortion would be wrong. On the contrary, there are some reasons to believe that emotional experiences can sometimes make a positive contribution to our activities in practical rationality.[55] So, there is a possibility that some emotions are not distorting factors. We are no longer justified in saying that emotions always distort our epistemic activities if this is right. Instead, emotions (construed as quasi-perceptual experiences) might have some cognitive elements assessable for rationality. Let me explain how emotional experiences can be assessable for rationality.

In different theories of emotion, including the quasi-perceptualist account of emotion, it is widely endorsed that emotions are representational states which can depict the world in a certain way (Doring, 2003 and 2007; Roeser, 2011). The emotion of fear, for instance, can represent something as dangerous. Therefore, emotional experiences can be rationally assessed as appropriate or inappropriate. For instance, when we say, 'his anger is not appropriate' or 'his fear is justified', we mean that the emotion is in a way representing the way the (evaluative) world happens to be. On the other hand, we can have non-inferential justification for believing moral propositions on the basis of having emotional experiences (construed as non-doxastic states). For example, our fear can justify us in believing that we are in danger. Furthermore, while emotions can form non-inferential beliefs, we can ask why we have some emotions, and thus we can offer sufficient reasons – if it is needed – for them. To better understand which kind of emotion we are dealing with, we can appeal to what Scanlon calls 'judgment-sensitive attitudes'. These attitudes, Scanlon writes, are ones that

> an ideally rational person would come to have whenever that person judged there to be sufficient reasons for them, and that would, in an ideally rational person, 'extinguish' when that person judged them not to be supported by reasons of the appropriate kind. (1998, 20)

Beliefs, fear, respect, anger and contempt, according to Scanlon, are all such judgement-sensitive attitudes. Just like judgement-sensitive attitudes, the emotions we deal with here are 'emotions as consequences of judgments' in the sense that, for example, fear is an emotion 'for which reasons can sensibly be asked or offered' (1998, 20). This must be distinguished from mere feelings such as hunger. Following Jones's (2003) discussion of *reason-tracking*, we can claim that emotions allow us to track reasons in the sense that we can register reasons so that we can behave in accordance with them.[56] For example, one can argue that we can provide reasons for emotions like perceptual experiences cases – if we see the car is red, we can say that it looks red to us.

So, emotions can be appropriate for rationality in three ways: emotions represent the way the (evaluative) world happens to be. Emotions form non-inferential moral beliefs. Furthermore, a rational person can offer reasons – if it is needed – for having some emotions.[57]

I am not claiming that we can have non-inferentially justified moral beliefs derived from intuition helped by a judgement-sensitive attitude. Judgement-sensitive attitudes do not create non-inferential moral beliefs. All I want to say is that insofar as moral intuition (construed as intellectual seeming) can form non-inferential moral beliefs, there can be some emotions that form non-inferential beliefs. In doing that, they are like moral intuitions because they both are similar to perceptual experiences.

However, suppose one objects that if this is the case, the general worry remains because these emotions can distort when they cause judgement. But this objection ignores the possibility of correction. Although emotions can distort, this does not entail that emotions cannot non-inferentially justify us in having judgements or beliefs. Suppose we become convinced that some particular emotion-based judgement or belief is distorted because the underlying emotion turns out to be unreliable in this case. We can then recover by adjusting our belief in response to other available evidence, for example, confirmation from a third party. Does this make our initial belief inferentially justified? No! While these emotions, without inference, can generate non-inferential beliefs, we need some inferences to keep these beliefs acceptable and plausible. In other words, although the generation of our initial belief is non-inferential, keeping the plausibility of our beliefs might be inferential. So, the generation of our initial belief is non-inferential, even if maintaining it under certain challenges requires inference. What I am arguing here is that some emotions, like moral intuitions, can generate non-inferential beliefs but not keep them acceptable and plausible. This places us in agreement there with moral intuitionists who think that emotional experience is not a distorting factor for our epistemic justification and can generate non-inferential justification.[58] Audi writes in this regard that

> [E]motions may reveal what is right or wrong before judgment articulates it; and they may both support ethical judgment and spur moral conduct. (2004, 57)

Let us go back to the main issue with which this section started. I asked whether emotional experiences can go hand in hand with our favoured theory of moral intuition, that is, seeming theory. My answer simply is yes.[59] Here is the reason: according to the seeming account of intuitions, moral intuitions are in some relevant ways similar to perceptual experiences that offer non-inferential justification. I also presented here the quasi-perceptualist account of emotion. This account treats emotions as non-doxastic states similar to perceptual states that can be assessable for rationality. The quasi-perceptualist account of emotion offers non-inferential justification for moral belief based on emotional experiences. Therefore, moral intuitions and some emotional experiences are similar to perceptual experiences in offering non-inferential justification. Moral intuition and emotion can be partners rather than contestants, with emotion as a source of insight rather than distortion.

To conclude, although moral intuition, emotion and perceptual experience are different, they are parallel at a certain level of abstraction. In the case of moral intuition, we can say that 'whereas x has the perceptual experience as if p iff it is translucently sensorily presented to x that p, x has the [moral] intuition that p iff it is translucently intellectually presented to x that p' (Bengson, 2010, 92). Likewise, while x has the *perceptual experience* as if p iff it is translucently sensorily presented to x that p, x has the *emotional experience* that p iff it is translucently emotionally presented to x that p. Of course, emotions *can* be misleading. So can moral intuitions. So can perceptual experiences. That they are misleading in some cases does not gainsay that they are sources of knowledge in other cases.

Therefore, the seeming account of moral intuition and the quasi-perceptualist account of emotion together offer integrated psychology and epistemology of moral intuition. These two accounts can explain what a moral intuition is, how emotion can be related to intuition, and how each of them can offer non-inferential justification for belief.

5 Conclusion

I have shown in this chapter that Singer's argument is not justified epistemologically. Some empirical results I outlined weaken the empirical psychologists' argument against moral intuition. I then argued that the seeming account of moral intuition could team up with an account of moral emotion. Not only intuition but also emotion can offer non-inferential justification. The fact that the quasi-perceptualist account of emotion treats emotions as potential (rational) sources of non-inferential beliefs offers a reply to criticisms raised by experimentalists that emotions are always distorting factors. Embracing the seeming account of moral intuition and the quasi-perceptualist account of emotion, we can explain that (i) moral intuitions are intellectual seemings similar to perceptual experiences, (ii) emotional experiences can be similar to perceptual experiences, (iii) the idea of non-inferentiality in moral intuition and emotional experiences is a presentational state of directness, and (iv) just as perceptual experiences provide non-inferential justification for belief, so do moral intuitions and emotions.

7

Scepticism about moral intuitionism
How my favoured account of epistemological intuitionism rebuts Sinnott-Armstrong's position

1 Introduction

In this chapter, I will examine whether my new account of modest epistemological intuitionism can be saved if we take into account Sinnott-Armstrong's argument against the epistemology of intuitionism. However, I need to clarify what I intend to do in this chapter. As I clearly explained before, the modest new account of epistemological intuitionism I advocated before has three parts. There is the ontological part, which mostly focuses on the idea that intuitions are seemings. The psychological part is about the relationship between emotional experiences and intuition (construed as seeming). And there is the epistemological part, which discusses the idea that non-inferential intuitive moral beliefs can get extra-inferential justification and that to adequately understand a proposition is to at least be able to draw some inferences *from* the proposition.

This chapter only examines the epistemological part of the modest new intuitionism against Sinnott-Armstrong's argument. One reason for this focus is that Sinnott-Armstrong's argument, which greatly influences the literature, focuses on the epistemological aspect of intuitionism. Another reason for this focus is that I already examined the ontological and psychological parts in the previous chapter. I examined how understanding moral intuitions in terms of seemings can help us to respond to neuroethicists who claim that emotions make moral intuitions unreliable. So, I will not comment extensively here on the ontology and psychology of moral intuitions. Instead, I focus on the epistemological idea of 'non-inferentiality'. I examine how the epistemological elements of my modest intuitionism can help us to save the idea of non-inferentiality.

In order to reject the epistemology of moral intuitionism, Sinnott-Armstrong's main target is to attack the Audian version of the intuitionist epistemology as the strongest form of epistemological intuitionism.[1] In his paper 'Framing Moral Intuitions', Sinnott-Armstrong explicitly defines a moral intuition 'as a strong immediate moral belief' (2008a, 47). He maintains that since moral intuitions are moral beliefs, they might arise after reflection. However, this does not entail that they have positive epistemic status. He writes,

> [I]t is better to define moral intuitions neutrally so that calling something a moral intuition does not entail by definition that it has any particular epistemic status, such as being true or probable or justified. (2008a, 75 in the notes)

Sinnott-Armstrong assumes that moral intuitions are belief-like states. However, things might change if our theory of moral intuition varies. Suppose our theory of moral intuitions holds that they are seeming states and that such seeming states and emotional experiences generate non-inferential justification for moral beliefs (*cf.* Chapter 6). With these suppositions, some of Sinnott-Armstrong's criticisms against the unreliability of moral intuitions misfire.

To elaborate, suppose moral intuitions are seeming states, formed via a non-inferential process and offering us some justification for corresponding moral beliefs, although our moral beliefs can be fallible. Suppose further that seeming states can be associated with some phenomenological features according to which emotional experiences do not necessarily cloud our moral beliefs. Sinnott-Armstrong's criticism, as we will see, is that, in all situations where our emotions are involved, our moral intuitions (read moral beliefs) fail to be non-inferentially justified since emotions distort them and they are formed in a cloudy situation.

However, believing that emotions can distort our moral intuition given that intuitions are beliefs is one thing, and believing that emotions can distort our moral intuitions given that intuitions are seemings is another. If we define moral intuition in terms of a doxastic state such as belief, we are readily excluding the discussion of emotion from moral intuition. Consequently, it is easy to say that emotion, as an external state, is a distorting source for our moral intuitions or beliefs. However, if we define moral intuitions in terms of seemings, we create an opportunity to admit that emotion can be associated with moral intuitions. And, as argued earlier, some emotions, far from being distorting factors, are enabling ones and bring epistemic benefits. There is the example of cases in which emotional experiences make salient otherwise obscured information and help us garner insights we would not have otherwise obtained. Furthermore, if we define moral intuitions in terms of seemings, our account of non-inferentiality might even change. As an illustration, Väyrynen writes that a non-inferentially justified belief is

> a belief that is based by some non-inferential mechanism on some kind of reasons or evidence, where non-doxastic states such as experiences and phenomenal and intellectual appearances are the relevant kind of reasons or evidence. (2008, 491)

Nevertheless, I am not saying it is *conceptually impossible* for our moral intuitions to be distorted by our emotions. Our emotions can make the world look different from how it is, for example, when we are depressed. Although emotions can distort our moral intuitions and render them unjustified, we can fix our moral intuitions to be justified after reflection and checking them with other people. But this does not entail that by reflecting and asking other people, we are not non-inferentially justified. I will talk more about this issue throughout this chapter.

Sinnott-Armstrong adopts the Audian style of epistemological intuitionism. However, as I argued before, the Audian accounts of moral intuition and self-evidence do not sound right to me. It would be pointless to raise my objection against Sinnott-Armstrong's Audian account of moral intuition as it is repetitive. So, in this chapter, I will not discuss Sinnott-Armstrong's definition of moral intuition, although I believe it is wrong. Rather, I argue that the epistemological elements of modest new intuitionism I advocated before show that Sinnott-Armstrong's argument against epistemological intuitionism is not strong enough to compel the rejection of moral intuitionist epistemology. Sinnott-Armstrong's account of epistemological intuitionism introduces a diluted version of the epistemology of moral intuitionism. In order to show this, I will focus solely on his definition of epistemological intuitionism and epistemic worries about the epistemology of moral intuitionism, not his theory of moral intuition.

2 Sinnott-Armstrong's central argument against epistemological intuitionism

In a series of papers, Sinnott-Armstrong (1996; 2002; 2006a; 2006b; 2008a; 2008b and 2010) has built up a number of objections against the epistemology of moral intuitionism on the grounds that moral intuitionism is committed to the view that at least some moral beliefs have a justification that does not come from their inferential relation with other beliefs.[2] He appeals to empirical premises and experiments in order to argue that many of our moral intuitions are unreliable because our emotions distort them. Sinnott-Armstrong claims that some confirmation is needed when we have a moral intuition or belief based on emotion. The need for confirmation leads to a problem for moral intuitionists since they need *inferential* confirmation before such beliefs could be justified. This might undermine the moral intuitionists' claim that some moral knowledge is justified non-inferentially.[3]

In the light of some criticisms made by Tolhurst (2008) and Shafer-Landau (2008), Sinnott-Armstrong backs away from some of the unjustified claims he made before.[4] However, in his paper, 'An Empirical Challenge to Moral Intuitionism', Sinnott-Armstrong develops his latest critique of the epistemology of moral intuitionism with a different formulation. Although he repeats some of his earlier claims, such as moral intuitions are subject to many distorting influences, and we cannot take moral intuitions as providing any justificatory support on their own, his new argument gets a lot of attention. In this new version of his critique, Sinnott-Armstrong carefully tries to lay out a novel and modified argument for the conclusion that no one can be justified non-inferentially and that, therefore, 'moral intuitionism is false' (2011, 25). Sinnott-Armstrong supports this conclusion by appealing to empirical studies and articulating epistemic premises. Sinnott-Armstrong's *central argument*, in his own words, against the epistemology of moral intuitionism is:

1. Informed adults are justified in believing that their own moral beliefs are in the class of moral beliefs.
2. Informed adults are justified in believing that a large percentage of moral beliefs are not true.
3. For any subject S, particular belief B, and a class of beliefs C, if S is justified in believing that B is in C and is also justified in believing that a large percentage of beliefs in C is not true, but S is not justified in believing that B falls into any class of beliefs C* of which a smaller percentage is not true, then S is justified in believing that B has a large probability of being untrue.
4. Therefore, if an informed adult is not justified in believing that a certain moral belief falls into any class of beliefs of which a smaller percentage is not true, then that adult is justified in believing that this particular moral belief has a large probability of being untrue.
5. A moral believer cannot be justified in holding a particular moral belief when that believer is justified in believing that the moral belief has a large probability of being untrue.

6. Therefore, if an informed adult is not justified in believing that a certain moral belief falls into any class of beliefs of which a smaller percentage is not true, then that adult is not justified in holding that moral belief.
7. If someone is justified in believing that a belief falls into a class of beliefs of which a smaller percentage is not true, then that person is committed to a justificatory inferential structure [a set of propositions where some propositions provide epistemic support for others] with that belief as a conclusion.
8. Therefore, an informed adult is not justified in holding a moral belief unless that adult is committed to a justificatory inferential structure with that belief as a conclusion.
9. If a believer is not justified in holding a belief unless the believer is committed to a justificatory inferential structure, then the believer is not justified non-inferentially in holding the belief.
10. Therefore, no informed adult is non-inferentially justified in holding any moral belief.
11. Moral intuitionism claims that some informed adults are non-inferentially justified in holding some moral belief.
12. Therefore, moral intuitionism is false (Sinnott-Armstrong, 2011, 22–5).

Ignoring the premises (1)–(3), Sinnott-Armstrong's argument, in fact, begins with an intermediate conditional conclusion, (4) if P then Q: if an informed adult is not justified in believing that a particular moral belief falls into at least one class of beliefs of which a smaller percentage is not true, then that adult is justified in believing that this particular moral belief has a large *probability* of being untrue. Then the argument makes another conditional claim, (5) if Q then R: if an informed adult is justified in believing that a particular moral belief has a large probability of being untrue, then that person cannot be justified in holding that belief. Then the argument draws the conclusion, (6) if P then R: if an informed adult is not justified in believing that a particular moral belief falls into at least one class of beliefs of which a smaller percentage is not true, then that adult is not justified in holding that moral belief. Then the argument goes (7) if ¬P then S: if someone is justified in believing that a moral belief falls into at least one class of beliefs of which a smaller percentage is not true, then that person has to have made at least an inference to that moral belief as a conclusion. And the argument concludes (8) if ¬S then R: an informed adult is not justified in holding a particular moral belief unless that adult is committed to at least an inference to that moral belief as a conclusion. Then the argument makes another conditional claim, (9) if (¬S then R) then K: if a believer is not justified in holding a moral belief unless the believer is committed to at least an inference to that belief as a conclusion, then the believer is not justified non-inferentially in holding the moral belief. So, the argument entails (10) K: no informed believer is non-inferentially justified in holding any moral belief. Then the argument presumes (11) ∃I∈¬K: [epistemological] moral intuitionism claims that some informed agents are non-inferentially justified in holding some moral belief. And the argument finally concludes, (12) ¬I: [epistemological] moral intuitionism must be false.

In short, Sinnott-Armstrong starts his argument against moral intuitionism by appealing to empirical studies, showing that moral beliefs are sometimes biased, are sometimes influenced by various irrelevant factors and are often subject to disagreement. Given these facts, Sinnott-Armstrong infers that we have two options regarding our moral beliefs: we either have reason to think that some of our moral beliefs are reliable or have no such reason. If we have no reason to believe that some of our moral beliefs are reliable, we are not justified in holding our moral beliefs. If we have reason to believe that some moral beliefs are reliable, then those beliefs are not non-inferentially justified because we need to have a 'countervailing reason' to accept that they are reliable. This entails that we have to have made at least an inference to those moral beliefs as a conclusion. If so, our moral beliefs are not non-inferentially justified, and so moral intuitionism is false.

Sinnott-Armstrong's argument consists of two main steps: in the first step, he suggests some empirical facts about moral beliefs derived from moral psychology, cognitive science and brain science. The initial epistemic consequences of those facts for moral beliefs are: we are partial, emotional and biased, and we have disagreements. Sinnott-Armstrong then concludes that these facts imply that 'a large percentage' of moral beliefs are false. Sinnott-Armstrong believes that this conclusion gives us evidence that our moral beliefs, taken as an entire class, are not reliable. In step two, Sinnott-Armstrong tries to derive his final epistemological conclusion from the first step. His main idea is that if we are aware of those empirical facts about moral belief and their epistemic consequences, then we should also believe that none of our moral beliefs are non-inferentially justified and so that moral intuitionism is false. Let me explain Sinnott-Armstrong's argument in more detail.

Sinnott-Armstrong uses different experiments to support his central argument. He states that empirical studies lead him to the idea that since 'informed adults are justified in believing that a large percentage of moral beliefs are not true' (2011, 22), they are committed to at least an inference to that belief as a conclusion. This is how he explains his central argument:

> The epistemic principles and empirical premises . . . combine to form an argument against moral intuitionism. The trick is to get from scientific evidence about moral judgments as a class to a conclusion about how any particular moral judgment needs to be justified. The path runs like this: empirical studies give informed moral believers reason to ascribe a large probability of error to moral beliefs in general. (2011, 21)

Sinnott-Armstrong supports this claim (i.e. moral believers have reason to ascribe a large probability of error to their moral belief) by saying that various empirical studies have shown that factors and effects such as 'order of presentation', 'wording' and 'sleep deprivation' have different impacts on different subjects' moral beliefs.[5]

Sinnott-Armstrong reasons for his empirical claim with the following examples.[6] He argues that our moral beliefs require confirmation in order to be justified, and this claim can be supported by empirical evidence. He maintains five 'framing effects' or circumstances in which confirmation is needed. After all, our moral beliefs are (i) partial, (ii) emotional, (iii) subject to disagreement, (iv) subject to illusion and (v) come from unreliable sources.[7]

Although Sinnott-Armstrong agrees with the moral intuitionists that belief in obvious principles could be justified, he believes that the important issue is 'whether it is justified in the strong non-inferential way' (2011, 25). Strong non-inferentiality, according to Sinnott-Armstrong, is

> when the believer is justified regardless of whether the believer is committed to any justificatory inferential structure. (2011, 13)

He then defines 'justificatory inferential structure' as

> a set of propositions where some propositions provide epistemic support for others. To be *committed* to such a structure is to accept or have a disposition to accept the supporting propositions in that structure or other propositions that entail or support the supporting propositions in that structure. (2011, 13)

It seems that the success of Sinnott-Armstrong's argument against the epistemology of moral intuitionism hinges on whether his 'strong way' of being non-inferentially justified in moral beliefs best fits with moral intuitionist epistemology. Let me explain Sinnott-Armstrong's empirical claims as supporting materials for his central argument. I then try to find out whether his argument's premises are sound. Next, I will show that what he pictures is not what moral intuitionists endorse.

Recall Sinnott-Armstrong's central claim that although most contemporary moral intuitionists believe that some of our moral beliefs are basic or foundational, that is, justified without *needing* to be inferred from other beliefs, moral or non-moral, many of our moral beliefs are formed in doubtful circumstances. Therefore, in his view, we cannot be non-inferentially justified in holding any moral beliefs simply on the basis that they are self-evident because the framing effects such as partiality (bias), disagreement and being emotional cast doubt on any non-inferential justification.

To illustrate his claim, Sinnott-Armstrong shows that, for example, disagreement, among other issues, can undermine the non-inferential justification for certain moral beliefs. He argues that, since there is a considerable disagreement in morality,

> if we know that many moral intuitions are unreliable because others hold conflicting intuitions, then we are not justified in trusting a particular moral intuition without some reason to believe that it is one of the reliable ones. (2006a, 350)

Sinnott-Armstrong appeals to a non-moral example, which could be called

> *The Tom Cruise Case*: Suppose that you see a man in Hollywood and you subsequently believe him to be Tom Cruise. However, your friend next to you disagrees; she does not think that the man is Tom Cruise.

Sinnott-Armstrong claims that when you see a man, in the case of Tom Cruise, you do not reach such a belief by drawing an inference.[8] Rather, the belief is made based on visual experience, that is, it is not mediated by explicit reasoning from premises. However, when your friend has another opinion, it seems that you need some additional confirmation that the man was, in fact, Tom Cruise before you could be justified in believing so. You should look at him carefully; ask him his name, etc. Sinnott-Armstrong, then, concludes that providing the relevant confirmation makes you draw an inference. So, you *ought* to be able to infer your belief on the basis of the confirming information. This entails that since most of our beliefs are formed in such dubitable circumstances, we need to get confirmation. Our beliefs, then, are not non-inferentially justified.

Let us now discuss the partiality case as another form of framing effect. Sinnott-Armstrong writes,

> because people's moral beliefs affect their self-interest so often in so many ways at least indirectly, and because people are so bad at telling when their own beliefs are partial, there is a presumption that moral beliefs are partial. (2006a, 197)

Take also his example of partiality, which can be called

> *The Piano-Playing Case*: Simply, the story is that a father cannot judge his daughter's performance in playing the piano in competition because he is partial and would judge unfairly.

In Sinnott-Armstrong's view, partiality renders the father's moral judgements unreliable. The father is partial when he forms the judgement that his daughter played excellently and her rival did not. By saying he is 'partial', Sinnott-Armstrong means that the judge's position is affected by the outcome of the case. The father is partial because maybe he has an interest in the outcome of his judgement. He then needs other people's confirmation in this respect. Sinnott-Armstrong writes that

> I still might be justified, if I am able to specify laudable features of her performance, or if I know that others agree, but some confirmation seems needed. (2006a, 343)

From the Piano-Playing and Tom Cruise cases, Sinnott-Armstrong concludes the principle that confirmation is required for a believer to be justified when the believer is partial or is in disagreement. This principle from the Piano-Playing and Tom Cruise cases is then applied to the moral case. We have a huge benefit in morality, that is, the truth or falsity of the various moral judgements we make affects our position. If we judge that some moral claims are true, we might face large costs (e.g. staying up all night for the sake of my mother in the event of an illness). Since we are partial, say, in cases such as helping others, we prefer to help our friends and family rather than strangers, we require a confirmation from other people for our moral beliefs, even for beliefs that moral intuitionists think properly basic or foundational, that is, those that we believe to be true on the basis that they seem to us to be true.

Sinnott-Armstrong goes further to contend: 'some recent research in psychology and brain science undermines moral intuitionism' (2006a, 340). In order to show this, he discusses bias (as a kind of partiality) and emotion to challenge moral intuitionism by empirical claims. For the discussion of bias, Sinnott-Armstrong talks about what psychologists identify as 'implicit bias' and 'cognitive illusion' that influence our moral beliefs. In the case of emotion, Sinnott-Armstrong refers to research from brain science that suggests that our moral judgement is often driven by the brain's emotional cortex. He concludes, then, that 'many moral judgements result from emotions that cloud judgment' (2006a, 350).[9]

The cases described earlier lead Sinnott-Armstrong to generalize the conclusion that partialities (biases), disagreements and emotion, among other things, create the need for confirmation for justification. In effect, he thinks that we are dealing with framing effects in a large percentage of such judgements, which create doubts and need to be confirmed by inference. He holds that for circumstances in which a belief comes from framing effects, this argument is applicable. If Sinnott-Armstrong is right about this, then any moral belief that is not inferred needs inferential confirmation to be justified. So, if the believer wants to be justified, he must draw inferences, and this falsifies the epistemology of moral intuitionism. Epistemological intuitionism, then, is unpersuasive.[10]

Sinnott-Armstrong surely knows that moral intuitionism, at least in one interpretation, does not claim that some moral beliefs that could not have originated in being inferred from other beliefs are justified. Moral intuitionists have zero interest in this claim because it is about the aetiology of moral beliefs, and their concern is not with that at all. Their concern is with justification. However, Sinnott-Armstrong believes that although the actual aetiology of moral beliefs is not the issue for moral intuitionists, the origin of a moral belief can undermine its justificatory power or change its justification from non-inferential to inferential.[11]

Although Sinnott-Armstrong's central argument is logically valid, that is, the premises entail such a conclusion, I believe his argument is not sound. The contents of some premises are problematic.[12] Since Sinnott-Armstrong's argument raised a lot of discussion in the literature, there are different strategies in which defenders of epistemological intuitionism have already responded to him. For example, some critics object that it is irrational to reject an epistemological idea in ethics by doing different empirical studies. Other critics tackle Sinnott-Armstrong's central argument by saying that many non-inferred moral beliefs are simply not subject to the sorts of errors he describes.[13] I try to respond to him in my own way, however.

I argue that Sinnott-Armstrong conflates the 'production of justification' and 'preservation of justification'. Although the preservation of justification is inferential, the production of justification can be non-inferential. One's justification for some self-evident proposition can be non-inferential, but this does not preclude the possibility that one can assess the proposition inferentially as well.

2.1 Attacking Sinnott-Armstrong's central argument

Before going through the content of the premises in more depth, let me discuss three general points on Sinnott-Armstrong's central argument that can raise doubts about its soundness.

(1) First of all, as I partly touched upon before, there is a subtle difference between belief and proposition. Belief is a sort of mental state, but a proposition is not (*cf.* Chapter 5). Epistemological intuitionists make use of 'self-evident moral propositions', not 'self-evident moral beliefs' because strictly speaking, the term 'self-evident' can only apply to a proposition or statement.[14] It can also apply to a belief when we have in mind the content of the belief – that is, what is believed – but not to a belief thought of as a certain cognitive attitude towards that content. When Sinnott-Armstrong uses the phrase 'non-inferential moral belief', he must denote the content of the belief, that is, 'belief as the fact or proposition represented'.[15] Although it seems that Sinnott-Armstrong talks about self-evident moral beliefs through his paper to proceed with his objections raised from empirical psychology, I prefer to read his account more charitably. So I assume by 'self-evident beliefs' that he must have meant the content of self-evident moral propositions.

The distinction between belief and proposition is important to understanding moral intuitionist epistemology. Almost all moral intuitionists just talk about moral propositions in their epistemology rather than talking about the psychological state of a believer who is in a position to believe that proposition. Saying that sometimes moral believers' psychological states are epistemologically unreliable and lead them to get confirmation from a third party is one thing, but saying that there are some moral propositions that do not need to be inferred from other propositions is another thing. And the latter epistemological point is what moral intuitionists are endorsing. Let me explain.

Generally, epistemological intuitionists make two kinds of claims. One is about *pro tanto* justified propositions, and the other is about our belief about self-evident (or independently credible) propositions. The history of moral intuitionism shows that although different moral intuitionists disagree about what these moral propositions are, it is widely accepted that there are at least a number of self-evident moral propositions, regardless of what people feel about them. Hence, there are at least some self-evident propositions that are not subject to framing effects, such as disagreement, emotions, and bias (partiality).

What Sinnott-Armstrong denies is our belief about self-evident propositions. Where belief about a self-evident moral proposition is concerned, the new moral intuitionists permit that psychological factors (e.g. framing effects) have an impact on our moral judgements.[16] In fact, empirical experiments cannot clearly show that self-evident moral propositions have been directly affected by these factors. This is because empirical studies cannot directly test that self-evident propositions like 'Breaking promises is *pro tanto* wrong' or 'Causing injury to others is *pro tanto* wrong' have been affected by framing effects. Although empirical studies might tell us something about the conditions under which people form various beliefs, for example, they might tell us that people's beliefs are liable to be influenced by framing effects, empirical studies could not possibly tell us which propositions are self-evident and which are not. It is not clear whether sleep-deprived subjects suddenly think that harming others is permissible or emotional, and biased subjects think it is permissible to break promises. Although for at least some moral beliefs, emotions can have an impact on them, moral intuitionists only think that some general *pro tanto* moral propositions are self-evident, not beliefs about them. It is far from clear that we have a partial interest, for example, in judging that the self-evident general propositions hold.

Yet Sinnott-Armstrong might object that we cannot ignore that these allegedly self-evident propositions have to be recovered from our beliefs because self-evidence surely has to be self-evidence to some believers, so framing effects cannot be put to one side. Of course, self-evident propositions need to be recovered from our beliefs, but moral intuitionists believe that at least some people can, under favourable conditions that framing effects do not reach, identify some true, self-evident propositions. These self-evident propositions purport to *describe*, or correspond to, moral facts.

(2) Second, inferring general normative conclusions about intuitionist epistemology from empirical studies could be problematic. Sinnott-Armstrong jumps from particular studies in neuroethics to a general conclusion in moral epistemology. He finishes off his argument by drawing a normative conclusion from empirical studies that give informed moral believers reason to ascribe a large probability of error to moral beliefs in general. In other words, he states that epistemological intuitionism is false because empirical findings show that we ought to commit to at least an inference for being justified.

There is no doubt that developments in neuroethics can affect moral philosophy. For instance, two people might have different opinions about whether it is morally permissible to boil lobsters alive. This is because they disagree about whether lobsters have a physiological neuro system to feel pain. Although the basis of their moral disagreement is an empirical–neurological disagreement, they can agree about the permissibility of boiling lobsters alive if they believe in the same non-moral, empirical–neurological facts.[17] Nevertheless, neuroethics cannot justify moving directly from empirical-natural sciences to a normative conclusion in meta-ethics (moral epistemology).[18] Although neuroethics can *explain* why in *some* cases emotions and biases affect our non-inferential moral judgement, it cannot epistemologically *justify* that almost *all* of our moral judgements cannot be non-inferentially justified because we are emotional or biased.

Sinnott-Armstrong might object that there is no problem with inferring normative conclusions from empirical premises. If our moral intuitions (read moral beliefs) are unreliable, we should not rely on them. Neuroethics can justify that our moral beliefs are not non-inferentially justified if it can show that framing effects distort or render our moral intuitions unreliable. These findings show that moral intuitions are unreliable and thereby need confirmation.

However, it is not acceptable to conclude that all moral intuitions are unreliable. Although empirical studies show that some of our moral intuitions are unreliable, this does not entail that we should not rely on *any* moral intuitions.[19] Saying that framing effects can distort *some* moral intuitions is one thing, but concluding that *all* moral intuitions are unreliable is another thing. Empirical studies on moral intuitions cannot prove that moral intuitions are systematically unreliable (*cf.* Chapter 6).

Sinnott-Armstrong might object again that if more of our moral intuitions are false than true, and we do not know which ones are true or false, then we need some processes to help us determine which to trust. This entails, he claims, that we can only be inferentially justified, so epistemological intuitionism is wrong. However, it is not true that we always have uncertainty about which ones are the reliable ones. Moral intuitionists do believe, that in normal situations without framing effects, there are at least some true moral propositions on the basis of our moral intuitions resulting from our adequate understanding of those propositions.[20] In these cases, we are non-inferentially justified.

(3) Third, it seems that Sinnott-Armstrong does not consider the difference between 'conflicts of duties' and 'conflicting intuitions'. In his discussion of disagreement, Sinnott-Armstrong conflates these two notions. On the one hand, although some moral duties or principles may conflict, this does not entail that we cannot know them non-inferentially. On the other hand, although people might have conflicting moral intuitions about our pro tanto duties, moral intuitionists such as Ross believe that moral intuitions cannot help us know what our all-things-considered duty is in these cases. Let me explicate this more.

Moral conflict occurs when, in one situation, we have at least two morally relevant non-moral properties or principles that oppose each other. This gives us conflicting *pro tanto* duties or principles. Ross believes that the conflicts between moral duties or principles are prone to cause some difficulties with which 'plain' people without 'sufficient mental maturity' cannot cope.

The first difficulty arises from a conflict between the moral principles of a given society at a given time. For example, consider the story of Jean-Paul Sartre's student, who came to him asking whether he should stay with his mother or join the Free French forces.[21] There are two principles or duties in this case, and it is not easy to make a decision.

Second, there are sometimes conflicts between the moral principles accepted by different societies. For instance, McNaughton talks about 'the case of the Eskimos who, it is said, used to leave old people to die on the ice once they had become too old to hunt or to make a contribution to the welfare of the tribe in other ways'.[22] Most people in Western societies probably take the Eskimos' act to be morally wrong. However, Eskimos themselves do not think that they are doing wrong. As another example, most Muslims (especially in Saudi Arabia) think that polygamy is right. But many Western people think that polygamy is wrong. These cases show that some principles that one society thinks are moral are taken to be immoral by another society.

Given these difficulties, people may get confused about the authority of general non-inferential moral principles and the right action they should do, for people often think that moral principles are absolute and should be free from conflicts and disagreements.

Although Ross thinks that it is the task of moral philosophy to remove such confusion as much as possible, he argues in the *Foundation of Ethics* that we can never know what we should do in complex situations. In Ross's view, we can only know the general non-inferential principles of *pro tanto* duty. We cannot know by moral intuition what we should do when many such principles conflict. In fact, he says that in particular situations, our all-things-considered duties cannot be *known* at all.[23]

Ross tries to explain where exactly, in a particular situation, moral conflicts can occur. According to him, moral conflict occurs only between moral principles of *pro tanto* duties. But this cannot ruin their generality and non-inferentiality.[24] According to him,

> If, as almost all moralists except Kant are agreed, and as most plain men think, it is sometimes right to tell a lie or break a promise, it must be mentioned that there is a difference between *prima facie* duty and actual or absolute duty. When we think ourselves justified in breaking, and indeed morally obliged to break, a promise in order to relieve someone's distress, we do not for a moment cease to recognize a *prima facie* duty to keep our promise, and this leads us to feel, not

indeed shame or repentance, but certainly compunction, for behaving as we do; we recognize further, that it is our duty to make up somehow to the promisee for the breaking of the promise. (1930, 2002, 28)

On this view, moral conflict is a real conflict, but not between all-things-considered duties. Ross thinks that this approach to the issue of conflicts of duties can survive the *authority* of general non-inferential moral principles. In other words, our general non-inferential *pro tanto* moral principles are taken to apply in every case without exception, but if they were to express all-things-considered duties, they would lose their authority about generality and non-inferentiality. Ross writes in this respect that

> The only way to save the authority of such rules is to recognize them not as rules guaranteeing the rightness of any act that falls under them, but as rules guaranteeing that any act which falls under them tends so far as that aspect of its nature goes, to be right, and can be rendered wrong only if in virtue of another aspect of its nature it comes under another rule by reason of which it tends more decidedly to be wrong. (1939, 313)

Hence, our general non-inferential moral rules have no exceptions if these rules are understood as expressing *pro tanto* duties, not all-things-considered duties. Although the real conflict occurs between the non-inferential *pro tanto* duties in a particular situation, the conflict does not ruin the non-inferentiality of moral rules.

Nonetheless, what can we generally say of conflicting intuitions about basic moral principles? Can we say that conflicts between moral duties originate from the conflict of moral intuitions? Duty conflicts are conflicts between principles of *pro tanto* duties about which we may agree. However, conflicts between moral intuitions can be conflicts between people in the sense that people might have conflicting intuitions about what *pro tanto* duties are. For example, Ross argues that some moral principles may be given up in a similar fashion as scientific theories are dropped when they contradict observations. This is the well-known passage from Ross:

> the moral convictions of thoughtful and well-educated people are the data of ethics, just as sense-perceptions are the data of natural science. Just as some of the latter have to be rejected as illusory, so have the former; but as the latter are rejected only when they conflict with other more accurate sense-perceptions, the former are rejected only when they conflict with convictions which stand better the test of reflection. (1930, 2002, 41)[25]

In this passage, Ross talks about moral intuition conflict rather than duty conflict. It seems that Ross appeals to moral intuition (convictions) to make a distinction between moral intuition conflict and duty conflict. What he means by moral intuition is the collective intuitions of well-educated people rather than personal moral intuitions. He writes,

> I should make it plain at this stage that I am *assuming* the correctness of some of our main convictions as to *prima facie* duties.... The main moral convictions of the plain men seem to me to be, not opinions which it is for philosophy to prove or disprove, but knowledge from the start; and in my own case I seem to find little difficulty in distinguishing these essential convictions from other moral convictions which I also have, which are merely fallible opinions based on an imperfect study of the working for good or evil of certain institutions or types of action. (1930, 2002, 20–1, fn. 1)

In Ross's view, moral intuitions are reflective and not naïve.[26] Of course, it is familiar that people's moral intuitions conflict with each other and their intuitions about *pro tanto* duty differ to some extent. Because some basic moral principles are not obvious, they need reflection and discussion. So, we should not expect a ready consensus on them.[27] Ross thought that moral intuitions could be rejected in favour of others' well-educated intuitions. This is, in fact, an example of the method of reflective equilibrium about moral intuitions that we talked about before.[28]

Saying that people have different moral intuitions, which may conflict is one thing, but saying that some people are non-inferentially justified in having a moral intuition about self-evident moral principles is another thing. When Sinnott-Armstrong talks about disagreement or conflicts between moral principles, he refers to the conflicting intuitions between people. This conflict is part of what leads him to reject the non-inferentiality of moral intuitions. However, conflicting intuitions about one particular situation do not undermine the idea that we non-inferentially believe in different *pro tanto* duties, which may conflict. For example, suppose that Jack and Jill might have different intuitions about what Sue should do, all-things-considered because Jack thinks that in this case, justice is more important than the avoidance of suffering, and Jill thinks that in this same case, the avoidance of suffering is more important than justice. So they disagree about all-things-considered duty, but they agree about what the relevant *pro tanto* duties are.

In the following, I will focus on the content of Sinnott-Armstrong's premises in much greater detail. I argue that his argument is not sound because the content of some of his premises is false.

2.2 Challenging premises (4) and (5)

There is a problem in premises (4) and (5) concerning particular moral beliefs and general moral principles. Sinnott-Armstrong writes, 'A moral believer cannot be justified in holding a particular moral belief when that believer is justified in believing that the moral belief has a large probability of being untrue.' When Sinnott-Armstrong tries to reject epistemological intuitionism, as he describes it, he refers to any sort of (non-inferential) moral belief, that is, either general or particular. However, it is evident from his various examples that his argument is directed against a particular kind of (non-inferential) moral belief.[29] Indeed, although he criticizes epistemological intuitionism just in *particular* cases, he concludes that moral agents cannot reach *any* sort of justified moral beliefs non-inferentially since they need confirmation to make their beliefs justified. Yet, I believe we can still have general non-inferentially justified self-evident moral propositions. Let me explain.

We can distinguish at least two kinds of epistemological intuitionism from each other: particularistic and generalistic intuitionism (*cf.* Chapter 3). According to the

> *Particularistic Account of Epistemological Intuitionism*: There are some justified self-evident moral propositions about particular situations which can be understood non-inferentially, but there are no self-evident general moral propositions.[30]

According to this account of epistemological intuitionism, we cannot know justified self-evident general principles. All we have are particular self-evident moral judgements that vary from case to case. However, there is an account of epistemological intuitionism in which general moral self-evident principles play a role. According to the

> *Generalistic Account of Epistemological Intuitionism*: There are some *general* self-evident moral propositions that can be justified non-inferentially.[31]

In this account of intuitionism, particular self-evident moral judgements are not important. All we have are general self-evident moral principles. These general principles can be used in every particular case. However, these two kinds of epistemological intuitionism can be combined.[32] According to the

> *Global Account of Epistemological Intuitionism*: There are some justified general self-evident non-inferential moral principles, and we can know some particular moral propositions non-inferentially through *matching* them with general moral principles by using our moral *imagination*.

There is a likely objection to this definition that matching involves finding similarities between two things, and indeed this is a kind of implicit inferential reasoning. I think we can reply to this objection by appealing to what scholars say in cognitive science. In fact, I put this psychological picture, that is, 'matching' and 'imagination', in my definition to provide an account in favour of the idea of non-inferentiality, both for general and particular moral knowledge. I know that some cognitive scientists might reject this psychological picture; however, I use it only as a possible explanation for non-inferential knowledge.

Yet Sinnott-Armstrong might rightly object that he did not say we do not have any non-inferential capacity in knowledge since a non-inferential capacity can be found, for example, in mathematics and logic. All he wants to reject is non-inferential *moral* knowledge.

However, cognitive psychology and linguistics can help us show that we might have a capacity for even non-inferential moral knowledge. George Lakoff (1999), following Eleanor Rosch's (1978) prototype theory of categorization, advocates a cognitive model as a way in which we organize knowledge by certain cognitive structures, through perceptual and conceptual processes, in the form of conceptual categories.[33] Suppose we have a category like birds. While we reflect on some kinds of birds as better examples than others, we can consider the best examples as *prototypes*. Now suppose we have the prototypical bird. How can we learn that, for instance, item A (e.g. parrot) is a bird? By matching an item to a prototype, we can judge that the item falls under a category through imagination.[34] If we see that the item is sufficiently similar to the prototype for the category, we can then categorize it as an instance of that category.

Although there can be different models for the matching process, the most important point here for cognitive psychologists and linguists is that the matching process is NOT inferential. The reason is that empirical evidence shows that this process is not consciously based on theory (principle) or other believed propositions.[35] In fact, experiments show that this process is not based on theory or other beliefs. The matching process is a process that happens (through imagination) unconsciously, and there is no premise-based reasoning involved.[36] Although someone might object that this empirical evidence seems unpersuasive and that the matching process looks like an argument, all these findings suggest is that there is a possibility of having a capacity for non-inferential judgement in terms of seeing similarities and dissimilarities of particular items to prototypes.[37] This cognitive picture can be applied to our moral beliefs and help us to see how matching some of our particular moral beliefs, as particular category items, to general self-evident moral principles, as prototypical principles, can be non-inferentially justified or independently credible.[38]

There is one more general worry about premises (4) and (5). It seems that Sinnott-Armstrong assumes that if a belief is improbable, we ought not to believe it. But that might be false. Suppose someone must choose among four mutually exclusive and jointly exhaustive hypotheses, A, B, C and D, about which one has the knowledge that A is 40 per cent probable, B 30 per cent, C 20 per cent and D 10 per cent. Our intuition plausibly says that one should believe A, even though one knows that A is probably false.

2.3 Rejecting step (7)

Sinnott-Armstrong argues that empirical studies suggest there is a *large probability* of error for *particular* moral beliefs and judgements.[39] He then argues in steps (4)–(7) that if a moral believer is justified in believing that a particular moral belief has a large probability of being untrue, then that moral believer has to have made at least an inference with that belief as a conclusion. 'If someone is justified in believing that a belief falls into a class of beliefs of which a smaller percentage is not true, then that person is committed to a justificatory inferential structure with that belief as a conclusion'. Although it is not clear what Sinnott-Armstrong means by 'large' probability, most moral intuitionists think that there are some *general* moral principles such as 'killing someone just for fun is *pro tanto* wrong' that are not distorted by emotions and biases (partiality). They think that some moral believers have at least a *reason* to believe that some of their general moral beliefs are not distorted by any such framing effects.

Sinnott-Armstrong grants that there is such reason and calls this reason that moral intuitionists believe in a 'countervailing reason' (2011, 22). Sinnott-Armstrong argues that if someone has a countervailing reason, that person has to ascribe a *low* probability of error to that particular moral belief.[40] Sinnott-Armstrong goes on to say that such a moral believer is justified – but inferentially. The reason that the justification is inferential is that it comes from and depends upon the information that the moral belief is not distorted by such factors. Thus, even a moral believer with a countervailing reason is committed to a justificatory inferential structure.

However, if we have a countervailing reason to believe that our moral beliefs are not distorted, we can still be justified non-inferentially because we did not commit to any inferential structure. Even if we do not have such countervailing reason and we are in a position with a 'high probability of error' because of, for example, being emotional, we can still be non-inferentially justified yet to a lesser degree of confidence. But this does not commit us to an inferential structure. Here is why.

To explain why Sinnott-Armstrong is wrong about being inferentially justified when we have some sort of reason such as countervailing reason, we need to appeal to the difference between 'production of justification' and 'preservation of justification'. Suppose that we have a proposition, P, and a reason to believe P. Suppose further that the reason to believe P comes from perceptual experience or seeming. If our justification for believing P is this reason, then we believe P non-inferentially. Although *preserving* the justification for believing P depends on inferences, this does not entail that the *production* of justification for believing P depends on inferences. Here our perceptual experience or seeming produces justification for believing P without our making inferences. However, to preserve the justification for believing P, we need to make inferences about other sources of support for believing P and about what, if anything, counts against believing P. All that epistemological intuitionists want to say is that the production of justification is non-inferential, not that the preservation is.[41]

Furthermore, recall that step (7) of Sinnott-Armstrong's argument is the premise that if someone is justified in believing that a moral belief falls into at least one class of beliefs of which a smaller percentage (of that class of beliefs) is not true, then that person has to have made at least an inference to that moral belief as a conclusion. In other words, this is the premise that someone who has a non-inferential moral belief has to have made at least one inference in order to be justified in forming this belief. This premise of Sinnott-Armstrong's argument is its Achilles' heel. The premise assumes that, in order to be justified in believing that a belief B is probably true, one must have made an inference to B. This assumption is utterly question-begging against the moral intuitionists. Moral intuitionists hold that it is not necessary for one to have made an inference to a moral belief in order for there to have been *production of justification* for forming the belief. Admittedly, once sources of unreliability are identified, one might need to make inferences in order to *preserve one's justification* for retaining the belief.

One might, however, object that although Sinnott-Armstrong can accept the distinction between production and preservation of justification, he would argue that the production of justification is unreliable. In other words, Sinnott-Armstrong would say that a belief is not *at all* justified unless the believer believes that their belief has a reliable source. However, Sinnott-Armstrong cannot endorse such a thing as this entails that we are not *at all* justified to believe something based on our perceptual experiences. Sinnott-Armstrong agrees that one can produce a non-inferential belief on the basis of, for example, visual experiences, but he thinks that one's belief cannot remain non-inferential because one needs to get confirmation and getting confirmation makes one's belief inferential. My answer is that, although one's production of justification might be unreliable, this does not entail that one's belief was not non-inferential.

2.4 Challenging steps (8) and (9)

Sinnott-Armstrong goes on and attacks in steps (8) – as an intermediate conclusion – and (9) the central idea of epistemological intuitionism, that is, non-inferentiality. He writes, 'If a believer is not justified in holding a belief unless the believer is committed to a justificatory inferential structure, then the believer is not justified non-inferentially in holding the belief'. I believe Sinnott-Armstrong's understanding of non-inferentiality is misguided. In order to show that, I will focus on the way in which he describes the notion of non-inferentiality based upon his description of epistemological intuitionism. Since Sinnott-Armstrong's description of epistemological intuitionism is weak, it allows him to support steps like (8) and (9). But I think a strong version of epistemological intuitionism does not support these steps. In the next section, I will show that Sinnott-Armstrong's conception of epistemological intuitionism is mistaken in a way that upsets his argument against this theory.

3 Sinnott-Armstrong's diluted description of epistemological intuitionism

The fundamental epistemological idea of moral intuitionism is that one is non-inferentially justified in believing some moral propositions – such as that killing someone just for fun is *pro tanto* wrong or that keeping one's promises, *ceteris paribus*, is morally right. Epistemological intuitionists believe that there are some self-evident moral principles we can know on the basis of a moral intuition generated by an adequate understanding of them but without any inferential reasoning.[42]

When Sinnott-Armstrong comes to the epistemology of moral intuitionism, he makes a distinction between two sorts of belief, that is, 'non-inferred' and 'non-inferable'. Non-inferred beliefs are beliefs that are not inferred from other beliefs, and non-inferable beliefs are beliefs that one is not *able* to infer them from other beliefs. Although Sinnott-Armstrong must have meant the 'propositions believed' as beliefs are odd things to be inferred, he tries to define epistemological intuitionism in terms of these two terms. Two possible versions of epistemological intuitionism, then, become

> *Non-Inferred Epistemological Intuitionism (Weak Position)*: Some people are justified in holding some non-inferred moral beliefs.

And

> *Non-Inferable Epistemological Intuitionism (Strong Position)*: Some people are justified in holding some non-inferable moral beliefs.

For Sinnott-Armstrong, a belief is inferred if it is the conclusion of an *explicit* reasoning process. By contrast, a belief is inferable when one

> already has enough information to go through a reasoning process that results in this belief if he had enough incentive to do so. (2002, 307)

The non-inferred account of epistemological intuitionism, Sinnott-Armstrong argues, cannot be the intuitionists' view. The trouble with the non-inferred intuitionism, in his view, is that it makes the idea of non-inferentiality too *weak* for the epistemological intuitionists' purpose. For him, non-inferred intuitionism makes fewer commitments and so is less controversial. Sinnott-Armstrong writes that

> A believer is justified non-inferentially in a *weak* way when the believer is justified regardless of whether the believer actually goes through any inference. (2011, 13)

In fact, Sinnott-Armstrong argues that it is a weak position because some moral beliefs can be non-inferred yet inferable. For example, the content of a belief might be so obvious to a mentally mature person that she does not need to go through any inference. In addition, one can accept the non-inferred version of epistemological intuitionism yet maintain that this justification is a matter of being able to construct certain inferences *to* what is believed.[43] For example, suppose one has a non-inferred moral belief according to which 'telling a lie is wrong'. Although this belief is non-inferred, it does not follow that it is not inferable. One can have certain inferences to reach such a conclusion, for example, telling a lie violates fidelity. Infidelity is morally wrong. So, telling a lie is wrong.

Furthermore, Sinnott-Armstrong rejects the non-inferred version of epistemological intuitionism since it cannot stop epistemic sceptical regress. He reasons that since weak intuitionism does not deny dependence on an inferential ability that leads to a skeptical regress, weak intuitionism is not strong enough to meet the skeptical challenge. (2006b, 190)

Sinnott-Armstrong believes that non-inferred intuitionism needs to deny an inferential ability to stop the sceptical challenge. However, one can rightly object that if we can be justified in holding a belief without inferring it from other beliefs we hold, then this can halt sceptical regress, although the belief might also be inferable. Therefore, despite Sinnott-Armstrong's view, I believe the weak version of intuitionism can stop sceptical regress.[44]

The non-inferable version of epistemological intuitionism, by contrast, reads non-inferentiality as being strong. Sinnott-Armstrong writes,

> a believer is justified non-inferentially in a *strong* way only when the believer is justified regardless of whether the believer is committed to any justificatory inferential structure. (2011, 13)

For the strong version of epistemological intuitionism, a belief is justified independently of any inferential structure and ability to infer it. In the stronger view, there is no dependence on inference or premise, according to Sinnott-Armstrong.

But what does such a commitment amount to? Is this just an obscure way of saying that the believer *cannot* infer this belief from any other beliefs he holds? Epistemological intuitionists, Sinnott-Armstrong argues, do not need to claim that. He writes,

> This [non-inferability] . . . does not require that such justified moral believers actually are not able to infer those moral beliefs from any other beliefs. The point instead is that, regardless of whether they happen to have that ability, such justified moral believers would remain justified even if they were not able to infer those moral beliefs from any other beliefs. (2002, 306)

Sinnott-Armstrong admits that the standard of a belief's being 'non-inferable' is too much for an epistemological intuitionist since it is not difficult for a person to be *able* to build at least some inferences. Nevertheless, he grants that only this stronger version of epistemological intuitionism could be enough to stop sceptical regress.[45] He thinks that the opponents of intuitionist epistemology need to deny only the stronger version of epistemological intuitionism.[46]

Although Sinnott-Armstrong believes that the opponents of intuitionist epistemology need to deny only the non-inferable version, he does not say that there are some propositions that *cannot* be inferred. What Sinnott-Armstrong must mean here is the view that there are some propositions that one can have justification to believe even when one is not *able* actually to infer them. We can generally doubt whether any proposition can be non-inferable at all. In fact, every proposition is inferable. From a contradiction, everything follows. And a proposition follows from itself. Since there cannot be non-inferable propositions, pretty much for the same reason, there cannot be non-inferable beliefs.[47]

Given what has been covered for the notions of 'non-inferred' and 'non-inferable' so far, Sinnott-Armstrong tries to give an account of a 'particular' and strong epistemological intuitionism based on the idea of 'non-inferability' but *in a different dress*.[48] In order to do this, he uses the idea of classic foundationalism. His idea is that some people's beliefs would be justified regardless of whether they had the 'ability' to form an inference from them. Thus, epistemological intuitionism in the hands of Sinnott-Armstrong becomes

> *Sinnott-Armstrong's Description of Epistemological Intuitionism*: Some believers are justified in holding some moral beliefs independently of whether the believers are *able* to infer those moral beliefs from any other beliefs. (2006b, 185)[49]

What is supposed to characterize non-inferential beliefs, according to Sinnott-Armstrong, is not that they are not inferred. Rather, the fact is that the justification of moral beliefs builds up independently of an 'ability' to infer them. Sinnott-Armstrong admits that we form many non-inferred moral beliefs; however, to reject epistemological intuitionism, he denies that such non-inferred beliefs are justified independently of an ability to infer them. However, I think Sinnott-Armstrong's distinction between non-inferred and non-inferable is not exhaustive, so an alternative account is needed. Here is why.

There is a worrying point in Sinnott-Armstrong's expression of his understanding of non-inferentiality. According to his understanding of epistemological intuitionism, we are justified in having a moral belief *independently of an ability* to infer it from any other beliefs. When he goes further and argues against moral intuitionism's epistemology, he refers to those moral beliefs that intuitionists think can be justified independently of inference as 'non-inferable'. This could not just be a slip of the pen when he writes, for example, that moral intuition is committed to 'strongly-held non-inferable moral belief'. In his view,

> Moral intuitionism claims that some strongly-held non-inferable moral beliefs are justified. Since such believers are justified but lack the ability to infer, they are justified non-inferentially. (2002, 308–9)[50]

He thinks that some people's moral beliefs or moral intuitions are, in fact, 'non-inferable', though he admits that it can be difficult to determine which beliefs fall into this category.[51]

Although Sinnott-Armstrong is well aware that Audi has long championed the idea that understanding a proposition entails the *ability* to draw some inferences from it, he refers to non-inferable intuitions as *intuitions that have no inferential relations with any other beliefs (propositions)*.[52] This is because, in his view, *only* such a category can halt the sceptical regress. Thus, Sinnott-Armstrong does not believe that the category of non-inferable intuitions can be interpreted as to be beliefs (propositions) *whose justification* is not (entirely) dependent on their being inferred or inferable *from other beliefs*. Rather, he believes one can remain justified even if one is *not able* to infer those moral beliefs from any other beliefs.

Given that, my criticism of Sinnott-Armstrong is that his understanding of moral non-inferentiality is based on some classic moral intuitionists' ideas, and it is a less plausible picture of new intuitionism, which I advocated. In my account of modest epistemological intuitionism, following Audi (2004), Shafer-Landau (2003), Stratton-Lake (2002) and Hooker (2000a), I have largely rejected the interpretation of non-inferentiality that is based on non-inferability (*cf.* Chapter 5). Although some classic moral intuitionists (e.g. Prichard) thought that moral agents could not say anything to prove their moral intuitions, some modest classic intuitionists (e.g. Ross) allowed inferentiality for moral intuitions.[53] According to the modest new epistemological intuitionism, having a self-evident moral belief does not entail that the belief *cannot* be inferred from other beliefs. It is a misconception of epistemological intuitionism to think that moral intuitions about self-evident propositions are non-inferable. As Audi points out, even if a moral believer reaches a moral belief non-inferentially, this does not entail that the agent is *not able* to infer the belief from other beliefs.[54]

Nonetheless, one can object that Sinnott-Armstrong's description of epistemological intuitionism can even be compatible with the new epistemological intuitionism: it does seem that, in my account of intuitionism, someone who *needs* not infer such a belief could be justified in holding it, non-inferentially. That is to say, if moral intuitions can be justified non-inferentially, then it can be true that someone who does not use the ability to infer them could be justified in believing them, and this would match Sinnott-Armstrong's description of epistemological intuitionism according to which someone is non-inferentially justified *independently* of the ability to infer.

Although Sinnott-Armstrong's understanding of epistemological intuitionism seems consistent with what most epistemological intuitionists say, I think he has a weak version of epistemological intuitionism in his sights. He does not present epistemological intuitionism in its *strongest form*. If epistemological intuitionists can show us that an agent can be non-inferentially justified in believing one moral belief even if he has the minimal *ability* to tie the belief to any other belief, with an inference or argument, this can *weaken* Sinnott-Armstrong's description of epistemological intuitionism. Epistemological intuitionists can argue that having the ability to infer something is necessary to have sufficient understanding.

The *ability* to form at least one argument for an allegedly self-evident principle, say that promise-breaking is pro tanto wrong, can be consistent with adequately and sufficiently understanding a moral proposition. In the next section, I shall try to explain why *inferential ability* can be parcelled with being justified in believing some moral propositions *non-inferentially*. Having this *ability* does not threaten the moral intuitionists' central epistemological idea, that is, one is justified in believing some self-evident moral propositions non-inferentially.

4 Adding fuel to the epistemological intuitionists' fire: An alternative version to Sinnott-Armstrong's epistemological intuitionism

Sinnott-Armstrong's interpretation of epistemological intuitionism is a *diluted* version of the epistemological intuitionist view of non-inferentiality. Since Sinnott-Armstrong's account of epistemological intuitionism is not strong enough, it is not immune to the empirical criticisms to which he is referring. But how can we have a stronger form of epistemological intuitionism to stand against Sinnott-Armstrong's criticisms derived from empirical psychology? To start with, let me first discuss some important points in the epistemology of modest new intuitionism, although I might need to repeat what I have discussed before (*cf.* Chapters 4 and 5).

Recall new epistemological intuitionism's central epistemic idea that distinguishes two claims from each other (*cf.* Chapter 5). Compare:

(1) We can justifiably believe some non-inferential propositions. Or we can know some self-evident propositions.
   And
(2) We can justifiably believe that some propositions are self-evident.

We have to make this distinction since one does not need to know that p is self-evident to know that p, self-evidently. To know that a proposition is *self-evidently justified*, one must be able to form an inference to the proposition's self-evidence; however, this does not exclude knowing a *self-evidently true* proposition based on *sufficient understanding* of it, non-inferentially. When we say that one's understanding of a proposition must be sufficient, this entails that one must know at least some logical entailments of the proposition, that is, be able to apply this knowledge in appropriate circumstances, comprehending the elements and at least some of their relations. Parfit, for example, writes about the self-evident truth that

> When Gödel writes that some beliefs force themselves upon us as true, Gödel may instead mean that these beliefs are self-evidently true, in the sense that, if we fully understand these beliefs, we can recognize that they are, or must be, true. (2011, Vol. 2, 508)

Proposition (1) states that certain propositions are self-evidently true, and we can know them self-evidently, that is, based on an *adequate understanding* of them. However, it does not follow that if one understands a self-evident proposition, one has to believe it. The point is that such propositions can be knowable only on the basis of an adequate understanding of them, not that understanding them requires believing them (much less that knowing them requires believing that they are self-evident). Although certain basic logical truths may be self-evident, someone without training in basic logic may understand them but not believe them on the basis of his understanding of them. Similarly, certain basic moral truths may be self-evident even though certain people do not believe them, even though they understand them.

However, proposition (2) holds that even if one can know some self-evident propositions based on adequate understanding, one can still form at least an inference or make an argument to show that the proposition is self-evident. And yet, one might not *need* to do so because self-evident propositions do not *require* proof.

Therefore, two important points must be considered here: (i) According to the new epistemological intuitionism, among the conditions for a moral proposition's being self-evidently true are that it need not be inferred from some other moral proposition and that by *sufficient understanding* of the proposition one can know it.[55] However, these conditions do not entail that one does not need any other propositions to know the self-evident proposition in question. To *sufficiently understand* self-evidently true propositions, one must be able to draw some inferences *from* them. (ii) Although some facts and *propositions believed to be self-evident* are morally basic, we can still say something to make them seem plausible. Even if there are some self-evidently true moral principles, a belief in those principles being true can be justified further by forming inferences *to* them. Understanding a proposition *does* require being *able* to draw inferences from it but does *not* require being able to make inferences to it.

Given all these points, I propose an alternative account of epistemological intuitionism, which is *stronger* than the one Sinnott-Armstrong attacks. In this version, the content of moral propositions is not at stake; rather, the *justificatory* role of believing these propositions is important. This version of epistemological intuitionism is:

> *Modest Account of Epistemological Intuitionism*: One is justified in holding some (self-evidently true) moral propositions based on *sufficient understanding* where this justification is not be based upon *inferences* but is adequate for knowledge of the propositions.[56] Yet, to have a sufficient understanding of propositions, one needs to have the *ability* to make at least some inferences *from* them. The possibility of knowing self-evident moral propositions based on some *argument* is not precluded.[57]

Although a moral proposition itself may be self-evident and non-inferentially justified, we do not *need* a higher-order belief about its status as self-evident in order to be inferentially justified in believing it. However, if we do not have the ability to infer something from the self-evident moral proposition, then we do not have a sufficient understanding of it. In that case, we do not have justification because we do not have sufficient understanding.

Based on the modest account of epistemological intuitionism, we can propose a modest account of non-inferentiality, as well:

> *Modest Account of Non-Inferentiality*: If P is the object of moral knowledge, then A knows that P non-inferentially at t if

(1) An understanding of P is sufficient justification for believing it and is sufficient for knowing the proposition, provided that A believes it on the basis of A's understanding of it.
(2) A is non-inferentially justified in his belief that P at t, whether or not he has an argument or inference for keeping the justification of P.
(3) A's ability to infer something from P is a necessary condition for A's having sufficient understanding of P, which is a necessary condition for A's being non-inferentially justified in believing P.

Sinnott-Armstrong cannot accept the modest accounts of epistemological intuitionism and non-inferentiality. What precludes his accepting them is that he thinks someone can be non-inferentially justified in believing some propositions independently of whether the believer is *able* to infer those propositions. But I think the way in which Sinnott-Armstrong focuses on inferential *ability* distorts the epistemological intuitionists' account because if one is totally unable to make any inferences *from* a proposition, one does not understand that proposition sufficiently. Let me explain this with an example.

Suppose that Tom's mother tells him strongly: 'it is absolutely wrong to abuse anyone in the school'. She then asks: 'Did you understand, Tom?' Probably Tom would answer, 'yes, Mum!' But how can Tom's mother make sure that her son really got the point? Tom's mother can ask again, 'tell me something to make me sure that you understood'. If Tom continues to say: 'I got the point, I don't have anything to say', his mother may doubt whether he understood it. But if Tom says, 'you're right, Mum! It is absolutely wrong to torture my friend, Jack', his mother would be happy. Tom shows that he understands 'abuse' and 'torture' and infers that a prohibition on abusing anyone in the school also prohibits torturing his friend (Jack) since torture is a kind of abuse.

Epistemological intuitionists can explain why having the inferential *ability* is necessary to be justified in believing a moral proposition. Here is my argument.

(1) According to my account of self-evidence, that is, the seeming account of self-evidence, having sufficient understanding is a necessary condition for being non-inferentially justified in believing a self-evident proposition (*cf.* Chapter 5).

(2) To have a sufficient understanding of a self-evident proposition, we need an ability to draw at least an inference *from* the self-evident proposition in question unless the proposition is too obvious.

(3) Thus, having the ability to infer something is a necessary condition for being non-inferentially justified in believing a self-evident proposition.

Having the ability to infer something does not entail that one is justified inferentially. Inferring B from A might not in any way be a justification of A. Yes, it is an inference. I think that the only way someone could think that seeing what A implies is part of the justification of A is that A's implications are attractive. But some of A's implications probably are neither attractive nor unattractive. When someone draws such an implication from A, perhaps in order to think through what A means, this really cannot be plausibly thought to be any part of the justification of A – and thus, though an inference, not an inferential justification.

What makes a justification inferential is explicit reasoning, not inferring a proposition for sufficient understanding.[58]

The difference between the modest account of intuitionism and Sinnott-Armstrong's description of epistemological intuitionism is that Sinnott-Armstrong's interpretation restricts the epistemological intuitionists' ideas of non-inferentiality because someone can be justified in believing a moral proposition non-inferentially while being *unable* to draw an inference, and this can fulfil Sinnott-Armstrong's description of intuitionism. However, when one is completely *unable* to infer something from the proposition, it is plausible to say that he does not understand the proposition adequately or sufficiently, so he is not actually justified in believing it.[59] People might be unable to point *to* inferences to a proposition P and yet very definitely understand the proposition. They do not understand the proposition unless they can make inferences *from* it.

In order to illustrate further the difference between a modest account of intuitionism and Sinnott-Armstrong's one, take the following case, which I call

The Flaming Cat: A man observes, on the street, that two kids want to set a poor cat on fire. He vehemently stops them from doing that.

Almost everyone admits that 'torturing a cat just for fun is *pro tanto* morally wrong' is self-evidently true in the sense that by reflecting on the constituted elements of the proposition, without needing other propositions, one can grant it. However, without having the ability to infer something from the self-evident proposition, it is hard to say that one understood the proposition. If we ask the man in the story why he stopped the kids from doing that, he probably would say because torturing a cat is *pro tanto* morally wrong and nothing else in the circumstances outweighed that consideration. He can illustrate his understanding of 'Torturing a cat is *pro tanto* morally wrong' by combining it with the proposition 'Tabby is a cat' and inferring from those two propositions, 'Torturing Tabby would be *pro tanto* morally wrong'.

Suppose further that someone asks the children in the story whether they sufficiently understand the judgement that it is *pro tanto* wrong to torture an innocent cat. How can they show that they did indeed understand the proposition? They should use their ability to infer something from it. For example, they might infer, 'it would be *pro tanto* wrong to torture any of Tabby, Felix, Kitty, or Tom for fun'. By offering an inference from the proposition, they have shown that they understood it.

But what would he say if someone further asks the man why torturing an innocent creature is (self-evidently) *pro tanto* morally wrong? He might form an inference or argument to the proposition to show that his belief is justified. Here is an example:

(1) Torturing a cat is an example of doing injury to others (maleficence).
(2) Doing injury to others is *pro tanto* morally wrong.
(3) Therefore, torturing a cat is *pro tanto* wrong.

One can object that the argument is not sound because of some premises. Although this objection might be correct, it does not have an impact on my point. All I wanted to show is that one can form at least one inference or argument to justify (3), even though (3) is itself a self-evident proposition.

A modest account of intuitionism maintains that the man in the story holds his proposition believed non-inferentially based on an adequate understanding of it. However, this man might also have an argument *for* the self-evident proposition. And the man might demonstrate his ability to infer something *from* the proposition in order to show that he sufficiently understood it. But neither the ability to make inferences *from* a proposition nor the ability to make inferences *to* this proposition precludes the man's having non-inferential justification for believing the self-evident proposition.

Sinnott-Armstrong might object that we have many disagreements about argument and reasoning, and we need to seek confirmation from other people's beliefs. But does any of this count against my account of modest non-inferentiality? I do not think it does. Disagreement is hardly something ignored by epistemological intuitionists. Advocates of modest epistemological intuitionists can accept fallibility. They can also acknowledge widespread disagreements about what is morally right, all-things-considered, in *particular* cases. But they point to greater consensus on *general* moral principles about *pro tanto* duties.

Let us end this section by highlighting the *weakness* of Sinnott-Armstrong's description of epistemological intuitionism. Sinnott-Armstrong describes epistemological intuitionism in terms of classic foundationalism, that is, the idea that we have two sorts of beliefs, basic and non-basic. Basic beliefs are non-inferable, and non-basic beliefs are inferred from basic ones. The relationship between basic and non-basic beliefs is unidirectional. However, as I have shown in Chapter 5, modest foundationalism holds that there can be a two-way justification between self-evident and non-self-evident moral propositions. This entails that even self-evident propositions can gain support from their fit with non-self-evident propositions. Self-evident propositions are not non-inferable, and we can argue for them by inference from non-self-evident propositions.

Epistemological intuitionism can be strengthened if it is defined in terms of *modest foundationalism*. Non-inferentiality and inferentiality can sit alongside each other without contradiction. Although we can know some moral propositions that are self-evidently true, this does not entail that we cannot form powerful inferences to them. Sinnott-Armstrong's description of epistemological intuitionism, then, in the light of these new insights, becomes

> *Revised Version of Sinnott-Armstrong's Description of Epistemological Intuitionism*: some believers are non-inferentially justified in holding some (self-evident) moral propositions based on an *adequate understanding* of them, which is dependent on the believer's *ability* to infer at least one proposition from them.

Even if the believer has the *ability* to *infer* those moral propositions from the propositions in question, the believer might still be non-inferentially justified. All I wanted to argue is that a believer must have the *minimal ability* to make inferences from the moral proposition, or they do not really understand it. But having the minimal ability to infer something for sufficient understanding does not alter the non-inferential justification of our beliefs to an inferential one. The revised version of Sinnott-Armstrong's description of intuitionism, then, is immune to his raised criticisms. If this is the case, the revised version of Sinnott-Armstrong's description of epistemological intuitionism does not support his central argument against moral intuitionism.[60]

5 Conclusion

In this chapter, I argued that Sinnott-Armstrong's central argument against epistemological intuitionism does not work. All he can show is that our beliefs in self-evident moral propositions can be distorted because we are emotional. And this is absolutely compatible with what most of the epistemological intuitionists say, that is, there are some self-evident propositions, independent of us. I also showed that step (7) in his argument – if someone is justified in believing that a moral belief falls into at least one class of beliefs of which a smaller percentage is not true, then that person has to have made at least an inference to that moral belief as a conclusion – is question-begging against intuitionists. I went on to argue that Sinnott-Armstrong's conception of epistemological intuitionism is mistaken. The best version of moral intuitionism can survive empirical criticisms. If we build 'having the ability to infer' into our account of understanding a proposition and if we distinguish between 'production of justification' and 'preservation of justification' in our version of epistemological intuitionism, we can explain why getting confirmation from a third party does not ruin the intuitionist epistemology of non-inferentiality. I believe Sinnott-Armstrong is mistaken to suggest that inference *from* the target proposition compromises the non-inferential element in the (production of) justification for the proposition.

If I am on the right track, Sinnott-Armstrong has two options. One is that he could abandon his argument against epistemological intuitionism. The other is that he could change his conception of epistemological intuitionism, but this change would have an impact on his conclusion. Having changed his conception of epistemological intuitionism, he should conclude that, even though some of our moral intuitions on particular occasions can be distorted by our emotions, there are some non-inferentially justified self-evident moral principles.

Afterword

In this book, I developed epistemological intuitionism by rethinking it in the light of empirical challenges. This book consists of three parts. In Part I of this book, I defended the non-doxastic seeming account of philosophical intuition. I demonstrated that the seeming account could provide us with a tenable mental ontology of *philosophical* intuition. For us to have the intuition that p, then, is for p to seem non-inferentially to us to be true. I also argued that the seeming account of philosophical intuition could be applied to *moral* intuitions as well: to have the moral intuition that p is to have the intellectual seeming that p. The seeming account of moral intuition gives us an explanation of why moral intuitions should be treated as evidence.

In Part II, I elucidated the most tenable elements of the classic moral intuitionist epistemology by focusing on Prichard's and Ross's intuitionist framework. I also defended the new modest moral intuitionist epistemology from various objections. I contended that non-inferential self-evident propositions might also have inferential justification. I also showed how reflection might work. Then I argued for what seems to me to be the strongest form of epistemological moral intuitionism, that is, modest seeming-based epistemological intuitionism. In my favoured account of epistemological intuitionism, since seemings (similar to perceptual experiences) have the upper hand, emotions (similar to perceptual experiences) can go hand in hand with intuition without creating any epistemic threat.

In Part III, I used my favoured account of moral intuition and epistemological intuitionism to offer responses to some empirical challenges that come from neuroethics. I showed that the empirical data which empirical moral psychologists provide to knock down moral intuition is not strong enough to do that. I argued then that thinking of moral intuitions as seemings can help us to have an account of emotion that fits with moral intuitions. I also argued that the strongest form of epistemological intuitionism could offer responses to the sceptics who believe that epistemological intuitionism is false because emotional experiences, among other things, always mislead intuition. The strongest form of epistemological intuitionism can also show that Sinnott-Armstrong's argument against epistemological intuitionism is question-begging, and his conception of epistemological intuitionism is mistaken.

Notes

Chapter 1

1. See Plato (*Republic*, 508e and 509d). Also see Gulley (1963). Throughout this book, I occasionally employ the terms 'non-inferential', 'direct' and 'immediate' justification interchangeably. For a similar view, see Pryor (2005).
2. For more details on Plato's and Aristotle's use of intuition, see Baltussen (2007), Gulley (1963) and Ross (1949).
3. Surely I am not denying that there is a rich literature on the topic with a variety of views on the nature of intuition and its role in cognition in medieval literature. As an example, see Wengert (1981).
4. It is important to note that Descartes thought of intuitive judgement as non-inferentially justified, but intuitive judgement is not intuition – it is the judgement that results from intuition. Intuition is the way of arriving at intuitive judgement, or the direct apprehension of truth. Moreover, I do not claim that every instance of intuitive judgement is the direct apprehension of truth. We can make intuitive judgements that appear to us to be direct apprehensions of truth but are actually mistaken.
5. This does not entail that intuitive propositions *cannot* be inferred. For further details about the distinction between inferential and non-inferential justification, see Streumer (2007).
6. I do not claim that the metaphysics of intuition and the psychology of intuition amount to the same thing. Perhaps they do, but this is a controversial view. Some might argue that what intuitions are is one thing and can be determined *a priori*; how intuitions are caused is another thing and can only be determined empirically. This matter however is not directly relevant to my main concern here.
7. For a summary of different theories about the nature of intuition, see Pust (2012), Chapman et al. (2013, esp. Ch. V), Chudnoff (2011, 2013), Bengson (2010) and Deutsch (2015, Chs. 1–2).
8. See also Wittgenstein (1979, §1).
9. See Cappelen (2012, Ch. 1) and Kasper (2012, 62–4).
10. Alternatively, most psychologists mean by the word 'intuition' a non-conscious state. They claim that intuitions are not necessarily conscious states. See Cushman, Young and Hauser (2006). For a sceptical view about intuition, that is, seeing intuitions as delusion, see Reimer (2010). However, in my book, I treat intuitions as conscious states.

11 Some critics of moral intuitionism believe that intuitionists are committed to such a mistake. This is not true, I believe. I will come to this issue in Chapters 3 and 4. Meanwhile, for more details on the criticism of the 'special faculty of intuition', see Stratton-Lake (2002b, 2002c and 2010). Moreover, for more details on different types of intuition, see Audi (2011, 172–3). He proposes five different characterizations, that is, cognitive, objectual, propositional, apprehensional intuition and intuitiveness.
12 See Cappelen (2012, 63–4 and Ch. 1) and Bengson (2014).
13 In Cappelen's view, intuition-talk is something generic like beliefs supported by 'some . . . evidence (of some kind)'. And such talk is argumentatively redundant and eliminable (2012, 44). Cappelen believes that intuitions as mental states do not have positive epistemic status (2012, Ch. 4). I will come to this issue in Chapter 3.
14 Reductionists can be of the view of doxastic and non-doxastic accounts of intuition, although I only deal with the reductionists who believe in doxastic account (i.e. belief-like state). I assume in this book that inclinations and dispositions, for the argument's sake, can be used interchangeably. Non-reductionists can also be of the view of doxastic and non-doxastic accounts of intuition. However, I only discuss the non-reductionists who believe in non-doxastic account of intuition (i.e. seeming state).
15 See Bealer (1998, 208–10).
16 See Lewis (1983, x) and Williamson (2007, 220). Based on another reading, Williamson (2004) is sceptical about using the word 'intuition' in our philosophical discussion as it is vague. He believes that intuitions cannot provide evidence. I talk about his account in Chapter 3.
17 See Plantinga (1993, 105–6).
18 See Nagel (2007, 2012). For further details of this classification, see Cappelen (2012, 7–11).
19 See Bealer (1998, 206f), Cummins (1998, 116), Kornblith (1998, 130), Miller (2000, 235), Pust (2000, Ch. 1), Williamson (2004, 110f), Baz (2012), Nagel (2007, 2012) and Kuntz and Kuntz (2011).
20 See Williamson (2007, Ch. 7).
21 See Brendel (2004), Dennett (1991, 1984), Williamson (2007, Ch. 6), Gendler (2007) and Brown (2011).
22 See Searle (1980, 1984), Parfit (1984) and Putnam (1975).
23 See also Dennett (1995 and 2013, Introduction); Dorbolo (2006) and Brendel (2004).
24 Some may think that Smith *does* know that (h). This does not change our claim that this is our intuition.
25 For an alternative view, see Weinberg, Gonnerman, Buckner and Alexander (2010); Nado (2014) and Miller (2000).

26 Although Audi is generally recognized as believing in a doxastic view of intuition, he sometimes accepts that an intuition is both a cognitive state and a feeling of conviction. Thus Audi sometimes seems to fuse the doxastic and non-doxastic accounts together. See Audi (2011, 175–7) and (1994).
27 See Nimtz (2010).
28 Kauppinen (2013) believes that classical intuitionists such as Price, Sidgwick and Ross take intuitions to be either dispositions-to-believe or just beliefs that result from mere understanding.
29 Pust (2000) also argues that the inclination or disposition-to-believe views fail to capture the occurrent nature of intuitions.
30 As an alternative, Earlenbaugh and Molyneux (2009) and Deutsch (2015) have developed positive arguments for doxastic views.
31 See also Bedke (2008, 2010) and Huemer (2005).
32 Bealer distinguishes rational intuition from the intuitions that are produced by scientific thought experiments. He calls the latter 'physical intuitions'. According to Bealer, physical intuitions, unlike rational intuitions, do not present themselves as necessary.
33 See Bealer (1996a, 123; 1996b, 7 and 1998, 207–11) and Bonjour (1998). See also Sidgwick (1967, 382) as a typical proponent of 'rational intuition'. For further details about rational intuition, see Singer and de Lazari-Radek (2012); Skelton (2008); Rawls (1996, 2007) and Grundmann (2007).
34 In this book, I am quiet about the judgement account (the Williamsonian view). The reason is that the judgement account has many similarities with other reductionist accounts.
35 See Bealer (1992, 101f), Pust (2000, 36&45) and Sosa (1998, 258f).
36 See also Pust (2000, 46) and Sosa (2009, 114f).
37 See Pust (2000, 38f).
38 See Bealer (1998, 207) and Pust (2000, 44).
39 See Bealer (1998, 207) and Sosa (2009, 114). For an alternative view, see Plantinga (1993).
40 There is a recent literature on 'cognitive phenomenology', which might lend support to Bealer's discussion of phenomenology of intuition as intellectual seeming. Advocates of cognitive phenomenology believe that conscious thought possesses a non-sensory phenomenology. So, cognitive phenomenology can be defined negatively as a kind of phenomenology over and above sensory phenomenology. However, for the sake of space, I am not going to discuss the idea of cognitive phenomenology. For more details, see Horgan (2012).
41 See McKay and Dennett (2009).
42 For more of these types of example, see Kahneman (2011, 44–6).
43 See Pust (2000, 32f) and Sosa (1998, 258f).
44 Koksvik (2011) also has developed detailed criticisms of doxastic views. He has explored the reasoning behind the intuition without belief argument in great detail.

45 In the inclination-to-believe model, for example, we will say I recognize that I used to believe that BLAH and perhaps I am even still inclined to believe BLAH, but I now believe not-BLAH. See Cappelen (2012, Ch. 1).

46 I said 'hard-to-solve' paradoxes because the reductionist might simply deny that one keeps having the intuition that p when one has solved the paradox and believes that not-p.

47 As another example, Nimtz (2010) says, we believe that Mary (in Jackson's thought experiment) does not learn anything new when she is released from her room. However, we might have the intuition that she does learn. Or you might believe that a man who just came in with his head covered (hooded man) is not your brother, but still you have the intuition (seeming) that he is your brother.

48 For further examples, see Katz (1981, 220); Plantinga (1993, 110); Pust (2000, 33); Dennett (1988) and Sosa (1998, 259).

49 See also Tucker (2013, Introduction). For an alternative view, that is, a defence of inclination or disposition account of intuition, see Werner (2013). For a defence of inclination or disposition account of intuition, see Earlenbaugh and Molyneux (2009) and Nimtz (2010).

50 Someone might object that Sosa would analyse the seeming as an inclination-to-believe, so my argument begs the question against him. But Sosa cannot analyse non-doxastic states as doxastic states. Because someone might have inclination-to-believe that something is not true, but this does not prevent its seeming to be true. There is also another charge against the disposition or inclination account in terms of is-ought: nothing about what we should believe can follow from the mere fact of a disposition. However, this objection can also be raised against the seeming account. Whether or not this objection works, all I want to highlight here is that although both the seeming and the dispositional or inclination account have some problems, the seeming account can better explain philosophical intuitions. Because the seeming account explains more fundamentally why we are inclined to believe that p while the dispositional or inclination account is uninformative about why we should believe that p.

51 My reasons here are inspired by Stratton-Lake's talk at Reading and Oxford University, 2013.

Chapter 2

1 There are also some metaphysically and epistemically significant differences between seemings accounts that have been discussed in the literature. For example, Chudnoff (2011; 2013) thinks there is significantly more to the phenomenology of presentation than mere seeming, Koksvik (2011; 2017) argues intuitions are

seemings with a felt pushiness rather than presentations; Tucker (2013) thinks in general seemings are accompanied by sensations but intuitions are special kind of seeming without accompanying sensations; Berghofer (2020) thinks intuitions are seemings with a kind of givenness quality.

2. In writing this section, I was influenced by the works of Dancy (2014b) and Bengson's doctoral thesis, 'The Intellectual Given'.
3. See Chappell (2008) and McGinn (2012).
4. See Bengson (2015).
5. See Williamson (2007, 217) and Sosa (2007, 48).
6. See Hintikka (1999, 137 ff.).
7. Directness is very important here because non-facticity does not favour the perceptual model over the idea that intuitions are beliefs, since beliefs are not factive either.
8. Note that although I see some similar shared common features between intuition (seeming) and perceptual experiences, I do not believe that intuitions are experiences as Chudnoff claims. See Chudnoff (2013). For more details on seeming and experiences, see Sosa (2014).
9. See Searle (1979).
10. We can also think of mere presentational states when we are in pain. Presentational states such as pain come to us non-voluntarily and without our conscious intention.
11. See Dancy (2014b).
12. See Wittgenstein (1976, 632).
13. The presentationality of intuition is even clearer if basic logical and mathematical axioms come into consideration. Kurt Gödel, for example, endorses such a view that sometimes logical and mathematical principles 'force themselves upon us as being true' (1964, 271). The geometrical axioms like 'the interior angles of a triangle always add up to 180' present themselves to us as being true.
14. It can be argued that intuitions can also provide us with a justificatory reason in addition to an explanatory one. For example, Stratton-Lake (2016a) believes that intuitions could justify us in having some beliefs. This entails that intuitions can provide us with reason or evidence to believe something. I will come to this issue in the next chapter.
15. For more examples, see Smith (2008).
16. For the sake of argument, this distinction is not at stake here. I treat 'translucent' as if it means 'transparent' in this book and use them interchangeably.
17. This example is inspired by Bengson (Dissertation).
18. For another example, see Dretske (1969, 153 ff.).
19. See Bengson (Dissertation). I do not deny that there is a tradition of philosophers such as Kant, Sellars and McDowell, etc. who think that perceptual states involve

the deployment of concepts. For example, when I see a tree in front of me I have deployed the concept of a tree. My claim here is compatible with what they said.
20 See Prinz (2004) for an alternative view.
21 This translucency is like non-inferentiality in the case of propositional belief.
22 I have used Lillehammer's (2011) various 'conceptions of ethical intuition' here.
23 This does not entail that, Audi believes, we cannot have intuitions about non-self-evident propositions. We can have intuitions that are not intuitions of self-evident propositions. See Audi (1996, 109–10). See also Shafer-Landau (2003).
24 See also Audi (1993, 299 and 1996, 109).
25 See also Audi (1993, 300 and 1996, 109–10).
26 See also Audi (1996, 110).
27 See also Audi (1993, 300 and 1996, 110). Audi elsewhere states that his focus on intuitions is on empirical quasi-perceptual intuitions: 'My concern will be only empirical intuitions and mainly quasi-perceptual intuitive moral judgments' (2007, 201). But how are moral intuitions empirical ones? I am not sure what Audi means by this, especially when he thinks intuitions are identified with *a priori* ones!
28 See also Audi (1993, 300 and 1996, 110).
29 For the discussion of reliability of intuitions, see Bealer (1998 and 2000) and E. Sosa (1998; 2006 and 2007).
30 See also Audi (1993, 303).
31 See Audi (1996, 116). Just to note, in the entirety of this book, I occasionally use the terms 'adequate understanding', 'sufficient reflection' and 'sufficient understanding' interchangeably. Although one can make a distinction between these, it is not at stake for me here.
32 See Audi (2004, 35–6; 1993, 305; 1996, 112 and 1998a, 23).
33 See Audi (2004, 45–7).
34 For example, Audi claims that even intuitive induction should be understood as a conclusion of reflection. He says: 'intuitionism does not have to view intuitive induction as inferential' (2004, 63). I will explain the idea of 'intuitive induction' in Chapter 4.
35 See Audi (1993, 302; 1996, 112; 1998a, 20 and 1999a, 281). Also, for more on the nature of intuition, see his (2008b, 476–8).
36 See Audi (2004, 32). Hudson (1967, 25) also considers the difference between psychological and logical senses of self-evidence.
37 See Boyd (1979).
38 See Audi (1996; 1998a; 1999b and 2004). See also Shafer-Landau (2003).
39 See also McMahan (2000, 93–4). For a discussion of two views on moral intuitions, see Bedke (2008).
40 See Sidgwick (1967, Book 3, Ch. 1, at 211).

41 Sidgwick believes that at least some intuitions can occur, in principle, without being true. He, for example, admits 'the possibility that any such "intuition" may turn out to have an element of error' (1967, Book 3, Ch. 1, §4).
42 Huemer (2007, at 30–5), for instance, believes that any epistemological theory which denies the justificatory power of seemings with moral content is self-defeating.
43 Although further investigation is needed to have an account of emotion, my conjecture would be that some emotions can be like seeming states, and in being so they are similar to moral intuitions; and among those, the moral ones are similar to moral intuitions. I will return to the issue of psychology of moral intuition and explain the theory of emotional experience with reference to seemings in Chapter 6.
44 See Prinz (2007).
45 See Kauppinen (2015 and 2014).
46 I was inspired by Kauppinen (2015, 180) to form this table.
47 Although intuitions can justify, they cannot be justified. One can explain why some intuitions (seeming) are true, but it is not plausible to say that intuitions (seeming) are justified.
48 Michael Huemer calls this 'the principle of phenomenal conservatism'. See Huemer (2007).

Chapter 3

1 For more details about *prima facie* reason, see Dancy (1993a, 609) and Feinberg and Shafer-Landau (2013, 521).
2 For more details on evidence and justification, see Kelley (1991) and Chisholm (1961).
3 For further details on different accounts of evidence, see Kelly (2014).
4 For a discussion that raises challenges to the view that intuition can justify belief, see Benacerraf (1973) and Field (1989). See also Ichikawa and Jarvis (2013, Ch. 13) and Ichikawa (2013).
5 Elsewhere, in a similar vein, Williamson writes: 'When contemporary analytic philosophers run out of arguments, they appeal to intuitions. It can seem, and is sometimes said, that any philosophical dispute, when pushed back far enough, turns into a conflict of intuitions about ultimate premises: "In the end, all we have to go on is our intuitions"' (2007, 214).
6 See Cappelen (2012, 5; 11; 12; 18 and 47).
7 For an alternative view, see Climenhaga (2018).

8   I borrowed the idea of the 'technical' use of intuition (seeming) along with two examples of Kripke and Chisholm from Bengson (2014).
9   See Williamson (2002, 186). See also Williamson (2007, 227–8) for an alternative account.
10 I do not mean to suggest that 'something known to be true' and 'true proposition' are equivalent! There are lots of true propositions that are not known to be true, since not everything true is known (unless there is an omniscient God).
11 See Williamson (2007, 210).
12 See also Chisholm (1957, 44–9).
13 See Chisholm (1957, Ch. 3 and 1989, 20–5) and Jackson (1977, 33–48).
14 See Bealer (1992, 101) and Huemer (2001, 90–91n39).
15 I will explain the idea of 'reflective equilibrium' in the next chapter.
16 It looks to me wrong that Bealer calls these cases 'concrete'. They are fairly *specific* cases, but they are all *fictional*. If they are fictional, then they are (technically) abstract rather than concrete.
17 See Deutsch (2010).
18 For more details, see Pust (2012).
19 For a comprehensive discussion about the justification of seeming states, see Tucker (2013, Ch. 4) and Chudnoff (2013. Ch. 5).
20 Note that I am not saying 'if intuitions are evidence, they cannot be beliefs' as there is no general problem about beliefs being evidence for beliefs. They can if their contents are not the same. So, if intuitions are beliefs, the intuition that p can be the basis for the belief that q. But this makes our belief in q inferential which is not my interest here.

Chapter 4

1   As commentators state, the Rossian moral intuitionism must be understood as in the rationalist tradition like Descartes or Aristotle. See Stratton-Lake (2013; 2010 and 2012). In the same vein, Cudworth thought that moral disagreements (and agreements) can be known by Cartesian intuition. See Hudson (1967, 24).
2   I will not talk about the tradition of intuitionism in the seventeenth and eighteenth century in more detail as it is not my concern here. To understand the ideas of these philosophers, see Sidgwick (1960), Darwall (1995), Schneewind (1997) and Stratton-Lake (2012). Interestingly, Thomas Aquinas held a similar idea in his *Summa Theologica* with different terminology. See Audi (2004, 203, fn. 1).
3   See McNaughton (2002) for an alternative view.
4   This idea was inspired in my mind by Hurka (2011, 1).

5 Needless to say, these classifications are not final and distinct. They can be revised in such a way that a philosopher like Ross can be classified as a modest classic intuitionist, and at the same time, some of his ideas are similar to those of contemporary philosophers.
6 For more details about classic foundationalism, see Dancy (1985b, 53–8).
7 For example, both Moore and Ross thought that certain intuitions may turn out to be false even though belief in them is non-inferentially justified. See Stratton-Lake (2005; 2002b and 2002c).
8 See Hurka (2011, 1 and 6). Also, for more details about the history of classic intuitionism, see Dancy (2003) and Sinnott-Armstrong (1992).
9 I have used 'knowledge' instead of 'belief' here because Prichard follows Cook Wilson in holding that knowledge is not belief and belief is not knowledge. Since he thinks we know certain moral truths, he would deny that we believe those truths. See Stratton-Lake (2005c).
10 Prichard is not clear as to what he means by moral thinking. Although it seems that moral thinking can be similar to moral intuition, they are not the same. Because thinking sounds like an activity, it does not sound like intuition.
11 Dancy, for example, believes that this interpretation is not comprehensive. See Dancy (2014a).
12 See Prichard (2002, 216–20).
13 See Moore (1903, 4.5.1 and 4.5.3.1).
14 See Moore (1912, 29–30).
15 See Prichard (1949, 4).
16 See Prichard (1949, 8). Although Prichard disagrees with this claim, new intuitionists can accept that. I will talk about this in the next chapter.
17 See Stratton-Lake (2002b, 2).
18 The interesting point here is Ross thought that this was possible. Although Ross historically belonged to the classic tradition, his epistemological ideas can be classified as moderate intuitionism.
19 For further details on this issue, see Stratton-Lake (2002b, 2–5). Also, for more elaboration on Sidgwick's three kinds of moral intuitionism, see Audi (2004, 5–11).
20 See Crisp (2002, 65–70). Also see Baldwin (2002) and Broad (1962, 151, 208–17).
21 See Stratton-Lake (2002b).
22 See Williams (1995, 182–91) and Rawls (1971, 34–40). See also Thomas (2006, 198–200) and Urmson (1975) for further details.
23 See Stratton-Lake (2002b, 2 and fn. 6 and 2002c, xii).
24 Dancy is not clear about this. Sometimes it seems that he is instead a moral intuitionist who prefers a coherentist epistemology. See Dancy (2004a).
25 The issue referred to is over the nature of intuitions – are they seemings or doxastic (most intuitionists would consider them, on either interpretation, 'epistemic' in

some sense of that flexible and sometimes elusive term)? All the major intuitionists consider some moral generalizations self-evident in some *a priori* way, but in recent literature the older conception of them as beliefs or belief-entailing is sometimes abandoned. A seemings-doxastic distinction is what I'm aiming at here.

26 Even if someone object that winning and losing can be a shared property of the above-mentioned games, in reply, we can refer to the case of a little boy or girl who is playing with his/her toys. We intuitively refer to this phenomenon as a kind of game even if no winning or losing is involved.

27 Luntley (2003, Ch. 3 and 4).

28 Although my account is a family resemblance one, it is not the case that none of these marks is a strictly necessary condition, hence we can call the marks 'defining' ones. Don't all the intuitionist views take intuitions to be both non-inferential (obviously for seemings) and to have some justificatory force? If so, then my account, as compared with Wittgenstein's, is qualifiedly a family resemblance one – or one that allows all family members to share one or two properties.

29 Dancy (2014b) also has suggested a similar list with slight changes. He lists realism, cognitivism, non-naturalism, metaphysical quietism, epistemology, pluralism in the theory of the right and the independence of the right. Moreover, Roeser, in her book, understands moral intuitionism as a combination of three marks which she calls 'core theory': cognitivism, foundationalism and non-reductive realism. See her (2011, 1–44).

30 For a critical view of Copp, see Tropman (2012). See also Sturgeon (2002), who compares ethical intuitionism with ethical naturalism.

31 See also Tropman (2008).

32 This claim however is not true of most of the modern moral intuitionists. I will discuss their ideas in the next chapter.

33 Both normative and meta-ethical aspects of Rossian ethics and criticism are discussed in the following: Audi (1993), Hooker (1996), McNaughton (2000 and 2002), Dancy (1991a; 1991b and 1993a, 92–108) and Stratton-Lake (2000, 78–91; 2012; 2013; 2002a; 2002b; 2002c; 1999; 2005b; 2010; 2011a; 1997; 2011b and 2007). Other sources are: Jones (1970), Rosen (1968), Jack (1966), Laird (1927), Baumrin (1965), Shope (1965), Atwell (1978), Clark (1971) and Snare (1974). Finally, Stratton-Lake (2002c, lii-lviii) lists many works about Ross and moral intuitionism in general.

34 See McNaughton (2000, 269; 2007 and 1998).

35 For a critical discussion of Ross's account about the relationship between 'right' and 'good', see Laird (1927).

36 Audi, for example, calls *prima facie* duties 'ineradicable but overridable'. See his (1997a, 34–5).

37 For more on the definition of *prima facie*, see Snare (1974, 237), who tries to propose an explicit definition of *prima facie* duties.

38 Ross usually talks about right-making features as ontological foundations of rightness. See Ross (1930, 46) and Stratton-Lake (2000, 82–7).
39 As far as I understand, when Ross says that moral situations usually have various morally relevant non-moral properties or features which can have an effect on our moral point of view (judgement), he probably means that there are right and wrong-making features of the possible acts, where some of these features provide reason for an act to be morally right and others provide reason for the act to be morally wrong. See Stratton-Lake (1997, 753). See also McNaughton (2000, 272–4) and Stratton-Lake (2013; 2010; 2000, 79–82 and 2002c, xxxiii–xxxviii).
40 See Ross (1930, 2002, 20).
41 See Ross (1930, 2002, 20).
42 Ross in the *Foundations of Ethics* prefers Carritt's terminology, that is, 'responsibility', to describe the idea of *prima facie*. See Ross (1939, 85) and Stratton-Lake (2000, 79–80).
43 See also Kagan (1989, 17) and Gaut (2002, 138 & fn. 1).
44 The term '*pro tanto* duty' was introduced by Broad in 1930. For further details, see also Broome (2004) and Dancy (1993a, 180). It seems that Stratton-Lake also accepts that using *pro tanto* presents no problems. See his (2011b, 149). For more details of this dispute, see McNaughton (2000, 273–4).
45 For more details, see Stratton-Lake (2002c, xxxiv and 1997, 752–3).
46 For more on this issue, see McNaughton (2000, 268–87).
47 See Hooker (2005, 631).
48 See Driver (2006, 122, fn. 1); Sidgwick (1967, 373–90); Broad (1962, 151) and Rawls (1971, 35).
49 See Stratton-Lake (2002c, xvi–xxvi). Typically, intuitionists believe that goodness (Moore), rightness (Ewing) or both of them (Ross) are indefinable.
50 Stratton-Lake has expressed such a view. See his (2002c and 2004). He believes that by adopting a buck-passing account of goodness and rightness, moral intuitionists can 'deny that moral properties must be entirely independent of us and our responses in order to be objective' (2002b, 12).
51 See Moore (1903, 192–272). Also, for more on moral pluralism, see Stratton-Lake (2002a, 135–6) and Gaut (2002, 137–41).
52 For a contemporary non-consequentialist approach to moral theory, see Oderberg (2000).
53 For more details, see Stratton-Lake (2013 and 2010). He uses the term 'good will view' for the intrinsic goodness of the action itself.
54 For more on this issue, see Ross (1930, 2002, 18–19 and 34–6). Stratton-Lake (2013) also considers the Rossian approach to analytic and synthetic consequentialistic claims.
55 Shaver (2011), however, believes that Ross's interpretation of 'ideal utilitarianism' is to some extent wrong because he fails to take pluralistic utilitarianism seriously.

For further details on Ross and utilitarianism, see Wiggins (1998) and Dancy (1998).

56 See Ross (1930, 2002, 5–6).
57 See Ross (1930, 2002, 43–7).
58 There is a controversy among scholars as to whether these duties are derivative or not. For further details of this discussion, see Stratton-Lake (2011b).
59 In the introduction to *Foundations of Ethics*, Ross says that by comparing one opinion with another, we can harmonize and purify them. See also Gaut (2002, 139).
60 The term 'complexity', often in the literature, refers to 'moral dilemmas'. See Williams (1965) and Sinnott-Armstrong (1988).
61 See Schaber (2005) and Audi (1999a, Ch. 12) for further clarifications on moral pluralism.
62 An intuitionist like Reid believes that morality is not like mathematics but rather like botany and mineralogy. See Roeser (2011, 19).
63 Ross claims that 'intuitive induction' can help us to catch general truths. I will talk about intuitive induction later in this chapter. For further details, see Broad (1962, 214) and Stratton-Lake (2002b, 6).
64 I did not say that propositions are infallibly true, since propositions cannot fail to do anything. It is our beliefs that are fallible, not the propositions which are their content.
65 See Ross (1927).
66 For a similar view, see Huemer (2005, 106).
67 See Ross (1930, 2002, 27).
68 Dancy, for example, believes that the valence can shift. See his (1981 and 1983). For a critical discussion, see Hooker and Little (2000).
69 I borrowed this example from Dabbagh, S. (2010).
70 See Ross (1930, 2002, 12, 20 and 33).
71 See Audi (1996, 105).
72 This example comes from Hooker (2002).
73 See Ross (1930, 2002, 29–30 and 40).
74 For more details, see Stratton-Lake (2002b, 21).
75 See Stratton-Lake (2016a).
76 See Hooker (2002, fn. 7) and Audi (1999). Self-evident propositions might be derivable from other propositions by deduction. See Roeser (2011, 19–20) who sees such an idea in Thomas Reid's works.
77 He refers in fn. 12 to Scanlon (1998, 70). For more on this issue, see Scanlon (forthcoming, Lecture 4).
78 See Hooker (2000a, 12).
79 See Aristotle (1908, 71b19–25).
80 See also Dabbagh (2021).

81 See Tropman (2009, at 449).
82 See McIntyre (1998, 254) and Davis (1985). Davis thinks of 'intuition' as an evident truth that we cannot argue for. The idea of self-evidence is one of the epistemic central ideas of moral intuitionism on account of which some philosophers reject moral intuitionism. Frankna (1988, 88) and Gensler (1998, 53–5) are examples. For more criticisms of moral intuitionism, see Warnock (1967, 12–17).
83 See Stratton-Lake (2002b, 19) and Audi (1998).
84 For more details about the objection of 'disagreement' and replies, see Stratton-Lake (2016a). Some objections to moral intuitionism, generally, such as the idea of self-evident moral propositions, subjectivism and dogmatism can be found here: Korsgaard (1998, 38), Nowell-Smith (1967, 46), Warnock (1960, 53), Hare (1989, 83), McIntyre (1998, 17), Raphael (1981, 43–7), Hare (1997, 82–102) and Popper (2001, 49–50). Moreover, Huemer (2005, 105–15) lists some objections and misunderstandings of intuitionism with replies. Roeser (2011, Ch. 3) has done the same job as well.
85 For more details about what it was Ross saw and what Moore missed, and how it resolves their differences, see Stratton-Lake (2002a).
86 Stratton-Lake (2002a, 114, fn. 6) also thinks about Ross in this way. However, Prichard used a similar phrase about moral maturity, that is, 'moral capacity'. See Warnock (1967, 15).
87 For more details, see Stratton-Lake (2002a, 115–16). Also, consider Ross's discussion about the universal principle of fidelity. See his (1930, 2002, 32).
88 For more details about Ross's thought experiment, see Stratton-Lake (2002a, 115–16 and fn. 10). Also see Brown (1993, 27–32) for the discussions of thought experiments in natural sciences. He stated some examples of moral thought experiments as well.
89 See Dancy (1985a). For more details, see also Sorensen (1992, 20). Dancy could hardly hold that *all* thought experiments in ethics are misguided, since his own work is full of them.
90 See Thomson (1971, 267–8).
91 See Tooley (1984). Also, for more details about Thomson's thought experiment, see Sorensen (1992, 210). For more on thought experiment as an argument, see Brown (1993, 27 and fn. 5) and Smith (2002). For a defence of using thought experiments in ethics, see Walsh (2011).
92 I have discussed this resemblance elsewhere. See Dabbagh, H. (2011).
93 See Ross (1939, 271–5).
94 For more details, see Stratton-Lake (2002a, 119–35).
95 See Ross (1930, 2002, 29).
96 See Ewing (1947, 91–2) and Stratton-Lake (2002c, 116–17).
97 Brink (1989, 117) holds that non-inferential justification basically amounts to the claim that some beliefs are self-justifying. See also Stratton-Lake (2002a, 117).
98 Audi also has used this terminology. I will explain it further in the next chapter.

99 I said 'may' because we do not 'need' such coherence to be justified in believing those intuitions.
100 See Dancy (1985b, 53–5).
101 There are three forms of particularism in the literature: metaphysical or normative particularism, epistemological particularism and methodological particularism. For more details, see Dancy (1981; 1983; 1993a, 114–15; 1999b; 1999a and 1999c) and McNaughton (1988, Ch. 13; 2000 and 2013). For criticism, see Audi (1998a), Sinnott-Armstrong (1999, at 3–8), Hooker (2000b), and Crisp (2000).
102 For further discussion of epistemological particularism, see Sinnott-Armstrong (1999, at 8) and Dancy (1993a, 57 and 60).
103 This example comes from Hooker (2002, Sec. 6). Hooker believes that we know some all-things-considered duties in some kinds of case where moral considerations conflict. His examples are: suppose my keeping my promise to you would benefit you slightly less than my breaking my promise to you would benefit someone else. We know that my all-things-considered moral duty in such cases is to keep my promise. For another example, suppose my physically harming one person without that person's consent would somehow result in a small net gain in utility for someone else. Again, we know that my all-things-considered moral duty is not to harm the person for the sake of such a small gain in utility for someone else. This is knowledge of general truths about all-things-considered duty.
104 See Stratton-Lake (2002c, x–xii) and Audi (2004, 21).
105 See Ross (1930, 2002, 21 and 27).
106 See Ross (1930, 2002, 22 and 30).
107 See Ross (1939, 188).
108 I picked out this point from Stratton-Lake (2002c, xxxvi–xxxvii).
109 Audi (2004, 28) prefers to read Ross based on the second metaphysical claim; however, Stratton-Lake (2002c, xxxvi–xxxvii) prefers to read Ross according to the revised version of second metaphysical claim.
110 Although Ross took all the *pro tanto* duties to be self-evident, we can ask why assume that they all are. However, since every system of morality takes some propositions to be self-evident, for the sake of argument, I assume that Ross is right and will not argue about this.
111 I say 'often' because as I stated before, Ross holds in one of his papers that we *can* arrive at intuitive judgements even inferentially. See Ross (1927, at 121).
112 Ross thinks that there are no principles for all-things-considered duties.
113 See Ross (1930, 2002, 29).
114 See Ross (1930, 2002, 29).
115 See Dancy (1981).
116 I am not alone in this interpretation. See Scanlon (1998, 1–13), Stratton-Lake (2013; 2011b, at 178) and Audi (2004, 23–4).

117 See Ewing (1959, 63, 110).
118 See the papers by Darwall, Wallace and Little in the festschrift for Dancy, edited by Hooker, Bakhurst, and Little (2013).
119 See Urmson (1975, 112–13) and Stratton-Lake (2011b, 147–50). Audi (2004, 104) also believes that Ross's basic *pro tanto* duties are not only self-evident but also provide independent moral reasons.
120 See Owens (2012 and 2013).
121 Talk of reasons can be classified into two categories as 'insistent' (obligatory) and 'good ground' reason. Likewise, Dancy (2004b), for example, talks about a distinction between two categories, that is, 'enticing' and 'peremptory' reasons, that capture different normative relations.
122 See Stratton-Lake (2002c, xliii).
123 Although 'looking away' might not be the best terminology, it does not make it sound as though one is ignoring the facts rather than thinking about them. This terminology came to my mind in the discussion with Soroush Dabbagh. For more details, see Dabbagh (Dissertation).
124 For more on practice theories, see Thompson (2008). For an alternative view, see Owens (2011).
125 See Ross (1930, 2002, 32–3). Also see Hooker (2002) for an alternative view.
126 Scanlon and Stratton-Lake believe that we can define moral concepts such as *good* and *bad* in terms of reasons. In the same way, I think, the more we are engaged in seeing different cases, the more we find reasons. In effect, reasoning is a kind of practice. See Scanlon (1998, 96 and 96ff and forthcoming) and Stratton-Lake (2002c, xx and 2004).

Chapter 5

1 See Audi (1993; 1996; 1997b; 1998a; 1999a; 1999b and 2001). Dancy is more Prichardian than Rossian. See his (2002; 2011; 1991a; 1991b; 1993a and forthcoming). In his *Moral Reasons*, Dancy writes that 'the prospects of a recognizable successor to the intuitionistic tradition began to seem much rosier' (1993a, ix). See also Hooker (2002 and 2000a, 9–13 and 104–7). McDowell is not happy to define himself as an intuitionist, but it is possible to characterize him as an epistemological intuitionist. See Dancy (2012). McDowell's 'sensible theory' often interpreted as a possible way between non-cognitivism and moral intuitionism. He believes in intuitionism as a realist position on values. See McDowell (1998 and 1988). Also see Tropman (2010) for an explanation of McDowell's position. See also McNaughton (2002 and 2000), Nagel (1986, 176–80 and 1997, 101–25), Parfit (2011, Vol. 2, 489–92 and 543–8 and Vol. 1, 366–70), Raz (1999), Scanlon (1998, Ch. 2; 98 and 206 and forthcoming), Stratton-Lake (2002a; 2002b and 2002c).

Stratton-Lake is a Rossian intuitionist in epistemology. Also see Wiggins (1991, 316 and 2006) who talks about 'new intuitionism'.
2. See McNaughton (2000, 269).
3. Audi's normative moral theory is discussed in Audi (2004, Ch. 3; 1997b, 279–80; 2008a, Ch. 9 and 2007). Also see Hurka's (2007) critical paper on Audi's marriage of Ross and Kant.
4. I follow Stratton-Lake (2002a and 2002c) in reading Ross this way.
5. See also Audi (1996, 116).
6. See Audi (1993, 305–6 and 1996, 119). Also Hooker (1996) has shown that Rule-Consequentialism is compatible with Rossian *pro tanto* duties.
7. See Audi (1993, 306).
8. Note that I am not saying that a reason not to believe P must be equivalent to a reason that P is false.
9. See Audi (1999, 19). For more on non-inferential justification, see Audi (2008b, 478–81 and 486–8).
10. See Audi (1993, 310), (1996, 120&126). For more on modest foundationalism, see Audi (1988a). Also, for a general idea of Audi on justification, see Audi (1988b).
11. See Audi (1993, 303; 1996, 114; 1998a, 20–2; 1999a, 283 and 1998b, 95).
12. See also Audi (1996, 106–7).
13. See Audi (1993, 286 and 1996, 107–8).
14. There is a further question whether all *a priori* propositions are self-evident. I will discuss this issue later in this chapter.
15. See Audi (1998a, 24).
16. See Audi (1998a, 22; 1993, 303; 1996, 284 and 2004, 48–54).
17. See Audi (1998a, 24 and 2004, 53). See also Bart Streumer's review of *The Good in the Right* in the electronic journal of *Notre Dame Philosophical Reviews*.
18. See Audi (1998a, 24).
19. See Audi (2004, 31).
20. See Audi (1993, 303 and 1996, 115).
21. For further details on self-evidence, see BonJour (1998). Also for the issue of self-evidence and rational disagreement, see Audi (2008b, 488–91). As a criticism of Audi's epistemological intuitionism particularly on self-evidence, see Kappel (2002).
22. See Audi (1993, 303).
23. See Stratton-Lake (2002a).
24. As another example, the Ptolemaic model of the solar system as being geocentric was 'self-evident', but was later overturned by the Copernican model of the solar system, a heliocentric model. Neither classical mechanics nor relativity disprove Copernican heliocentric model. Rather heliocentricity disproves the Ptolemaic model.
25. I said 'apparently self-evident moral propositions' here because in Audi's view a proposition cannot really be self-evident without being true. If Audi's account of self-evident is correct, a self-evident proposition cannot turn out to be false. An

apparently self-evident one can, however. Compare this with the claim made by Hooker, who wrote that a proposition can seem to be self-evidently true and yet turn out to be false. See Hooker (2000a and 2002). Audi's account of self-evidence has some shortcomings, I believe. I will explain my criticisms at end of this chapter.

26 See Reichenbach (1949).
27 See Popper (1959 [1934], 31).
28 See Audi (1993, 310 and 1996, 107–8, 120 and 126).
29 See Audi (1993, 311).
30 See also Audi (1996, 121).
31 See Audi (1993, 308). This method, according to Audi, can be compatible with many ethical theories such as cognitivism, non-cognitivism, rationalism, empiricism, naturalism, non-naturalism, particularism and generalism, though it is not compatible with divine command theory and instinctual moral theory, since reflection plays no role in the justification of their moral principles. See Audi (1993, 308–10; 1996, 122–3 and 1998a, 25–6).
32 Recall that in Audi's view, although epistemological intuitionism is the view that there is no need for justified moral beliefs to be inferential, some premises 'may' be found for direct moral knowledge and justification. However, some philosophers do not believe this. See Sinnott-Armstrong (2007, Ch. 2).
33 See Shafer-Landau (2003, 57–9); Tolhurst (1990) and Timmons (1999, 59).
34 See Sinnott-Armstrong (2007, 19).
35 For a good summary of this book, see Shafer-Landau (2007).
36 See Korsgaard (1998, 38&32) and Nowell-Smith (1967, 46).
37 See Audi (1999a, 290; 1996, 125–6 and 1998a, 31 and 33). Korsgaard also makes another point according to which appealing to intuitions does not solve the basic problem of why we should see moral reasons as reasons.
38 See Audi (1996, 124).
39 I believe it is 'intuition' (construed as seeming) that is doing all the work. I will talk about this later in this chapter.
40 Another objection relates to moral pluralism. Critics say that pluralism leads to the incommensurability of all-things-considered duties. They believe that moral intuitionism only says something about basic *pro tanto* duties and it cannot say anything about our all-things-considered duties, which can conflict. However, Audi believes that the idea of incommensurability of all-things-considered duties in the case of moral conflict only shows that acquiring justified belief about all-things-considered duties is more difficult than that of *pro tanto* duties, and so we need some further reflections on them. It does not follow from this that all-things-considered duties are epistemologically incommensurable. See Audi (1998a, 30 and 1999a, 289–90). For further responses to critics of moral intuitionism, see Nelson

(1990; 1991 and 1999); McNaughton (2000 and 2002) and Stratton-Lake (2002a and 2002b).

41 Sidgwick also says that self-evident propositions must be agreed upon or at least agreed upon by experts, but he does not explain why experts should have any special weight here.
42 See Audi (1993, 303; 1996, 114; 1998a, 20–2; 1999a, 283; 2004, 49; 2008b, 478 and 2011, 174). Also see Shafer-Landau (2003, 247).
43 See Audi (2004, 69 and 1996, 109).
44 See Audi (2004, 55 & 49 and 2011, 172).
45 See Clarke (1706, 226) and Prichard (2002, 28). This claim might be complex in Prichard. For more on this, see Hurka (2014, Ch. 5).
46 See Ross (1930, 2002, 33 and 1939, Ch. 8).
47 For an alternative view, see Hooker (2000a).
48 Audi thinks that non-self-evident propositions can also be intuitive. See Audi (2008, 477–8). Also see Bedke (2010, at 1071).
49 It seems that Audi himself understood that something has to be developed with respect to his framework. He claims in his (2011, 7) that he wants to advance his model by providing a conception of moral experience and emotions.
50 It seems that Audi is also somehow talking about self-evident particular moral propositions when he talks about the moral properties of fittingness and unfittingness. See Audi (2008, 482 and 2011, 5–7 and 181–4).
51 See Tropman (2009).
52 See Audi (1993, 305–6; 1996, 119; 1997a, 285 and 2001). For another example, see Audi (2007, 204).
53 I occasionally use 'reflection' and 'adequate understanding' interchangeably here (*cf.* Chapter 2). Although it is possible that one reflect on something without having adequate understanding, I assume here that to reflect on something is to understand it adequately and vice versa.
54 See Price (1969 [1758], 187).
55 See also Audi (1997a, 216 and 2004, 48–9).
56 See Stratton-Lake (2016a). Kirchin (2015) also maintains that intuitionists need to develop a positive account of what understanding of self-evident propositions amount to.
57 Loosely speaking, by justification I mean the reason or argument that someone (properly) holds a belief. To (properly) hold beliefs is having good reasons to think that they are true. A justified belief is one that we are epistemologically or intellectually right in holding.
58 This also can be true of analytic conditionals, for example, 'If Holmes killed Sikes, then Sikes is dead.'
59 See Copp (2007, 40) and Tropman (2012).

60 See Chudnoff (2013, 68–9). He thinks it can become intuitive after reflection.
61 For the relationship between intuition and *a priori*, see Jenkins (2014).
62 Audi has updated his account of self-evidence recently. See Audi (2018).
63 Stratton-Lake's (2016b) account of self-evidence, which is also based on the non-doxastic account of moral intuition is similar to mine, though they have important differences. Stratton-Lake believes that 'intuitionists should give up talk of self-evident moral propositions' and that the notion of self-evidence 'has no important epistemic role to play' (p. 42). I don't think so. In my account, as I argued, self-evidence still has important epistemic role, though intuiting self-evident propositions, construed as seeming, is more basic.
64 Note, I am not claiming that what is most *basic* in terms of normative justification must also be *self-evident*, which is an epistemological matter. Must the first principle be self-evident? Well, it must be attractive in its own right, but various alternative candidate first principles are attractive in their own right and yet are not consistent with one another. If self-evident propositions have to be consistent with one another, then not all these attractive alternative candidate first principles are self-evident; indeed, it remains an open question whether any of these are. We should bear in mind that being basic or foundational can be an epistemic matter or a matter of normative metaphysics. Contractualism and Rule-Consequentialism, for example, cannot be plausibly claimed to be epistemologically basic but they are claimed to be foundational in terms of the normative justification of rules and actions.
65 See Audi (2015) who suggests that in ethics intuitions were until recent years 'convictions' (Ross's term), whereas in epistemology – at least since the 1990s – they have been non-beliefs.
66 See Ross (1930, 29–30). As a possible similarity, Chappell (2015), for example, seems to read W. D. Ross's view as quasi-perceptual, although Chappell does not mention the seeming account.

Chapter 6

1 For more details about the scepticism debate, see Williamson (2004).
2 We can also think of two sorts of scepticisms: global and selective. Sinnott-Armstrong, for example, is a global sceptic about the epistemology of moral intuition. Singer, however, is a selective one with regard to moral intuition. In the same vein, Sinnott-Armstrong (2006b) distinguishes between 'everyday' and 'philosophical' justification. He believes that we have some everyday justification for moral beliefs but not a philosophical one.
3 See Knobe and Nichols (2008), Sinnott-Armstrong (2006a and 2008a), Petrinovich and O'Neill (1996) and Greene (2008).

4 See Appiah (2008, Ch. 3) and Cushman, Young and Hauser (2006).
5 See Singer (1981, Ch. 3). For an alternative view, see Austin (2003).
6 Both consequentialists and deontologists think that consequences are important, but act-consequentialists believe that consequences are the only things that ultimately matter, while deontologists believe that morality both requires and allows us to do things that do not produce the best possible consequences.
7 It is not clear to me, however, whether Greene's psychological remarks have anything to do with the soundness of the philosophy.
8 For a brief and concise summary of the trolley problem, see Appiah (2008, 89–96).
9 In a different manner, there are some philosophers such as Kamm (1991) who interpret the trolley problems as a matter of the doctrine of double effect rather than utilitarianism vs. deontology. Judith Thomson (1976 and 1985) also tries to give an account of 'the doctrine of double effect' to provide a justification for these two opposing responses. See also Kahane et al. (2018). They argue that trolley moral dilemmas which study utilitarian vs. non-utilitarian decision-making ignore the altruistic side of utilitarianism.
10 See Fischer and Ravizza (1992), Petrinovich and O'Neill (1996) and Petrinovich, O'Neill and Jorgensen (1993).
11 See Fischer and Ravizza (1992) and Greene et al. (2001).
12 See Haidt (2001) and Wilson (2002).
13 See Bargh and Chartrand (1999).
14 Just to note that Greene does not claim that deontological judgement cannot be cognitive, and does not claim that consequentialism is emotionless.
15 As an alternative view and criticism of Greene, see Sauer (2012a).
16 See Kahane et al. (2010 and 2012). See also Greene et al. (2013) as a reply to Kahane.
17 See also Kahane et al. (2015). They argue that there is no necessary connection between the intuitions commonly considered as utilitarian and utilitarian attitudes.
18 See Sauer (2012a and 2012b).
19 Timmons, for example, embraces sentimentalism and still develops a deontological theory. This form of deontology can be saved from Greene's argument. Timmons writes: 'Sentimentalism is a metaethical account about the nature of moral judgement; deontology is a normative theory about the right, the good and their relation to one another. Although sentimentalism may seem to fit most comfortably with consequentialism, accepting the former metaethical view does not commit one to the latter normative moral theory' (2008, 102).
20 See Haidt (2001 and 2007) and Haidt and Björklund (2008).
21 See Bargh (1994), Bargh and Chartrand (1999), Sloman (1996), Stanovich and West (2000) and Wilson (2002).
22 We should be aware that 'reasoning' cannot produce moral intuitions. For, as I argued before, moral intuitions stand on their own feet and cannot be justified by something else.

23 Greene (2013; 2014; 2015) makes clearer in his formulation of his argument that the VMPFC is not just associated with emotions but with automatic heuristics which are often emotional.
24 For alternative views and criticism of Haidt, see Pizarro and Bloom (2003), Salzstein and Kasachkoff (2004), Sauer (2012b), Railton (2014) and Musschenga (2008 and 2009).
25 Haidt, unlike Greene, does not think emotional moral intuitions are specifically deontological. However, they both think that commonsense moral intuitions are largely emotion-driven.
26 For an alternative view, see Kahane (2011 and 2014) and Tropman (2014).
27 See Singer and de Lazari-Radek (2014, Ch. 3 and 7). For an alternative view, see Hooker (2016).
28 See Mason (2011). Lenman (2015) also responds to Singer, although I do not agree with him in construing intuitions as a species of desire.
29 See Nichols and Prinz (2010, 118). It cannot be right that emotions are all truth-apt.
30 Note that Singer is not just saying commonsense intuitions are emotionally driven but that they are driven by morally irrelevant factors. Singer (and Greene) have recently come to emphasize it. For a related argument, see Street (2006) and Joyce (2000).
31 Singer might object that it is not emotions as such, but emotions that are sensitive to distance that are a problem. I can also imagine that intuition sceptics (Singer, Greene, etc.) would likely reply that there is an important difference between these cases (where emotion is known to increase our reliability) and the case of *purely* moral intuitions: there are good reasons why evolution would have designed our emotional mechanism to be a reliable guide to our self-interest (including taking account of descriptive facts that bear on our interests), but no obvious reason why that mechanism would be calibrated to the objective moral facts. This argument may or may not be right, but in the rest of this chapter I will argue that the standard *contrast* between intuition and emotion is a mistake and moral intuitions and emotions can be partners.
32 See Fine (2006) and Kennett and Fine (2009).
33 See Lazarus (1991), Scherer (1997), Prinz and Nichols (2010, 118).
34 For it cannot be right that emotions are all truth-apt. It is absurd to claim that emotions can be inserted into valid forms of argument like *modus ponens*.
35 For more details of Gage's case, see also Damasio (1994, Chs. 1 and 2).
36 Again, the VMPFC is not just associated with emotion and an emotional deficit is not what's distinctive of patients with VMPFC damage. It's the attenuation of 'somatic markers' that inform personal decision-making.
37 For more details about emotions and feelings, see Damasio (1999, Ch. 2 and 9).
38 See Hareli and Parkinson (2008).

39 See Dijksterhuis et al. (2006).
40 For another explanation of two systems of thinking, see Kahneman (2011, Ch. 1).
41 People who describe intuition in terms of belief can appeal to reliabilism to justify their account. Reliabilists such as Goldman, Dertske and Nozick claim that what makes beliefs probably true and justified is the dependability of the process by which the belief comes to be held or is sustained. So, reliabilism then is: 'one knows that P iff P is true and one believes that P seems true, and one has arrived at the belief that P through some reliable process'. If reliabilism is true, it might be possible to argue that since intuition is a reliable source, we are justified in appealing to our intuitive judgements.
42 Roeser (2011) also tries to give an account of integration of psychology and epistemology of intuition. I will not discuss it here though.
43 See Audi (2008, 478). Some seeming theorists such as Bedke (2008, 255) think that the doxastic view is inadequate to the extent that it introduces a truth condition on having an intuition at all. Alternatively, Stratton-Lake does not deny truth conditions. Intuitions, on his view, have truth conditions and are truth-apt states.
44 There are some other moral intuitionists such as John Greco, Justin McBrayer and David McNaughton who believe that we can have non-inferential justification for believing on the basis of having moral perceptual experiences. See Greco (2000). Ernest Sosa (1998) also advocates an account of intuitions as dispositions-to-believe. He reads intuition as disposition-to-believe merely on the basis of adequate understanding.
45 See Musschenga (2010). Note that this does not entail that doxastic views do not have a *psychological* theory of intuition. Rather, Audi for example endorses that we have to distinguish two different things: believing in a proposition as a psychological state, and believing that the content of that proposition is justified. See Audi (1997a, 44–9).
46 Hanno Sauer (2012c and 2017) also made similar point that emotional moral intuitions can be analogous to perceptual experiences in justifying moral beliefs non-inferentially. However, my point here is that moral intuition is like intellectual seemings and moral emotion is like perceptual experiences. Seemings and perceptual experiences can justify moral belief non-inferentially.
47 Some moral intuitionists like Ross allow that a moral judgement can express a feeling of approval. See Stratton-Lake (2002b, 14).
48 It is not true that all feelings are emotions. See Damasio (1999, Ch. 2).
49 I retrieved this quote from Musschenga (2010).
50 This perceptual view differs from the James-Lange's perceptual theory of emotions in which emotions are constituted by perceptions of bodily changes. See James (1884).
51 Gibbard (2002) also argues that ethical expressivism needs moral intuitions.

52 We can also make a distinction between literal perceptual theories and non-literal ones. Literal ones hold that emotions literally are perceptual states, while non-literal theories hold that there are deep and explanatory analogies between perception and emotion. This distinction is drawn in Brady (2013).
53 They believe that the existence of 'recalcitrant emotions' give us reason to reject theories of emotion that treat judgements as necessary components of emotions. However, as Roberts writes, recalcitrant emotions cannot be in tension with the cognitive part of our judgements unless they have 'a character that can be expressed in thoughts' (2003, 111).
54 Compare Gendler's idea of alief, which may be in tension with explicit belief. See Gendler (2008).
55 I do not deny that some emotions can distort. But how do we tell the difference between the distorting ones and the non-distorting ones? Although this question is very important, I will not discuss it in this chapter as it needs much more psychological background than can be provided in this space. For current purposes, it is enough to show that at least *some* emotions are not distorting.
56 In Jones's words, a reason-tracker is 'capable of registering reasons and behaving in accordance with them, but it need possess neither the concept of a reason nor have a self-conception. It thus need not have the higher-order reflective capacities characteristic of reason responders' (2003, 190).
57 For an alternative view see Brady (2010). Although Brady defends a perceptual theory of emotion, he criticizes the epistemological use of emotion as justifying beliefs.
58 See McCann (2007).
59 Robert Cowan (2012) also in his PhD thesis defended an account of emotion for moral intuitionism.

Chapter 7

1 See Sinnott-Armstrong (2011, 14–15).
2 For a visual understanding of Sinnott-Armstrong's objections against epistemological intuitionism, see his interview with Matt Bedke on TV: http://sinnott-armstrong.com/press/news/2011/08/22/philostv-matt-bedke-and-walter-sinnott-armstrong
3 For an understanding of different types of criticisms against epistemology of moral intuitionism, see Sinnott-Armstrong (1992) and Zimmerman (2010, Ch. 4).
4 See also Sinnott-Armstrong's response (2008b) to them in the same volume.
5 See Sinnott-Armstrong (2011, 15–16).
6 See Sinnott-Armstrong (2002; 2006a and 2008a).

7   See Sinnott-Armstrong (2006a, 343–6).
8   See Sinnott-Armstrong (2002, 311–12).
9   See also Nadelhoffer and Feltz (2008).
10 Sinnott-Armstrong puts these examples together and makes a 'master argument' against epistemological intuitionism. For more details, see his (2006a and 2008a, 52). However, since I have discussed his more recent argument, I will not talk about his master argument any more.
11 I do not believe that Sinnott-Armstrong is committed to the 'genetic fallacy'. Because the genetic fallacy is the fallacy of assuming that a belief that comes from an unreliable source must be a bad belief, or that a belief that comes from a good source must be good. Lots of moral beliefs come from discarded religious systems of thought. These moral beliefs might be good or not.
12 See Zamzow and Nicholas (2009).
13 See Tolhurst (2008), Shafer-Landau (2008), Smith (2010), Tropman (2011), Huemer (2008), Väyrynen (2008) and Dabbagh, H. (2011). See also Bengson (2013), Nagel (1997, 124–5) and Roojen (2014) for a general worry about the experimental attack on moral intuition and moral intuitionism.
14 See Stratton-Lake (2016a). He is careful about this distinction. However, Shafer-Landau (2003) sometimes uses 'self-evident belief' when he means the content of belief.
15 See Schwitzgebel (2011).
16 See Audi (2011), Dancy (2014b), Lillehammer (2011) and Bedke (2010).
17 I borrowed the lobster example from Stratton-Lake (2016a).
18 For an alternative view, see Joyce (2006) and Sinnott-Armstrong (2000 and 2006a, 339–40).
19 See for example Dabbagh (2021). In this chapter, I empirically argue in favour of the reliability of some moral intuitions.
20 In Audi's view, of course we believe some true self-evident moral proposition only if we have adequate understanding for believing them.
21 See Sartre (1975).
22 See McNaughton (1988, 202). For more details on conflicts between principles, see Warnock (1960, 40–1).
23 See Ross (1939, 312).
24 For an alternative view, see Trigg (1971).
25 For further details, see also Audi (2004, 27–9 and Chapter 2).
26 See Ross (1930, 2002, 41).
27 This idea of disagreement and conflict is one of the most common objections to intuitionism. I addressed this objection before and provided an answer to that in the discussion of Audi (*cf.* Chapter. 4).
28 For more details, see McNaughton (2000).
29 See Sinnott-Armstrong (2006a and 2011). The reason might be that Sinnott-Armstrong is an epistemological particularist. See his (1999). Although I can

criticize particularism here, that is not the duty of this book. For more details on particularism and its criticisms, see Hooker and Little (2000).
30 See Dancy (2004a); McNaughton (1998) and McDowell (1998). McDowell does not use such terms as 'particularism'. He deals with the epistemological aspect of moral reasoning.
31 See Hooker (1996 and 2000a).
32 See Stratton-Lake (2000, 9–10).
33 See Cienki (2007).
34 For further details on moral imagination, see Johnson (1993, Ch. 8) and Lovibond (1983).
35 See Rosch (1978).
36 See Smith (1995).
37 If Sinnott-Armstrong objects that our empirical evidences about the non-inferentiality of matching process do not have a justificatory power, we can reply: 'we are in the same boat!'
38 For further details, see Dworkin (1995) and Tropman (2009). Tropman shows in her paper that prototype theory might provide a plausible psychological evidence to the intuitionist epistemology that there are some non-inferential moral beliefs (propositions).
39 See Sinnott-Armstrong (2011, 21).
40 See Sinnott-Armstrong (2011, 22).
41 For further details on this objection, see Ballantyne and Thurow (2013).
42 See Audi (2004), Stratton-Lake (2002b) and Arrington (1989, 159).
43 See Sinnott-Armstrong (2002, 309).
44 Sinnott-Armstrong's argument can only work against the weak version, I think. However, I will be focusing on the strong version (non-inferable intuitionism) which he thinks can halt sceptical regress.
45 See Sinnott-Armstrong (2006a, 187).
46 See Sinnott-Armstrong (2002, 310).
47 I guess, just as perceptions are not inferable, neither are intellectual seemings. But this is not what Sinnott-Armstrong is considering.
48 He writes, for example, 'My target is a particular version of moral intuitionism . . . ' (2002, 305).
49 He elsewhere similarly understands epistemological intuitionism to be the claim that 'some people are adequately epistemologically justified in holding some moral beliefs independently of whether those people are able to infer those moral beliefs from any other beliefs' (2006a, 341).
50 For more examples, see Sinnott-Armstrong (2002, 317, 320, 322, 232 and 324).
51 See Sinnott-Armstrong (2006b, 187–8).
52 Although Sinnott-Armstrong accepts that Audi's version of epistemological intuitionism is a strong one, he thinks this strong sort is false. See Sinnott-Armstrong (2011, 14–15).

53 See Prichard (1949, 8).
54 See Audi (2004, 42–8). Also see Stratton-Lake (2002b, 21).
55 I said one of the conditions because, as I argued before, the Audian account of self-evidence is not sufficient for having a self-evident proposition.
56 In fact, a sufficient reason to hold them is provided by the nature of what is believed.
57 By 'argument', here, I mean explicit premise-based inferential reasoning.
58 The ability to infer something to have sufficient understanding of a proposition can be similar to the 'fast thinking' process that Kahneman (2011) refers to. As I have already discussed, Kahneman believes that the fast thinking process is a non-inferential process (*cf.* Chapter 1).
59 See Audi (1999a; 1999b and 2004) who made a similar point.
60 In this chapter, I did not intent to defeat all different arguments against moral intuitionism to opt for 'modest epistemological intuitionism'. All I wanted to show is that Sinnott-Armstrong's argument, as a significant argument against moral intuitionism, cannot digest what seems to me the strongest alterative form of epistemological intuitionism.

Bibliography

Andow, J. (2018). 'Are Intuitions About Moral Relevance Susceptible to Framing Effects?', *Review of Philosophy and Psychology*, 9 (1): 115–41.
Appiah, K. (2008). *Experiments in Ethics*. Cambridge, MA: Harvard University Press.
Aristotle (1908). *Metaphysics*, ed. W. D. Ross. Oxford: Clarendon Press.
Aristotle (1960). *Posterior Analytics*, Greek text with translation by Hugh Tredennick. Loeb Classical Library. Cambridge, MA: Harvard University Press.
Arrington, R. L. (1989). *Rationalism, Realism, and Relativism: Perspectives in Contemporary Moral Epistemology*. Ithaca, NY: Cornell University Press.
Atwell, J. (1978). 'Ross and Prima Facie Duties', *Ethics*, 88 (3): 240–9.
Audi, R. (1988a). 'Foundationalism, Coherentism, and Epistemological Dogmatism', *Philosophical Perspectives*, 2, Epistemology: 417–32.
Audi, R. (1988b). 'Justification, Truth, and Reliability', *Philosophy and Phenomenological Research*, 49 (1): 1–29.
Audi, R. (1993). 'Ethical Reflectionism', *The Monist*, 76: 296–315.
Audi, R. (1994). 'Dispositional Beliefs and Dispositions to Believe', *Noûs*, 28 (4): 419–34.
Audi, R. (1996). 'Intuitionism, Pluralism, and the Foundation of Ethics', in W. Sinnott-Armstrong, and M. Timmons (eds), *Moral Knowledge?: New Readings in Moral Epistemology*, 101–36. Oxford: Oxford University Press.
Audi, R. (1997a). *Moral Knowledge and Ethical Character*. New York: Oxford University Press.
Audi, R. (1997b). 'The Moral Justification of Actions and the Ethical Character of Persons', in his *Moral Knowledge and Ethical Character*. Oxford: Oxford University Press.
Audi, R. (1998a). 'Moderate Intuitionism and the Epistemology of Moral Judgment', *Ethical Theory and Moral Practice*, 1: 15–44.
Audi, R. (1998b). *Epistemology: A Contemporary Introduction to the Theory of Knowledge*. London: Routledge.
Audi, R. (1999a). 'Moral Knowledge and Ethical Pluralism', in J. Greco and E. Sosa (eds), *The Blackwell Guide to Epistemology*, 271–302. Oxford: Wiley-Blackwell.
Audi, R. (1999b). 'Self-Evidence', *Philosophical Perspectives*, 13: 205–28.
Audi, R. (2001). 'A Kantian Intuitionism', *Mind*, 110 (439): 601–35.
Audi, R. (2004). *The Good in the Right: A Theory of Intuition and Intrinsic Value*. Princeton: Princeton University Press.
Audi, R. (2007). 'Intuition, Reflection and Justification', in Mark Timmons, John Greco, and Alfred Mele (eds), *Rationality and the Good*, 201–21. New York: Oxford University Press.

Audi, R. (2008a). 'Rational Disagreement as a Challenge to Practical Ethics and Moral Theory: An Essay in Moral Epistemology', in Quentin Smith (ed.), *Epistemology: New Essays*, 225–419. Oxford: Oxford University Press.

Audi, R. (2008b). 'Intuition, Inference, and Rational Disagreement in Ethics', *Ethical Theory and Moral Practice*, 11 (5): 475–92.

Audi, R. (2011). 'Introduction' and 'Conclusion', in Jill Graper Hernandez (ed.), *The New Intuitionism*, 1–10 and 171–90. London: Continuum Publisher.

Audi, R. (2015). 'Intuition and Its Place in Ethics', *Journal of the American Philosophical Association*, 1 (1): 57–77.

Audi, R. (2018). 'Understanding, Self-Evidence, and Justification', *Philosophy and Phenomenological Research*, 99 (2): 358–81.

Austin, M. W. (2003). 'On the Alleged Irrationality of Ethical Intuitionism', *Southwest Philosophy Review*, 19 (1): 205–13.

Baldwin, T. (2002). 'The Three Phases of Intuitionism', in P. Stratton-Lake (ed.), *Ethical Intuitionism: Re-evaluations*, 92–112. Oxford: Oxford University Press.

Ballantyne, N. and C. T. Thurow (2013). 'Moral Intuitionism Defeated?', *American Philosophical Quarterly*, 50 (4): 411–21.

Baltussen, H. (2007). 'Did Aristotle Have a Concept of "intuition"? Some Thoughts on Translating "nous"', in E. Close, M. Tsianikas, and G. Couvalis (eds), *Greek Research in Australia: Proceedings of the Sixth Biennial International Conference of Greek Studies, Flinders University*, 53–62. Flinders University Department of Languages-Modern Greek: Adelaide.

Bargh, J. A. (1994). 'The Four Horsemen of Automaticity: Awareness, Intention, Efficiency, and Control in Social Cognition', in R. S. Wyer Jr. and T. K. Srull (eds), *Handbook of Social Cognition*, 1–40. Hillsdale, NJ: Lawrence Erlbaum.

Bargh, J. A. and T. L. Chartrand (1999). 'The Unbearable Automaticity of Being', *American Psychologist*, 54 (7): 462–79.

Baumrin, B. H. (1965). 'Prima Facie Duties', *The Journal of Philosophy*, 62 (24): 736–9.

Baz, A. (2012). 'Must Philosophers Rely On Intuitions?', *Journal of Philosophy*, 109 (4): 316–37.

Bealer, G. (1992). 'The Incoherence of Empiricism', *Proceedings of the Aristotelian Society*, 66: 99–138.

Bealer, G. (1996a). 'A Priori Knowledge: Replies to William Lycan and Ernest Sosa', *Philosophical Studies*, 81: 163–74.

Bealer, G. (1996b). 'A Priori Knowledge and the Scope of Philosophy', *Philosophical Studies*, 81: 121–142.

Bealer, G. (1998). 'Intuition and the Autonomy of Philosophy', in M. Depaul and W. Ramsey (eds), *Rethinking Intuition: The Psychology of Intuition and its Role in Philosophical Inquiry*, 201–40. New York: Rowman and Littlefield Publishers, Inc.

Bealer, G. (2000). 'A Theory of the a Priori', *Pacific Philosophical Quarterly Journal*, 81: 1–30.

Bealer, G. (2002). 'Modal Epistemology and the Rationalist Renaissance', in T. S. Gendler and J. Hawthorne (eds), *Conceivability and Possibility*, 71–125. Oxford: Oxford University Press.

Bedke, M. (2008). 'Ethical Intuitions: What They Are, What They Are Not, and How They Justify', *American Philosophical Quarterly*, 45 (3): 253–70.

Bedke, M. (2010). 'Intuitional Epistemology in Ethics', *Philosophy Compass*, 5 (12): 1069–83.

Bedke, M. (2013). 'Ethics Makes Strange Bedfellows: Intuitions and Quasi-realism', in Matthew C. Haug (ed.), *Philosophical Methodology: The Armchair or the Laboratory?* 416. London: Routledge.

Bedke, M. (2014). 'A Menagerie of Duties?: Normative Judgments are Not Beliefs About Non-Natural Properties', *American Philosophical Quarterly*, 51 (3): 189–201.

Benacerraf, P. (1973). 'Mathematical Truth', *Journal of Philosophy*, 70: 661–79.

Bengson, J. (2010). *The Intellectual Given*. Dissertation, University of Texas at Austin.

Bengson, J. (2013). 'Experimental Attacks on Intuitions and Answers', *Philosophy and Phenomenological Research*, 86 (3): 495–532.

Bengson, J. (2014). 'How Philosophers Use Intuition and "Intuition"', *Philosophical Studies*, 171 (3): 555–76.

Bengson, J. (2015). 'The Intellectual Given', *Mind*, 124 (495): 707–60.

Berghofer, P. (2020). 'Towards a Phenomenological Conception of Experiential Justification', *Synthese*, 197: 155–83.

BonJour, L. (1998). *In Defense of Pure Reason: A Rationalistic Account of A Priori Justification*. New York: Cambridge University Press.

Boyd, R. (1979). 'Metaphor and Theory Change: What is "Metaphor" a Metaphor for?', in Ortony, A. (ed.), *Metaphor and Thought*, 481–532. Cambridge: Cambridge University Press.

Brady, M. S. (2009). 'The Irrationality of Recalcitrant Emotions', *Philosophical Studies*, 145 (3): 413–30.

Brady, M. S. (2010). 'Virtue, Emotion, and Attention', *Metaphilosophy*, 41 (1): 115–31.

Brady, M. S. (2013). *Emotional Insight: The Epistemic Role of Emotional Experience*. Oxford: Oxford University Press.

Brendel, E. (2004). 'Intuition Pumps and the Proper Use of Thought Experiments', *Dialectica*, 58: 89–108.

Brink, D. (1989). *Moral Realism and the Foundations of Ethics*. Cambridge: Cambridge University Press.

Broad, C. D. (1940). 'Review of Foundations of Ethics by W. D. Ross', *Mind*, 49: 228–39.

Broad, C. D. (1962). *Five Types of Ethical Theory*. London: Routledge & Kegan Paul Ltd.

Broome, J. (2004). 'Reasons', in Philip Pettit, Samuel Scheffler, Michael Smith, and Jay Wallace (eds), *Reason and Value*, 28–55. Oxford: Oxford University Press.

Brown, J. (1993). *The Laboratory of the Mind: Thought Experiments in the Natural Sciences*. London: Routledge.

Brown, J. (2011). 'Thought Experiments, Intuitions and Philosophical Evidence', *Dialectica*, 65 (4): 493–516.

Cappelen, H. (2012). *Philosophy Without Intuitions*. Oxford: Oxford University Press.

Chapman, A., A. Ellis, R. Hanna, T. Hildebrand, and H. Pickford (2013): *In Defense of Intuitions; A New Rationalist Manifesto*. London: Palgrave Macmillan.

Chappell, T. (2008). 'Moral Perception', *Philosophy*, 83 (4): 421–37.

Chappell, S. G. (2015). 'Introduction', in Chappell, S. G. (ed.), *Intuition, Theory, and Anti-Theory in Ethics*. Oxford: Oxford University Press.

Chisholm, R. (1957). *Perceiving: A Philosophical Study*. Cornell University Press.

Chisholm, R. (1961). 'Evidence as Justification', *Journal of Philosophy*, 58 (23): 739–48.

Chisholm, R. (1989). *Theory of Knowledge*. 3rd ed. Englewood Cliffs, NJ: Prentice-Hall.

Chudnoff, E. (2011). 'What Intuitions are Like', *Philosophy and Phenomenological Research*, 82: 625–54.

Chudnoff, E. (2013). *Intuition*. New York: Oxford University Press.

Cienki, A. (2007). 'Frames, Idealized Cognitive Models, and Domains', in D. Geeraerts and H. Cuyckens (eds), *The Oxford Handbook of Cognitive Linguistics*. Oxford and New York: Oxford University Press.

Clark, G. N. (1971). 'Sir David Ross: 1877–1971', *Proceedings of the British National Academy*, 57: 525–43.

Clarke, S. (1706 [1969]). 'Discourse on Natural Religion', in Raphael, D. D. (ed.), *The British Moralists 1650–1800, I*, 224–61. Oxford: Clarendon Press.

Climenhaga, N. (2018). 'Intuitions are Used as Evidence in Philosophy', *Mind*, 127 (505): 69–104.

Copp, D. (2003). 'Why Naturalism?', *Ethical Theory and Moral Practice*, 6: 179–200.

Copp, D. (2007). *Morality in a Natural World: Selected Essays in Metaethics*. Cambridge: Cambridge University Press.

Cowan, R. (2012). *Intuition, Perception and Emotion*. Dissertation, University of Glasgow.

Crisp, R. (2000). 'Particularizing Particularism', in B. Hooker and M. O. Little (eds), *Moral Particularism*, 23–47. Oxford: Clarendon Press.

Crisp, R. (2002). 'Sidgwick and the Boundaries of Intuitionism', in P. Stratton-Lake (ed.), *Ethical Intuitionism: Re-evaluations*, 56–75. Oxford: Oxford University Press.

Cullison, A. (2010). 'What are Seemings?', *Ratio*, 23 (3): 260–74.

Cummins, R. (1998). 'Reflection on Reflective Equilibrium', in M. Depaul and W. Ramsey (eds), *Rethinking Intuition: The Psychology of Intuition and its Role in Philosophical Inquiry*, 113–28. New York: Rowman and Littlefield Publishers, Inc.

Cushman, F. A., L. Young, and M. D. Hauser (2006). 'The Role of Reasoning and Intuition in Moral Judgments: Testing Three Principles of Harm', *Psychological Science*, 17 (12): 1082–9.

D'Arms, J. and D. Jacobson (2003). 'The Significance of Recalcitrant Emotion', *Royal Institute of Philosophy Supplement*, 52: 127–45.

Dabbagh, H. (2011). 'Wittgensteinian Approach to Partiality', *The Proceeding of 34rd International Wittgenstein Symposium*, Kirchberg, 56–8.

Dabbagh, H. (2021). 'Intuitions About Moral Relevance—Good News for Moral Intuitionism', *Philosophical Psychology*, forthcoming. doi:10.1080/09515089.2021.1960297.

Dabbagh, S. (2006). *Moral Reasons: Particularism, Patterns and Practice*. Dissertation, Warwick University.

Dabbagh, S. (2010). 'Emerging Moral Patterns: Reading Ross in the Light of Wittgenstein', *The Proceedings of 33th International Wittgenstein Symposium*, Kirchberg, 23–5.

Damasio, A. (1994). *Descartes' Error: Emotion, Reason and the Human Brain*. New York: Putnam Publisher.

Damasio, A. (1999). *The Feeling of What Happens: Body and Emotion in the Making of Consciousness*. New York: Harcourt Brace.

Dancy, J. (1981). 'On Moral Properties', *Mind*, 90: 367–83.

Dancy, J. (1983). 'Ethical Particularism and Morally Relevant Properties', *Mind*, 92: 530–47.

Dancy, J. (1985a). 'The Role of Imaginary Cases in Ethics', *Pacific Philosophical Quarterly*, 6: 141–53.

Dancy, J. (1985b). *An Introduction to Contemporary Epistemology*. Oxford: Wiley-Blackwell Publishing.

Dancy, J. (1991a). 'An Ethics of Prima Facie Duties', in P. Singer (ed.), *A Companion to Ethics*, 219–29. Oxford: Blackwell.

Dancy, J. (1991b). 'Intuitionism', in P. Singer (ed.), *A Companion to Ethics*, 411–20. Oxford: Blackwell.

Dancy, J. (1993a). *Moral Reasons*. Oxford: Blackwell Publisher.

Dancy, J. (1993b). 'Prima Facie Reasons', in, J. Dancy and E. Sosa (eds), *A Companion to Epistemology*. Oxford: Wiley-Blackwell Publishing Inc.

Dancy, J. (1998). 'Wiggins and Ross', *Utilitas*, 10 (3): 281–5.

Dancy, J. (1999a). 'Can a Particularist Learn the Difference Between Right and Wrong?', in K. Brinkmann (ed.), *The Proceedings of the Twentieth World Congress of Philosophy, Vol. 1: Ethics*, 59–72. Bowling Green: Philosophy-Doc-Ctr.

Dancy, J. (1999b). 'Defending Particularism', *Metaphilosophy*, 30 (1–2): 25–32.

Dancy, J. (1999c). 'On the Logical and Moral Adequacy of Particularism', *Theoria*, 65 (2–3): 144–55.

Dancy, J. (2002). 'Prichard on Duty and Ignorance of Fact', in P. Stratton-Lake (ed.), *Ethical Intuitionism: Re-evaluations*, 229–47. Oxford: Clarendon Press.

Dancy, J. (2003). 'From Intuitionism to Emotivism', in Baldwin (ed.), *The Cambridge History of Philosophy 1870–1945*, 695–705. Cambridge: Cambridge University Press.

Dancy, J. (2004a). *Ethics Without Principles*. New York: Oxford University Press.

Dancy, J. (2004b). 'Enticing Reasons', in R. Jay Wallace, Phillip Pettit, Samuel Scheffler, and Michael Smith (eds), *Reason and Value: Themes From the Moral Philosophy of Joseph Raz*, 91–118. Oxford: Oxford University Press.

Dancy, J. (2011). 'Has Anyone Ever Been a Non-Intuitionist?', in T. Hurka (ed.), *Underivative Duty: British Moral Philosophers From Sidgwick to Ewing*, 87–105. Oxford: Oxford University Press.

Dancy, J. (2012). 'McDowell, Williams and Intuitionism', in U. Heuer and G. Lang (eds), *Luck, Value and Commitment: Themes From the Ethics of Bernard Williams*, 269–90. Oxford: Oxford University Press.

Dancy, J. (2013). 'Meta-ethics in the Twentieth Century', in Beaney (ed.), *Oxford Handbook of the History of Analytic Philosophy*, 729–49. Oxford: Oxford University Press.

Dancy, J. (2014a). 'Harold Arthur Prichard', in Edward N. Zalta (ed.), *The Stanford Encyclopedia of Philosophy*. http://plato.stanford.edu/archives/spr2014/entries/prichard/

Dancy, J. (2014b). 'Intuition and Emotion', *Ethics*, 124 (4): 787–812.

Darwall, S. (1995). *The British Moralists and the Internal 'Ought': 1640–1740*. Cambridge: Cambridge University Press.

Davis, W. H. (1985). 'The Moral Obvious', *The Journal of Value Inquiry*, 19: 263–77.

Dennett, D. (1984). *Elbow Room: The Varieties of Free Will Worth Wanting*. Cambridge, MA: The MIT Press.

Dennett, D. (1988). 'Quining Qualia', in Anthony J. Marcel and E. Bisiach (eds), *Consciousness in Contemporary Society*, 42–77. New York: Oxford University Press.

Dennett, D. (1991). *Consciousness Explained*. Allen Lane: The Penguin Press.

Dennett, D. (1995). 'Intuition Pumps', in Brockman, J. (ed.), *The Third Culture: Beyond the Scientific Revolution*, 181. New York: Simon & Schuster.

Dennett, D. (2013). *Intuition Pumps and Other Tools for Thinking*. New York: W. W. Norton & Company.

Descartes, R. (1628/2000). *Rules for the Direction of the Mind*. Indianapolis: Bobbs-Merrill Co Publisher.

Deutch, M. (2010). 'Intuitions, Counterexamples, and Experimental Philosophy', *Review of Philosophy and Psychology*, 1: 447–60.

Deutsch, M. (2015). *The Myth of the Intuitive: Experimental Philosophy and Philosophical Method*. Cambridge, MA: The MIT Press.

Dijksterhuis, A. (2004). 'Think Different: The Merits of Unconscious Thought in Preference Development and Decision Making', *Journal of Personality and Social Psychology*, 87 (5): 586–98.

Dijksterhuis, A., M. W. Bos, L. F. Nordgren, and R. B. van Baaren (2006). 'On Making the Right Choice: The Deliberation-without-attention Effect', *Science*, 311 (5763): 1005–7.

Dorbolo, J. (2006). 'Intuition Pumps', *Minds and Machines*, 16 (1): 81–6.

Döring, S. (2003). 'Explaining Action by Emotion', *Philosophical Quarterly*, 53 (211): 214–30.

Döring, S. (2007). 'Seeing What To Do: Affective Perception and Rational Motivation', *Dialectica*, 61: 363–94.

Doring, S. A. (2008). 'Conflict Without Contradiction', in G. Brun, U. Doğuoğlue, and D. Kuenzle (eds.), *Epistemology and Emotions*, 83–103. Aldershot: Ashgate.

Dretske, F. (1969). *Seeing and Knowing*. Chicago, IL: University of Chicago Press.

Driver, J. (2006). *Ethics: The Fundamentals*. Malden, MA: Wiley-Blackwell Publisher.

Dworkin, G. (1995). 'Unprincipled Ethics', *Midwest Studies in Philosophy*, 20: 224–39.

Earlenbaugh, J. and B. Molyneux (2009). 'Intuitions are Inclinations to Believe', *Philosophical Studies*, 145: 89–109.

Ewing, A. C. (1947). *The Definition of Good*. London: Routledge.

Ewing, A. C. (1959). *Second Thoughts in Moral Philosophy*. London: Routledge & Kegan Paul.

Feinberg, J. and R. Shafer-Landau (2013). *Reason and Responsibility: Readings in Some Basic Problems of Philosophy*. 15th edn. Andover: Cengage Learning Publisher.

Field, H. (1989). *Realism, Mathematics, and Modality*. Oxford: Basil Blackwell.

Fine, C. (2006). 'Is the Emotional Dog Wagging its Rational Tail, or Chasing it? Reason in Moral Judgment', *Philosophical Explorations*, 9 (1): 83–98.

Fischer, J. M. and Ravizza, M. (1992). *Ethics: Problems and Principles*. New York: Holt, Rinehart & Winston.

Frankna, W. (1988). *Ethics*. 2nd edn. Lebanon: Indiana Pearson.

Gaut, B. (2002). 'Justifying Moral Pluralism', in P. Stratton-Lake (ed.), *Ethical Intuitionism: Re-evaluations*, 137–60. Oxford: Oxford University Press.

Gendler, T. (2007). 'Philosophical Thought Experiments, Intuitions, and Cognitive Equilibrium', *Midwest Studies in Philosophy*, 31: 68–89.

Gendler, T. (2008). 'Alief and Belief', *Journal of Philosophy*, 105 (10): 634–63.

Gendler, T. (2010). *Intuition, Imagination, and Philosophical Methodology*. Oxford: Oxford University Press.

Gensler, H. (1998). *Ethics: A Contemporary Introduction*. London: Routledge.

Gettier, E. (1963). 'Is Justified True Belief Knowledge?', *Analysis*, 23 (6): 121–3.

Gibbard, A. (2002). 'Knowing What to Do, Seeing What to Do', in P. Stratton-Lake (ed.), *Ethical Intuitionism: Re-evaluations*, 213–28. Oxford: Oxford University Press.

Gödel, K. (1964). 'What is Cantor's Continuum Problem?', in P. Benacerraf and H. Putnam (eds), *Philosophy of Mathematics: Selected Readings*, 470–85. Englewood Cliffs, NJ: Prentice-Hall.

Goodman, N. (1955). *Fact, Fiction, and Forecast*. Cambridge, MA: Harvard University Press.

Greco, John (2000). *Putting Skeptics in Their Place: The Nature of Skeptical Arguments and Their Role in Philosophical Inquiry*. Cambridge: Cambridge University Press.

Greene, Joshua D. (2008). 'The Secret Joke of Kant's Soul', in W. Sinnott-Armstrong (ed.), *Moral Psychology*, 35–80. Vol. 3. Cambridge, MA: The MIT Press.

Greene, Joshua D. (2013). *Moral Tribes: Emotion, Reason, and the Gap Between Us and Them*. New York: Penguin.

Greene, Joshua D. (2014). 'Beyond Point-and-Shoot Morality: Why Cognitive (Neuro) Science Matters for Ethics', *Ethics*, 124 (4): 695–726.

Greene, Joshua D. (2015). 'The Cognitive Neuroscience of Moral Judgment and Decision Making', in Jean Decety and Thalia Wheatley (eds), *The Moral Brain: A Multidisciplinary Perspective*, 197–220. Cambridge, MA: The MIT Press.

Greene, Joshua D. and Haidt, J. (2002). 'How (and Where) Does Moral Judgment Work?', *Trends Cognitive Science*, 6: 517–23.

Greene, Joshua D., R. B. Sommerville, L. E. Nystrom, J. M. Darley, and J. D. Cohen (2001). 'An fMRI Investigation of Emotional Engagement in Moral Judgment', *Science*, 293: 2105–8.

Greene, Joshua D., L. Nystrom et al. (2004). 'The Neural Bases of Cognitive Conflict and Control in Moral Judgment', *Neuron*, 44: 389–400.

Greene, Joshua D., S. A. Morelli, K. Lowenberg, L. E. Nystrom, and J. D. Cohen (2008). 'Cognitive Load Selectively Interferes With Utilitarian Moral Judgment', *Cognition*, 107 (3): 1144–54.

Greene, Joshua D., J. M. Paxton, and L. Ungar (2011). 'Reflection and Reasoning in Moral Judgment', *Cognitive Science*, 36 (1): 163–77.

Greene, Joshua D., J. M. Paxton, and T. Bruni (2013). 'Are "counter Intuitive" Deontological Judgments Really Counter Intuitive? An Empirical Reply to Kahane', *Social Cognitive and Affective Neuroscience*, Advance Access.

Grundmann, T. (2007). 'The Nature of Rational Intuitions and a Fresh Look at the Explanationist Objection', *Grazer Philosophische Studien*, 74: 69–87.

Gulley, N. (1963). 'Theories of Intuition in Plato and Aristotle', *Journal of The Classical Review*, 13 (3): 285–7.

Haidt, J. (2001). 'The Emotional Dog and Its Rational Tail: A Social Intuitionist Approach to Moral Judgment', *Psychological Review*, 108 (4): 814–34.

Haidt, J. (2007). 'The New Synthesis in Moral Psychology', *Science*, 316: 998–1002.

Haidt, J. (2013). *The Righteous Mind: Why Good People Are Divided by Politics and Religion*. New York: Vintage Books.

Haidt, J. and F. Bjorklund (2008). 'Social Intuitionists Answer Six Questions About Moral Psychology', in W. Sinnott-Armstrong (ed.), *Moral Psychology: The Cognitive Science of Morality: Intuition and Diversity*. Vol. 2, 181–217. Cambridge, MA: The MIT Press.

Hare, R. M. (1989). 'Rawls' Theory of Justice', in N. Daniels (ed.), *Reading Rawls*. Stanford University Press. First published in Philosophical Quarterly, 1973, 23 (91): 144–55.

Hare, R. M. (1997). *Sorting out Ethics*. Oxford and New York: Oxford University Press.

Hareli, S. and Parkinson, B. (2008). 'What's Social About Social Emotions?', *Journal for the Theory of Social Behaviour*, 38: 131–56.

Hintikka, J. (1999). 'The Emperor's New Intuitions', *Journal of Philosophy*, 96: 127–47.

Hooker, B. (1996). 'Ross-Style Pluralism vs. Rule-Consequentialism', *Mind*, 105: 531–52.

Hooker, B. (2000a). *Ideal Code, Real World*. Oxford: Oxford University Press.

Hooker, B. (2000b). 'Moral Particularism: Wrong and Bad', in B. Hooker and M. Little (eds), *Moral Particularism*, 1–22. Oxford: Oxford University Press.

Hooker, B. (2002). 'Intuitions and Moral Theorizing', in P. Stratton-Lake (ed.), *Ethical Intuitionism: Re-evaluations*, 161–83. Oxford: Oxford University Press.

Hooker, B. (2005). 'Moral Pluralism', in Honderich (ed.), *Oxford Companion to Philosophy*. 2nd ed., 631. Oxford: Oxford University Press.

Hooker, B. (2016). 'Wrongness, Evolutionary Debunking, Public Rules', *Etica & Politica / Ethics & Politics*, XVIII (1): 135–49.

Hooker, B. and M. Little (2000). *Moral Particularism*. Oxford: Clarendon Press.

Hooker, B., D. Bakhurst, and M. Little (2013). *Thinking About Reasons: Themes From the Philosophy of Jonathan Dancy*. Oxford: Oxford University Press.

Horgan, T. (2012). 'From Agentive Phenomenology to Cognitive Phenomenology: A Guide for the Perplexed', in Bayne, T. and M. Montague (eds), *Cognitive Phenomenology*, 57–78. New York: Oxford University Press.

Hudson, W. D. (1967). *Ethical Intuitionism*. London: Macmillan.

Huemer, M. (2001). *Skepticism and the Veil of Perception*. New York: Rowman and Littlefield Publishers, Inc.

Huemer, M. (2005). *Ethical Intuitionism*. New York: Palgrave MacMillan.

Huemer, M. (2007). 'Compassionate Phenomenal Conservatism', *Philosophy and Phenomenological Research*, 74: 30–55.

Huemer, M. (2008). 'Revisionary Intuitionism', *Social Philosophy and Policy*, 1: 368–92.

Hurka, T. (2007). 'Audi's Marriage of Ross and Kant', in Mark Timmons, John Greco, and Alfred Mele (eds), *Rationality and the Good*, 64–72. Oxford: Oxford University Press.

Hurka, T. (2011). 'Introduction', in T. Hurka (ed.), *Underivative Duty: British Moral Philosophers From Sidgwick to Ewing*, 1–5. Oxford: Oxford University Press.

Hurka, T. (2014). *British Ethical Theorists From Sidgwick to Ewing*. Oxford: Oxford University Press.

Ichikawa, J. (2013). 'Virtue, Intuition, and Philosophical Methodology', in John Turri (ed.), *Virtuous Thoughts: Essays on the Philosophy of Ernest Sosa*, 1–20. Dordrecht: Springer Publishing.

Ichikawa, J. and B. Jarvis (2013). *The Rules of Thought*. Oxford: Oxford University Press.

Jack, H. (1966). 'More on Prima Facie Duties', *The Journal of Philosophy*, 63 (18): 521–4.

Jackson, F. (1977). *Perception: A Representative Theory*. Cambridge: Cambridge University Press.

Jackson, F. (1982). 'Epiphenomenal Qualia', *Philosophical Quarterly*, 32: 127–36.

James, W. (1884). 'What is an Emotion?', *Mind*, 9: 188–205.

Jenkins, C. S. I. (2014). 'Intuition, "Intuition", Concepts and the A Priori', in Booth, A. R. and Rowbottom, D. P. (eds), *Intuitions*, 91–115. New York: Oxford University Press.

Johnson, M. (1993). *Moral Imagination*. Chicago: The University of Chicago Press.

Jones, K. (2003). 'Emotion, Weakness of Will, and the Normative Conception of Agency', in A. Hatzimoysis (ed.), *Philosophy and the Emotions*, 181–200. Cambridge: Cambridge University Press.

Jones, P. (1970). 'Doubts About Prima Facie Duties', *Philosophy*, XLV: 39–54.

Joyce, R. (2000). 'Darwinian Ethics and Error', *Biology and Philosophy*, 15: 713–32.

Joyce, R. (2006). *The Evolution of Morality*. Cambridge, MA: The MIT Press.

Kagan, S. (1989). *The Limits of Morality*. New York: Oxford University Press.

Kahane, G. (2011). 'Evolutionary Debunking Arguments', *Noûs*, 45: 103–25.

Kahane, G. (2014). 'Evolution and Impartiality', *Ethics*, 124 (2): 327–41.

Kahane, G. and N. Shackel (2010). 'Methodological Issues in the Neuroscience of Moral Judgement', *Mind & Language*, 25 (5): 561–82.

Kahane, G., K. Wiech, N. Shackel, M. Farias, J. Savulescu, and I. Tracey (2012). 'The Neural Basis of Intuitive and Counterintuitive Moral Judgement', *Social, Cognitive and Affective Neuroscience*, 7 (4): 393–402.

Kahane, G., J. A. Everett, B. D. Earp, M. Farias, and J. Savulescu (2015). '"Utilitarian" Judgments in Sacrificial Moral Dilemmas Do Not Reflect Impartial Concern for the Greater Good', *Cognition*, 134: 193–209.

Kahane, G., J. A. Everett, B. D. Earp, L. Caviola, N. S. Faber, M. J. Crockett, and J. Savulescu (2018). 'Beyond Sacrificial Harm: A Two-dimensional Model of Utilitarian Psychology', *Psychological Review*, 125 (2): 131–64.

Kahneman, D. (2011). *Thinking Fast and Slow*. New York: Farrar, Straus and Giroux.

Kamm, Frances M. (1991). 'The Doctrine of Double Effect: Reflections on Theoretical and Practical Issues', *Journal of Medicine and Philosophy*, 16 (5): 571–85.

Kappel, K. (2002). 'Challenges to Audi's Ethical Intuitionism', *Ethical Theory and Moral Practice*, 5 (4): 391–413.

Kasper, D. (2012). *Intuitionism*. New York: Bloomsbury Academic Publisher.

Katz, J. (1981). *Language and Other Abstract Objects*. Oxford: Blackwell.

Kauppinen, A. (2013). 'A Humean Theory of Moral Intuition', *Canadian Journal of Philosophy*, 43 (3): 360–81.

Kauppinen, A. (2014). 'Ethics and Empirical Psychology', in M. Christen, C. van Schaik, J. Fischer, M. Huppenbauer, and C. Tanner (eds), *Empirically Informed Ethics: Morality Between Facts and Norms*, 279–305. Switzerland: Springer Publisher.

Kauppinen, A. (2015). 'Moral Intuition in Philosophy and Psychology', in Neil Levy and Jens Clausen (eds), *Springer Handbook of Neuroethics*, 169–83. New York: Springer Publisher.

Kelley, D. (1991). 'Evidence and Justification', *Reason Papers*, 16: 165–79.

Kelly, T. (2014). 'Evidence', in Edward N. Zalta (ed.), *The Stanford Encyclopedia of Philosophy*. http://plato.stanford.edu/archives/fall2014/entries/evidence/.

Kennett, J. and C. Fine (2009). 'Will the Real Moral Judgment Please Stand Up? The Implications of Social Intuitionist Models of Cognition for Meta-ethics and Moral Psychology', *Ethical Theory and Moral Practice*, 12 (1): 77–96.

Kirchin, S. (2015). 'Self-evidence, Theory, and Anti-theory', in S. G. Chappell (ed.), *Intuition, Theory, and Anti-theory in Ethics*, 167–85. Oxford: Oxford University Press.

Knobe, J. and S. Nichols (2008). *Experimental Philosophy*. New York: Oxford University Press.

Koksvik, O. (2011). *Intuition*. PhD Dissertation, The Australian National University.

Koksvik, O. (2017). 'The Phenomenology of Intuition', *Philosophy Compass*, 12: e12387.

Kornblith, H. (1998). 'The Role of Intuition in Philosophical Inquiry', in M. DePaul and W. Ramsey (eds), *Rethinking Intuition*, 129–41. Lanham, MD: Rowman and Littlefield.

Korsgaard, C. M. (1998). *The Sources of Normativity*. Cambridge: Cambridge University Press.

Kripke, S. (1980). *Naming and Necessity*. Cambridge, MA: Harvard University Press.

Kuntz, J. R. and J. R. C. Kuntz (2011). 'Surveying Philosophers About Philosophical Intuition', *Review of Philosophy and Psychology*, 2 (4): 643–65.

Laird, J. (1927). 'Of "Right" and "good" and of Mr. Ross's Views', *International Journal of Ethics*, 37: 337–48.

Lakoff, G. (1999). 'Cognitive Models and Prototype Theory', in E. Margolis and S. Laurence (eds), *Concepts: Core Readings*, 391–421. Cambridge, MA: The MIT Press.

Lazarus, R. (1991). *Emotions and Adaption*. New York: Oxford University Press.

Lenman, J. (2015). 'Scepticism About Intuition', in S. G. Chappell (ed.), *Intuition, Theory, and Anti-theory in Ethics*, 24–39. Oxford: Oxford University Press.

Lewis, D. (1983). *Philosophical Papers: Volume I*. New York: Oxford University Press.

Lillehammer, H. (2011). 'The Epistemology of Ethical Intuitions', *Philosophy*, 86: 181–4.

Locke, J. (1969). *An Essay Concerning Human Understanding*. Oxford: Clarendon Press.

Lovibond, S. (1983). *Realism and Imagination in Ethics*. Oxford: Basil Blackwell Publisher.

Luntley, M. (2003). *Wittgenstein: Meaning and Judgment*. Oxford: Blackwell.

MacIntyre, A. (1984). *After Virtue: A Study in Moral Theory*. Notre Dame, IN: University of Notre Dame Press.

Mason, K. (2011). 'Moral Psychology and Moral Intuition: A Pox on All Your Houses', *Australasian Journal of Philosophy*, 89 (3): 441–58.

McCann, H. (2007). 'Metaethical Reflections on Robert Audi's Moral Intuitionism', in Mark Timmons, John Greco, and Alfred Mele (eds), *Rationality and the Good*, 40–51. : Oxford University Press.

McDowell, J. (1988). *Mind, Value and Reality*. Cambridge, MA: Harvard University Press.

McDowell, J. (1998). *Meaning, Knowledge and Reality*. Cambridge, MA: Harvard University Press.

McGinn, M. (2012). 'Non-Inferential Knowledge', *Proceedings of the Aristotelian Society (Hardback)*, 112: 1–28.

McIntyre, A. (1998). *A Short History of Ethics*. London: Routledge.

McKay, R. T. and D. Dennett (2009). 'The Evolution of Misbelief', *Behavioral and Brain Sciences*, 32: 493–510.
McMahan, J. (2000). 'Moral Intuition', in H. LaFollette (ed.), *The Blackwell Guide to Ethical Theory*, 92–110. Oxford: Blackwell Publisher.
McNaughton, D. (1988). *Moral Vision*. Cambridge: Blackwell Publisher.
McNaughton, D. (2000). 'Intuitionism', in H. Lafollette (ed.), *The Blackwell Guide to Ethical Theory*, 268–87. : Blackwell Publisher.
McNaughton, D. (2002). 'An Unconnected Heap of Duties', in P. Stratton-Lake (ed.), *Ethical Intuitionism: Re-evaluations*, 76–91. Oxford and New York: Oxford University Press.
McNaughton, D. and P. Rawling (1998). 'On Defending Deontology', *Ratio*, 11: 37–54.
McNaughton, D. and P. Rawling (2000). 'Unprincipled Ethics', in B. Hooker and M. Little (eds), *Moral Particularism*, 256–75. Oxford: Oxford University Press.
McNaughton, D. and P. Rawling (2007). 'Deontology', in R. Ashcroft, A. Dawson, H. Draper, and J. McMillan (eds), *Principles of Health Care Ethics*, 65–72. Chichester, West Sussex and Hoboken: John Wiley & Sons, Ltd.
McNaughton, D. and P. Rawling (2013). 'Particularism', in H. Lafollette (ed.), *The International Encyclopaedia of Ethics*, 3811–20. Malden, MA: Wiley-Blackwell.
Miller, R. B. (2000). 'Without Intuitions', *Metaphilosophy*, 31: 231–50.
Moore, G. E. (1903 [1993]). *Principia Ethica*. Cambridge: Cambridge University Press.
Moore, G. E. (1912 [1966]). *Ethics*. London: Oxford University Press.
Musschenga, A. W. (2008). 'Moral Judgment and Moral Reasoning', *International Library of Ethics, Law, and the New Medicine*, 39: 131–46.
Musschenga, A. W. (2009). 'Moral Intuitions, Moral Expertise and Moral Reasoning', *Journal of Philosophy of Education*, 43: 597–613.
Musschenga, Albert W. (2010). 'The Epistemic Value of Intuitive Moral Judgments', *Philosophical Explorations: An International Journal for the Philosophy of Mind and Action*, 13 (2): 113–28.
Nadelhoffer, T. and A. Feltz (2008). 'The Actor–Observer Bias and Moral Intuitions: Adding Fuel to Sinnott-Armstrong's Fire', *Neuroethics*, 1: 133–44.
Nado, J. (2014). 'Why Intuition?', *Philosophy and Phenomenological Research*, 89 (1): 15–41.
Nagel, J. (2007). 'Epistemic Intuitions', *Philosophy Compass*, 2: 792–819.
Nagel, J. (2012). 'Intuitions and Experiments: A Defense of the Case Method in Epistemology', *Philosophy and Phenomenological Research*, 85: 495–527.
Nagel, T. (1970). *The Possibility of Altruism*. Oxford: Oxford University Press.
Nagel, T. (1986). *The View From Nowhere*. Oxford: Oxford University Press.
Nelson, M. (1991). 'Intuitionism and Subjectivism', *Metaphilosophy*, 22 (1–2): 115–21.
Nagel, T. (1997). *The Last Word*. Oxford: Oxford University Press.
Nelson, M. (1999). 'Morally Serious Critics of Moral Intuitions', *Ratio*, 12: 54–79.
Nelson, M. (1990). 'Intuitionism and Conservatism', *Metaphilosophy*, 21 (3): 282–93.

Nimtz, C. (2010). 'Saving the Doxastic Account of Intuitions', *Journal of Philosophical Psychology*, 23: 357–75.

Nowell-Smith, P. H. (1967). *Ethics*. New York: Penguin.

Nussbaum, M. C. (2001). *Upheavals of Thought: The Intelligence of Emotions*. Cambridge: Cambridge University Press.

Oderberg, D. (2000). *Moral Theory: A Non-Consequentialist Approach*. Oxford: Blackwell Publisher.

Owens, D. (2011). 'The Problem With Promising', in Hanoch Sheinman (ed.), *Understanding Promises: Philosophical Essays*, 58–79. Oxford: Oxford University Press.

Owens, D. (2012). 'The Value of Duty', *Proceedings of the Aristotelian Society Supplementary*, 86 (1): 199–215.

Owens, D. (2013). 'Promises', in H. LaFollette (ed.), *The International Encyclopedia of Ethics*, 4143–55. Malden, MA: Wiley-Blackwell.

Parfit, D. (1984). *Reasons and Persons*. Oxford: Clarendon Press.

Parfit, D. (2011). *On What Matters*. Oxford: Oxford University Press.

Petrinovich, L., and O'Neill, P. (1996). 'Influence of Wording and Framing Effects on Moral Intuitions', *Ethology and Sociobiology*, 17: 145–71.

Petrinovich, L., O'Neill, P., and Jorgensen, M. J. (1993). 'An Empirical Study of Moral Intuitions: Towards an Evolutionary Ethics', *Journal of Personality and Social Psychology*, 64 (3): 467–78.

Pizarro, D. A. and Bloom, P. (2003). 'The Intelligence of the Moral Intuitions: A Comment on Haidt', *Psychological Review*, 110: 193–6.

Plantinga, A. (1993). *Warrant and Proper Function*. New York: Oxford University Press.

Plato (2000). *The Republic*, ed. G. R. F. Ferrari, trans. Tom Griffith. Cambridge: Cambridge University Press.

Popper, K. (1959 [1934]). *The Logic of Scientific Discovery*. London: Hutchinson.

Popper, K. (2001 [1971]). 'Facts, Standards, and Truth: A Further Criticism of Relativism', in T. Moser and T. Carson (eds), *Moral Relativism: A Reader*, 32–52. Oxford: Oxford University Press.

Price, H. H. (1932). *Perception*. London: Methuen and Co. Ltd.

Price, R. (1969 [1758]). 'A Review of the Principle Questions in Morals', in D. D. Raphael (ed.), *The British Moralists 1650–1800, II*, 131–98. Oxford: Clarendon Press.

Prichard, H. A. (1949). 'Does Moral Philosophy Rest on a Mistake?', in his *Moral Obligation*, 1–18. Oxford: Clarendon Press.

Prichard, H. A. (2002). *Moral Writings*, ed. J. MacAdam. Oxford: Clarendon Press.

Prinz, J. (2004). *Gut Reactions: A Perceptual Theory of the Emotions*. Oxford: Oxford University Press.

Prinz, J. (2006). 'The Emotional Basis of Moral Judgment', *Philosophical Explorations*, 9 (1): 29–43.

Prinz, J. (2007). 'Can Moral Obligations Be Empirically Discovered?', *Midwest Studies in Philosophy*, 31 (1): 271–91.

Prinz, J. (2008). 'Is Emotion a Form of Perception?', in Luc Faucher and Christine Tappolet (eds), *The Modularity of Emotions*, 137–60. Calgary: University of Calgary Press.

Prinz, J. and S. Nichols (2010). 'Moral Emotions', in John Michael Doris (ed.), *The Moral Psychology Handbook*, 111–48. Oxford: Oxford University Press.

Pryor, J. (2000). 'The Skeptic and the Dogmatist', *Noûs*, 34: 517–49.

Pryor, J. (2005). 'There Is Immediate Justification', in M. Steup and E. Sosa (eds), *Contemporary Debates in Epistemology*, 181–202. Oxford: Blackwell Publisher.

Pust, J. (2000). *Intuitions as Evidence*. New York: Garland, Routledge Publisher.

Pust, J. (2012). 'Intuition', in Edward N. Zalta (ed.), *The Stanford Encyclopedia of Philosophy*. http://plato.stanford.edu/archives/spr2014/entries/intuition/.

Putnam, H. (1975). 'The Meaning of "meaning"', in his *Philosophical Papers, Vol. 2: Mind, Language and Reality*, 215–71. Cambridge: Cambridge University Press.

Railton, P. (2014). 'The Affective Dog and Its Rational Tale: Intuition and Attunement', *Ethics*, 124 (4): 813–59.

Raphael, D. D. (1981). *Moral Philosophy*. Oxford and New York: Oxford University Press.

Rawls, J. (1971). *A Theory of Justice*. Cambridge, MA: Belknap Press of Harvard University Press.

Rawls, J. (1996). *Political Liberalism*. New York: Columbia University Press.

Rawls, J. (2007). *Lectures on the History of Political Philosophy*. Cambridge, MA: Harvard University Press.

Raz, J. (1999). *Engaging Reason*. Oxford: Oxford University Press.

Reichenbach, H. (1949). 'The Philosophical Significance of the Theory of Relativity', in Schilpp, P. A. (ed.), *Albert Einstein: Philosopher-Scientist*, 287–311. Evanston: The Library of Living Philosophers.

Reimer, M. (2010). 'Only a Philosopher or a Madman: Impractical Delusions in Philosophy and Psychiatry', *Philosophy, Psychiatry, & Psychology*, 17 (4): 315–28.

Roberts, R. C. (2003). *Emotions: An Essay in Aid of Moral Psychology*. Cambridge: Cambridge University Press.

Roeser, S. (2011). *Moral Intuitions and Emotions*. Basingstoke: Palgrave Macmillan.

Roojen, M. (2014). 'Moral Intuitionism, Experiments, and Skeptical Arguments', in A. R. Booth and D. P. Rowbottom (eds), *Intuitions*, 148–64. New York: Oxford University Press.

Rosen, B. (1968). 'In Defense of W. D. Ross', *Ethics*, 79 (3): 237–41.

Rosch, E. (1978). 'Principles of Categorization', in E. Rosch and B. B. Lloyd (eds), *Cognition and Categorization*, 27–48. Hillsdale, NJ: Erlbaum.

Ross, W. D. (1927). 'The Basis of Objective Judgments in Ethics', *International Journal of Ethics*, 37: 113–27.

Ross, W. D. (1930 [2002]). *The Right and the Good*, ed. P. Stratton-Lake. Oxford: Clarendon Press.

Ross, W. D. (1939). *The Foundations of Ethics*. Oxford: Clarendon Press.

Ross, W. D. (1949). 'Introduction', in *Aristotle's Prior and Posterior Analytics*, 1–93. Oxford: Clarendon Press.
Russell, B. (1912 [1997]). *The Problems of Philosophy*. New York: Oxford University Press.
Saltzstein, H. D. and T. Kasachkoff (2004). 'Haidt's Moral Intuitionist Theory: A Psychological and Philosophical Critique', *Review of General Psychology*, 8: 273–82.
Sartre, J. (1975). 'Existentialism is a Humanism', in W. Kaufmann (ed.), *Existentialism From Dostoyevsky to Sartre*, 345–68. New York: New American Library.
Sauer, H. (2012a). 'Moral Irrelevant Factors: What's Left of the Dual Process-model of Moral Cognition?', *Philosophical Psychology*, 25 (6): 783–811.
Sauer, H. (2012b). 'Educated Intuitions. Automaticity and Rationality in Moral Judgment', *Philosophical Explorations*, 15 (3): 255–75.
Sauer, H. (2012c). 'Psychopaths and Filthy Desks', *Ethical Theory and Moral Practice*, 15 (1): 95–115.
Sauer, H. (2017). *Moral Judgments as Educated Intuitions*. Cambridge, MA: The MIT Press.
Scanlon, T. (1998). *What We Owe To Each Other*. Cambridge, MA: Harvard University Press.
Scanlon, T. (2014). *Being Realistic About Reasons*. Oxford: Oxford University Press.
Schaber, P. (2005). 'Ethical Pluralism', in T. Nitta (ed.), *Studies into the Foundations of an Integral Theory of Practice and Cognition*, 139–56. Sapporo: Hokkaido University Press.
Scherer, K. R. (1997). 'The Role of Culture in Emotion-antecedent Appraisal', *Journal of Personality and Social Psychology*, 73: 902–22.
Schneewind, J. B. (1997). *The Invention of Autonomy: A History of Modern Moral Philosophy*. Cambridge: Cambridge University Press.
Schwitzgebel, E. (2011). 'Belief', in Edward N. Zalta (ed.), *The Stanford Encyclopedia of Philosophy*. http://plato.stanford.edu/archives/spr2014/entries/belief/.
Searle, J. (1979). 'A Taxonomy of Illocutionary Acts', in J. Searle (ed.), *Expression and Meaning: Studies in the Theory of Speech Acts*, 1–29. Cambridge and New York: Cambridge University Press.
Searle, J. (1980). 'Mind, Brains, and Programs', *The Behavioral and Brain Sciences*, 3: 417–457.
Searle, J. (1984). 'Can Computers Think?', in J. Searle (ed.), *Minds, Brains, and Science*, 28–41. Cambridge, MA: Harvard University Press.
Searle, J. (1987). 'Prima Facie Obligations', in J. Raz (ed.), *Practical Reasoning*, 81–90. Oxford: Oxford University Press.
Shafer-Landau, R. (2003). *Moral Realism: A Defence*. Oxford: Oxford University Press.
Shafer-Landau, R. (2007). 'Audi's Intuitionism', *Philosophy and Phenomenological Research*, LXXIV (1): 250–61.
Shafer-Landau, R. (2008). 'Defending Ethical Intuitionism', in W. Sinnott-Armstrong (ed.), *Moral Psychology*. Vol. 2, 83–95. Cambridge, MA: The MIT Press.

Shaver, R. (2011). 'The Birth of Deontology', in T. Hurka (ed.), *Underivative Duty: British Moral Philosophers From Sidgwick to Ewing*, 126–45. Oxford: Oxford University Press.

Shope, R. K. (1965). 'Prima Facie Duty', *The Journal of Philosophy*, 62 (11): 279–87.

Sidgwick, H. (1960 [1866]). *Outlines of the History of Ethics*. Boston: Beacon Hill.

Sidgwick, H. (1967 [1874]). *The Methods of Ethics*. 7th ed. London: Macmillan.

Singer, P. (1981). *The Expanding Circle: Ethics and Sociobiology*. New York: Farrar, Straus and Giroux.

Singer, P. (2005). 'Intuitions and Ethics', *Journal of Ethics*, 9: 331–52.

Singer, P. and K. de Lazari-Radek (2012). 'The Objectivity of Ethics and the Unity of Practical Reason', *Ethics*, 123 (1): 9–31.

Singer, P. and K. de Lazari-Radek (2014). *The Point of View of the Universe*. Oxford: Oxford University Press.

Sinnott-Armstrong, W. (1988). *Moral Dilemmas*. Oxford and New York: Basil Blackwell.

Sinnott-Armstrong, W. (1992). 'Intuitionism', in L. C. Becker (ed.), *Encyclopedia of Ethics*, Vol. I, 628–30. New York and London: Garland Publishing Co.

Sinnott-Armstrong, W. (1996). 'Moral Skepticism and Justification', in W. Sinnott-Armstrong and M. Timmons (eds), *Moral Knowledge? New Readings in Moral Epistemology*, 3–48. New York: Oxford University Press.

Sinnott-Armstrong, W. (1999). 'Some Varieties of Particularism', *Metaphilosophy*, 30: 1–2.

Sinnott-Armstrong, W. (2000). 'From "Is" to "Ought" in Moral Epistemology', *Argumentation*, 14 (2): 159–74.

Sinnott-Armstrong, W. (2002). 'Moral Relativity and Intuitionism', *Philosophical Issues*, 12, Realism and Relativism: 305–28.

Sinnott-Armstrong, W. (2006a). 'Moral Intuitionism Meets Empirical Psychology', in T. Horgan and M. Timmons (eds), *Metaethics After Moore*, 339–65. New York: Oxford University Press.

Sinnott-Armstrong, W. (2006b). *Moral Skepticisms*. New York: Oxford University Press.

Sinnott-Armstrong, W. (2007). 'Reflections on Reflection in Audi's Moral Intuitionism', in Mark Timmons, John Greco, and Alfred Mele (eds), *Rationality and the Good*, 19–30. New York: Oxford University Press.

Sinnott-Armstrong, W. (2008a). 'Framing Moral Intuitions', in W. Sinnott-Armstrong (ed.), *Moral Psychology*. Vol. 2, 47–76. Cambridge, MA: The MIT Press.

Sinnott-Armstrong, W. (2008b). 'How to Apply Generalities: Reply to Tolhurst and Shafer-Landau', in W. Sinnott-Armstrong (ed.), *Moral Psychology*. Vol. 2, 97–105. Cambridge, MA: The MIT Press.

Sinnott-Armstrong, W. (2011). 'An Empirical Challenge to Moral Intuitionism', in J. Graper Hernandez (ed.), *The New Intuitionism*, 11–28 and 200–3. London: Continuum.

Sinnott-Armstrong, W., L. Young, and F. Cushman (2010). 'Moral Intuitions', in J. Doris and the Moral Psychology Research Group (ed.), *The Moral Psychology Handbook*, 246–72. Oxford and New York: Oxford University Press.

Skelton, A. (2008). 'Sidgwick's Philosophical Intuitions', *Ethics & Politics*, X (2): 185–209.

Skorupski, J. (1999). 'Irrealist Cognitivism', *Ratio*, 12: 436–59.

Sloman, S. A. (1996). 'The Empirical Case for Two Systems of Reasoning', *Psychological Bulletin*, 119: 3–22.

Smith, A. D. (2008). 'Translucent Experiences', *Philosophical Studies*, 140 (2): 197–212.

Smith, B. (2002). 'Analogy in Moral Deliberation: The Role of Imagination and Theory in Ethics', *Journal of Med Ethics*, 28: 244–8.

Smith, E. E. (1995). 'Concepts and Categorization', in E. E. Smith and D. N. Osherson (eds), *Thinking: An Invitation to Cognitive Science*, 3–33. The MIT Press.

Smith, J. (2010). 'On Sinnott-Armstrong's Case Against Moral Intuitionism', *Ethical Theory and Moral Practice*, 13(1): 75–88.

Snare, F. (1974). 'The Definition of Prima Facie Duties', *The Philosophical Quarterly*, 24 (96): 235–44.

Solomon, Robert C. (1977). 'The Rationality of the Emotions', *Southwestern Journal of Philosophy*, 8 (2): 105–14.

Sorensen, R. A. (1992). *Thought Experiments*. Oxford: Oxford University Press.

Sosa, D. (2006). 'Skepticism About Intuition', *Philosophy*, 81: 633–47.

Sosa, E. (1998). 'Minimal Intuition', in M. Depaul and W. Ramsey (eds), *Rethinking Intuition*, 257–69. New York: Rowman and Littlefield Publishers, Inc.

Sosa, E. (2006). 'Intuitions and Truth', in P. Greenough and M. Lynch (eds), *Truth and Realism*, 208–26. Oxford: Oxford University Press.

Sosa, E. (2007). 'Experimental Philosophy and Philosophical Intuition', *Philosophical Studies*, 132: 99–107.

Sosa, E. (2009). 'Replies to Commentators on A Virtue Epistemology', *Philosophical Studies*, 144: 137–47.

Sosa, E. (2014). 'Intuitions: Their Nature and Probative Value', in A. R. Booth and D. P. Rowbottom (eds), *Intuitions*, 36–49. Oxford: Oxford University Press.

Spinoza, B. (1677). *Ethics*.

Stanovich, K. E. and R. F. West (2000). 'Individual Differences in Reasoning: Implications for the Rationality Debate?', *Behavioral and Brain Sciences*, 23: 645–65.

Stratton-Lake, P. (1997). 'Can Hooker's Rule-Concequentialist Principle Justify Rossian Prima Facie Duties?', *Mind*, 106: 751–8.

Stratton-Lake, P. (1999). 'Why Externalism is Not a Problem for Ethical Intuitionists', *Proceedings of the Aristotelian Society*, XCIX (Part 1): 77–90.

Stratton-Lake, P. (2000). *Kant, Duty and Moral Worth*. London: Routledge.

Stratton-Lake, P. (2002a). 'Pleasure and Reflection in Ross', in P. Stratton-Lake (ed.) *Ethical Intuitionism: Re-evaluations*, 113–36. Oxford: Oxford University Press.

Stratton-Lake, P. (2002b). 'Introduction', in P. Stratton-Lake (ed.), *Ethical Intuitionism: Re-evaluations*, 1–28. Oxford: Oxford University Press.
Stratton-Lake, P. (2002c). 'Introduction', in P. Stratton-Lake (ed.), *The Right and the Good*. ix–xlix. Oxford: Clarendon Press.
Stratton-Lake, P. (2004). 'Introduction', in P. Stratton-Lake (ed.), *On What We Owe to Each Other*, 1–17. Oxford: Blackwell.
Stratton-Lake, P. (2005a). 'G. E. Moore: Principia Ethica', in J. Shand (ed.), *The Central Works of Philosophy*. Vol. 4, 20–37. Chesham: Acumen.
Stratton-Lake, P. (2005b). 'Ross, William David (1877–1971)', in A. Ellis (ed.), *Dictionary of Twentieth-century British Philosophers*, 1200. Bristol: Thoemmes Press.
Stratton-Lake, P. (2005c). 'Prichard, Harold Arthur (1871–1947)', in A. Ellis (ed.), *Dictionary of Twentieth-century British Philosophers*, 1200. Bristol: Thoemmes Press.
Stratton-Lake, P. (2007). 'Ross and Kant on Right-Making', in Z. Movahed (ed.), *Proceedings of Kant's Seminar*, 129–46. Tehran: Iranian Institute of Philosophy.
Stratton-Lake, P. (2010). 'Intuitionism', in J. Skorupski (ed.), *The Routledge Companion to Ethics*, 467–77. Oxford: Routledge.
Stratton-Lake, P. (2011a). 'Recalcitrant Pluralism', *Ratio*, 24 (4): 364–83.
Stratton-Lake, P. (2011b). 'Eliminativism About Derivative Prima Facie Duties', in T. Hurka (ed.), *Underivative Duty*, 146–65. Oxford: Oxford University Press.
Stratton-Lake, P. (2012). 'Rational Intuitionism', in *The Oxford Handbook of the History of Ethics*, 337–57. Oxford: Oxford University Press.
Stratton-Lake, P. (2013). 'Ross, W. D.', in H. LaFollette (ed.), *The International Encyclopedia of Ethics*, 4082–6. Malden, MA: Wiley-Blackwell.
Stratton-Lake, P. (2016a). 'Intuitionism in Ethics', in Edward N. Zalta (ed.), *The Stanford Encyclopedia of Philosophy*. https://plato.stanford.edu/archives/win2016/entries/intuitionism-ethics/.
Stratton-Lake, P. (2016b). 'Intuition, Self-Evidence, and Understanding', in Russ Shafer-Landau (ed.), *Oxford Studies in Metaethics* 28–44. Vol. 11. Oxford: Oxford University Press.
Street, S. (2006). 'A Darwinian Dilemma for Realist Theories of Value', *Philosophical Studies*, 127 (1): 109–66.
Streumer, B. (2007). 'Inferential and Non-Inferential Reasoning', *Philosophy and Phenomenological Research*, 74: 1–29.
Sturgeon, N. (2002). 'Ethical Intuitionism and Ethical Naturalism', in P. Stratton-Lake (ed.), *Ethical Intuitionism: Re-evaluations*, 184–211. Oxford: Oxford University Press.
Swain, S., J. Alexander, and J. Weinberg (2008). 'The Instability of Philosophical Intuitions: Running Hot and Cold on Truetemp', *Philosophy and Phenomenological Research*, 76: 138 155.
Thomas, A. (2006). *Value and Context: The Nature of Moral and Political Knowledge*. Oxford: Oxford University Press.
Thompson, M. (2008). *Life and Action: Elementary Structures of Practice and Practical Thought*. Cambridge, MA: Harvard University Press.

Thomson, J. J. (1971). 'A Defence of Abortion', *Philosophy & Public Affairs*, 1 (1): 47–66.
Thomson, J. J. (1976). 'Killing, Letting Die, and the Trolley Problem', *The Monist*, 59: 204–17.
Thomson, J. J. (1985). 'The Trolley Problem', *Yale Law Journal*, 94: 1395–415.
Timmons, M. (1999). *Morality Without Foundations*. New York: Oxford University Press.
Timmons, M. (2008). 'Toward a Sentimentalist Deontology', in W. Sinnott-Armstrong (ed.), *Moral Psychology*, 93–104. Vol. 3. Cambridge, MA: The MIT Press.
Timmons, M., J. Greco, and A. Mele (2007). *Rationality and the Good: Critical Essays on the Ethics and Epistemology of Robert Audi*. New York: Oxford University Press.
Tolhurst, W. (1990). 'On the Epistemic Value of Moral Experience', *Southern Journal of Philosophy*, 29: 67–87.
Tolhurst, W. (1998). 'Seemings', *American Philosophical Quarterly*, 35 (3): 293–302.
Tolhurst, W. (2008). 'Moral Intuitions Framed', in W. Sinnott-Armstrong (ed.), *Moral Psychology*, 47–76. Vol. 2. Cambridge, MA: The MIT Press.
Tooley, M (1984). 'A Defence of Abortion and Infanticide', in J. Feinberg (ed.), *The Problem of Abortion*, 51–91. California: Wadsworth Publication Company.
Trigg, R. (1971). 'Moral Conflict', *Mind*, 80 (317): 41–55.
Tropman, E. (2008). 'Naturalism and the New Moral Intuitionism', *Journal of Philosophical Research*, 33: 163–84.
Tropman, E. (2009). 'Renewing Moral Intuitionism', *Journal of Moral Philosophy*, 6: 450.
Tropman, E. (2010). 'Intuitionism and the Secondary-Quality Analogy in Ethics', *The Journal of Value Inquiry*, 44 (1): 31–45.
Tropman, E. (2011). 'Non-Inferential Moral Knowledge', *Acta Analytica*, 26 (4): 355–66.
Tropman, E. (2012). 'Self-Evidence and A Priori Moral Knowledge', *Disputatio*, 4 (33): 459–67.
Tropman, E. (2014). 'Evolutionary Debunking Arguments: Moral Realism, Constructivism, and Explaining Moral Knowledge', *Philosophical Explorations: An International Journal for the Philosophy of Mind and Action*, 17 (2): 126–40.
Tucker, C. (2013). *Seemings and Justification: New Essays on Dogmatism and Phenomenal Conservatism*. Oxford and New York: Oxford University Press.
Urmson, J. O. (1975). 'A Defence of Intuitionism', *Proceedings of the Aristotelian Society*, 75: 111–19.
Van Inwagen, P. (1997). 'Materialism and the Psychological-Continuity Account of Personal Identity', *Philosophical Perspectives*, 11: 305–19.
Vayrynen, P. (2008). 'Some Good and Bad News for Ethical Intuitionism', *The Philosophical Quarterly*, 58 (232): 489–511.
Walsh, A. (2011). 'A Moderate Defence of the Use of Thought Experiments in Applied Ethics', *Ethical Theory and Moral Practice*, 14 (4): 467–81.
Warnock, G. (1967). *Contemporary Moral Philosophy*. London: Melbourne Macmillan.
Warnock, M. (1960). *Ethics Since 1900*. London and New York: Oxford University Press.

Weinberg, J., C. Gonnerman, C. Buckner, and J. Alexander (2010). 'Are Philosophers Expert Intuiters?', *Philosophical Psychology*, 23 (3): 331–55.

Wengert, R. (1981). 'The Sources of Intuitive Cognition in William of Ockham', *Franciscan Studies*, 41: 415–47.

Werner, P. J. (2013). 'Seemings: Still Dispositions to Believe', *Synthese*, 191 (8): 1761–74.

Wiggins, D (1991). *Needs, Value and Truth*. Oxford: Clarendon Press.

Wiggins, D. (1998). '"The Right and the Good" and W. D. Ross's Criticism of Consequentialism', *Utilitas*, 10 (3): 261–80.

Wiggins, D (2006). *Ethics: Twelve Lectures on the Philosophy of Morality*. Cambridge, MA: Harvard University Press.

Williams, B. (1965). 'Ethical Consistency', *Proceedings of the Aristotelian Society*, 39: 103–24.

Williams, B. (1995). *Making Sense of Humanity*. Cambridge: Cambridge University Press.

Williamson, T. (2002). *Knowledge and its Limits*. Oxford: Oxford University Press.

Williamson, T. (2004). 'Philosophical 'Intuitions' and Scepticism About Judgement', *Dialectica*, 58 (1): 109–53.

Williamson, T. (2007). *The Philosophy of Philosophy*. Oxford: Blackwell.

Wilson, T. D. (2002). *Strangers to Ourselves: Discovering the Adaptive Unconscious*. Cambridge, MA: Harvard University Press.

Wittgenstein, L. (1953). *Philosophical Investigation*, tran. G. E. M. Anscomb. Oxford: Basil Blackwell Publisher.

Wittgenstein, L. (1976). 'Cause and Effect; Intuitive Awareness', trans. P. Winch, *Philosophia*, 6 (3–4): 409–25.

Wittgenstein, L. (1979). *On Certainty*, ed. G. E. M. Anscombe and G. H. Von Wright, trans. Denis Paul and G. E. M. Anscombe. Oxford: Basil Blackwell.

Woodward, J. and Allman, J. (2007). 'Moral Intuition: Its Neural Substrates and Normative Significance', *Journal of Physiology–Paris*, 101: 179–202.

Wrangham, R. and Peterson, D. (1996). *Demonic Males*. Boston. Houghton Mifflin.

Wright, J. (2006). *The Role of Reason and Intuition in Moral Judgment: A Review*. Submitted to the Department of Psychology, University of Wyoming in partial fulfilment of the Comprehensive Exam.

Zamzow, J. and N. Nicholas (2009). 'Variations in Ethical Intuitions', *Philosophical Issues*, 19, Metaethics ed. Ernest Sosa: 368–88.

Zimmerman, A. (2010). *Moral Epistemology*. New York: Routledge.

Index

abortion, moral permissibility of   85–6
actual duties. *See also* all-things-
    considered duties
    vs. prima facie duties   72–4
act-utilitarianism   27, 93
    and evolution   148–9
Adelson's checker shadow illusion   24–5
adequate understanding   4, 18, 40–1,
    109–11, 122–9, 132–3, 192–3,
    206 n.31
Alexander, J.   137–8
alief   25, 223 n.54
Allman, J.   155–6
all-things-considered duties   73–4,
    179–80, 214 n.103
    beliefs about   78–80, 90–1
    epistemological accounts of   96–8
    particularist view of   91–4
    and pluralism   217 n.40
analytic propositions   125–6
archai   82
Aristotle   9, 82–3, 208 n.1
Audi, R.
    evaluation of moral intuitionism
        of   116–23
    method of reflection   113–14, 217 n.32
    modest foundationalism of   107–8
    on nature of moral intuition   4, 40–3,
        119–20, 203 n.26, 206 nn.23, 27,
        218 n.49
    notion of moral intuitionism   64–5,
        70, 105–7, 113–16
    notion of self-evidence   105, 108–11,
        116–18, 216 n.25, 218 n.50
axioms   82–4, 112, 205

Bealer, G.   208 n.16
    argument against reductionist
        account   2, 3, 24–5, 27–8
    on intuition as evidence   53
    non-reductionist account of   13, 14,
        19–24, 31–3, 39, 44, 46, 203 n.40

    on physical intuitions   203 n.32
Bedke, M.   14, 67, 70, 222 n.43
beliefs   5, 177–8. *See also* doxastic
    account
    about *pro tanto* and all-things-
        considered duties   78–80, 90–1
    differences between propositions
        and   176–7
    evidence for   208 n.20
    non-inferred and non-
        inferable   186–7
    tentative   51
Benacerraf, P.   138
beneficence   73, 95–7
Bengson, J.   2, 49
    on distinction between intuition and
        intuitive   11–12
    seeming account of intuition   3–4,
        13, 14, 32–9, 44–7
Berghofer, P.   205 n.1
Berlin, I.   66
bias   171, 174, 177–8
Boyd, Richard   42
Brady, M. S.   160, 223 n.57
Brink, D.   213 n.97
British moral philosophers   59–61

Cappelen, H.   12, 49–50, 52, 54–5,
    202 n.13
Centrality   49–52, 54–5
Chisholm, R.   51, 53, 55
Chudnoff, E.   205 n.1
Clarke, S.   118
classic foundationalism   104–5, 189, 196
classic moral intuitionism   60–4, 68, 69,
    97, 102, 199, 203 n.28
cognition, and emotion   150–4
cognitive illusion   174
cognitive phenomenology   203 n.40
cognitive psychology   183–4
cognitivism   69–70, 77, 210 n.29
coherence   70, 87

commonsense 221 nn.25, 30
conceptual scepticism 138
conclusion of inference 41–2, 120–3
conclusion of reflection 41–2, 120–3
conclusive reason 98
confirmation 46
conflicting intuitions 179–81
conscious thought 144–5, 155–6
consequentialism 62–4, 75, 220 n.6
consistency 46, 87
contemporary new moral
  intuitionism 60, 64–5, 67,
  104–5, 113–14, 199
context of discovery 113
context of justification 113
continuous seeing 86
Copp, D. 70
corroboration 46
countervailing reason 171, 184–5
Crisp, R. 70
Cudworth, R. 208 n.1

Damasio, A. 153
Dancy, J. 70, 85, 94–5, 209 n.24,
  201 n.29, 215 n.121(Ch 4),
  215 n.1 (Ch 5)
Davis, W. H. 213 n.82
dawning of an aspect 86
deduction 9
De Lazari-Radek, K. 148
Dennett, Daniel 14–15
deontic valence 79–80, 93, 99
deontology. *See* normative theory
Descartes, R. 10, 201 n.4, 208 n.1
Dijksterhuis, A. 155
directness 37–8, 40, 47
disjunction 126
disposition 36–7
disposition-to-believe account 3, 16–18,
  203 nn.28–9, 204 n.50, 222 n.44
  critique of 28–30
dogmatism 65–6, 114–15
Döring, S. 160, 161
doxastic model 2, 3
  of moral intuition 4, 33, 40–3
  of philosophical intuition 13–19,
  30–1, 202 n.14

emotion

and cognition 150–4
and moral intuition 5, 158–60, 164–
  8, 207 n.43, 221 nn.25, 30–1
and moral judgement 138, 140–5
and moral judgement, empirical
  evidence 151–6
and perception 222 n.46, 223 n.52
quasi-perceptualist account of 133,
  160–4
empirical evidence 151–6, 171–2, 176–8,
  225 n.37
empirical induction 82–3
empirical scepticism 137, 138
epistemic access 42
epistemic foundationalism 104–5
epistemological particularism 92
epistemology of moral intuitionism 1–3,
  32, 55, 66–7, 104, 124, 215 n.1
  Audi's account of 64–5, 105–7,
    113–14
  Audi's account of, evaluation of 116–
    23
  Cartesian sense of 9–10
  critique of 114–16
  defence of 175
  integration with psychology of moral
    intuition 157–64
  and moral intuition distinguished 39
  new account of (*see* modest
    epistemological intuitionism)
  Sinnott-Armstrong's account
    of 186–91, 195–8, 225 n.49
  Sinnott-Armstrong's argument
    against 5, 166–75, 182,
    226 n.60
  stronger form of 191–7
ethical egoism 75–8
ethical reflectionism 105, 108, 112
evidence. *See also* self-evidence
  for beliefs 208 n.20
  facticity of 50–1
  intuitings and intuited as 54
  intuition as 4, 14, 20, 44–6, 48–9
  intuition as, scepticism against 49–
    54
  notion of 50–1, 124–5
evolutionary debunking argument 5,
  138–9, 164
  Greene's 139–44

Haidt's 144–7
  Singer's 147–51
Ewing, A. C. 98
experiential seemings, and intellectual
      seemings distinguished 20–1
explanation problem 94–103

fallibility 78, 79, 106–7
falsity 106–7, 112, 174, 184
family resemblance 4, 60, 68, 71,
      210 n.28
fast thinking 25, 46, 226 n.58
feeling of veridicality 159
fidelity 73, 76, 78–9, 95–7, 99
firmness 40
foundationalism-coherentism 88
framing effects 5, 172–6
further reflection 77–8, 86–7
  on intuitive beliefs 106–7
  on self-evident propositions 110–12

Gage, P. 153
game 4, 60, 68
Gendler, T. 25
generalism 52–3, 91–4, 132, 182–4
  epistemic status of 149–50
  self-evident 117–19
genetic fallacy 224 n.11
Gettier case 15–17
goodness 215 n.126
  pluralism about 74–6
  and rightness 62–4, 70, 72, 211 n.50
good reason 98
good will view 75–6
gratitude 76, 78–9, 96–7, 102
Greene, J. D.
  moral psychology of 5, 139–43, 151
  moral psychology of, critique
      of 143–4, 156
gut feeling 39, 46, 47

Haidt, J. 221 n.25
  social psychology of 5, 144–7, 151,
      156
hard self-evidence 109–11
harm, personal and impersonal forms
      of 140–2
Hooker, B. 67, 81–2, 129, 214 n.103,
      217 n.25

Huemer, M. 14, 28, 43, 51, 67, 162,
      207 n.42
Hutcheson, F. 59

ideal utilitarianism 75–6, 211 n.55
immediately and mediately self-evident
      propositions 109–10, 112, 115
implicit bias 174
inclination-to-believe account. *See*
      disposition-to-believe account
inconsistent beliefs 28
independently credible proposition 82,
      176
inference 166, 194–6
  conclusion of inference 41–2, 120–3
  notions of 10
  perceptual experiences distinguished
      from 33
inferentiality 63–5, 81–2, 105–6, 108,
      110–12, 132–3, 194–5, 199
intellectual appearances 28
intellectual seeming 2–4, 132, 222 n.46
  account of moral intuition 33,
      39–40, 43–6
  account of philosophical
      intuition 13, 19–24, 44–5
  as felt givenness 35
  superiority of 28–30, 42
  translucent state of 38–9
intuition
  primary notion of 2, 17
  psychology of 11–24, 37, 201 nn.6,
      10
  similarities between perceptual
      experience and 33–8
  technical use of 4, 49–50, 53
  types of 202 n.11
intuition pumps 14–19, 53
intuitive 12
intuitive induction 82–4, 206 n.34,
      212 n.62
intuitive judgement 9–10, 152–4,
      201 n.4
intuitive justification 105–8
irrealist cognitivism 69–70

Jackson, F. 15, 37, 51, 204 n.47
Jones, K. 163
judgement 40, 59

in moral conflict cases 95–101
psychology of 139–44
role of emotions in 151–4, 157, 161–4
truth of 61–2, 174
judgement-sensitive attitudes 162–3
justification 48–9, 219 n.2
context of justification 113
of moral judgements 95–101
notion of 218 n.57
prima facie 53–4
production and preservation of 175, 185–6, 197–8
Ross's theory of 87–91
of self-evident proposition 77–8, 80–2
justification from above 106
justification from below 106
justificatory inferential structure 172–3

Kahane, G. 143
Kahneman, D. 25, 46, 226 n.58
Kamm, F. M. 220 n.9
Kantianism 75, 105
Kauppinen, A. 161, 203 n.28
Koksvik, O. 203 n.44 205 n.1
Korsgaard, C. M. 11, 217 n.37
Kripke, S. 51–2, 55

Lakoff, G. 183–4
Lewis, J. 13, 16
literal and non-literal perceptual theories 223 n.52
Locke, J. 10, 124
looking away 99–102, 132

McDowell, J. 215 n.1, 225 n.30
McNaughton, D. 67, 179, 222 n.44
mathematics 12
and ethics compared 77
and hard self-evidence 110, 111
naïve comprehension principles of set theory 204 n.48
and presentationality 205 n.13
mental maturity 85, 102
mental ontology 2, 11, 44–5, 132, 156, 199
meta-ethics 66
moral epistemology in 77–94

methodological intuitionism 66–8, 71
mode of thought/deliberation 155–6
moderate contemporary moral intuitionism 60, 104–5, 110, 199
modest classic moral intuitionism 60–1, 65
and Rossian ethics 71–94
modest epistemological intuitionism 131–4, 166, 168, 190–7, 199, 209 n.18, 226 n.60
modest foundationalism 87–91, 93–4, 107–8, 132, 196–7
modest non-inferentiality 193–4
monism 59, 75–6, 101
Moore, G. E. 59, 63, 64, 66, 67, 84–5, 209 n.7
moral conflicts 224 n.27
of pro tanto duties 96–101, 178–81
moral dumbfounding 145–7
moral epistemology
Prichard's 61–4
Ross's 71–2, 77–94
moral foundationalism 60, 70
moral inferentialism/evidentialism 63–4
moral intuition 1–2, 30, 206 n.27, 209 n.25, 222 n.46
disagreement about 115–16, 224 n.27
doxastic account of 3–4, 40–3, 47, 119–20, 203 n.26
epistemic status of 4, 14, 20, 42, 44–6, 48–54, 68, 138, 144–51, 156, 161–2, 167–8, 202 n.13
non-doxastic account of 1, 3–4, 33, 39–40, 43–7, 138, 158–9, 164–5, 167–8
non-doxastic account of, and emotions 158–60
reliability of 1, 41, 46, 106–7, 115, 166, 168–71
Singer's notion of 139
Sinnott-Armstrong's notion of 167
moral intuitionism 59–60. *See also* epistemology of moral intuitionism
history and classification of 59–61, 65–9
properties/marks of 68–71

rejection of   213 n.82
moral naturalism   63
moral thinking   209 n.10
moral weight   79–80, 93
Müller-Lyer illusion   35
mystical intuitions   17

Nado, J.   39, 202 n.25
Nagel, J.   14, 67
naïve comprehension axiom   27
naturalism   70
natural science, and ethics   88
necessary truths   21–2
neuroethics   3, 131, 138, 156, 177–8
neurophysiology of vision   15
Nimtz, C.   3, 22–3, 204 n.47
nóêsis (νόησις)   9
non-doxastic seeming model   202 n.14
   of moral intuition   1, 3–4, 33,
      39–40, 43–7, 138, 158–9, 164–5,
      203 n.26
   of philosophical intuition   3, 30–1,
      199
non-inferable beliefs   186–7, 225 n.38
non-inferable epistemological
      intuitionism   187–90
non-inferentiality   2–3, 5, 9–11, 65,
      158, 213 n.97, 222 nn.44, 46,
      225 n.37
   and emotions   163–4, 167–8
   epistemological intuitionist view
      of   170–91
   modest account of   191–7
   and reflection   85–7, 113
   and self-evidence   105–6, 109–12,
      128–9, 132
non-inferred beliefs   186–7
non-inferred epistemological
      intuitionism   187–90
non-maleficence   76, 78–9, 95
non-naturalism   70, 77, 210 n.29
non-reductionism   19–22, 44, 202 n.14.
      See also non-doxastic seeming
      model
   critique of   22–4
   notion of   13
   superiority of   24–31
normative theory   66–7, 149–51,
      220 nn.6, 19

Rossian   71–94

occurrent account   16–17
ontological particularism   92
opinions   16

Parfit, D.   14, 67, 107, 109, 129, 192
partiality   173–5
particularism   52–3, 91–4, 132, 182–4
   forms of   214 n.101
   probability of error for   184–6
   self-evident   117–21
perception   9–11, 23–4, 32, 158, 160–1,
      165, 222 n.46, 223 n.52. See also
      quasi-perceptualism
perceptual illusions   24–5
perceptual intuitionism   65–6
perceptualism, presentational and
      representational states of   33–
      8, 44
philosophical consequentialism   139–40,
      142, 143
philosophical deontology   139–43
philosophical intuition
   categorization of   12–13
   doxastic and non-doxastic accounts
      of   2–4, 199, 204 n.50
   non-reductionist account of   13,
      19–24, 44
   quasi-perceptualist account of   3–4,
      13, 32–9, 46–7
   reductionist account of   13–19
philosophical intuitionism   65–6
physicalism   15, 203 n.32
Plantinga, A.   14
Plato   9
pluralism   66–7, 69
   critique of   217 n.40
   Ross's   74–7, 211 n.55
practice   101–2
presentationality   205 nn.10, 13
   of perceptual experiences   34–6, 44
   of philosophical intuition   36–8,
      46–7
   psychological element of   119–20
preservation of justification   175, 185–6,
      197–8
pre-theoretical requirement   40
Price, H. H.   10

Price, R. 124
Prichard, H. A. 59–60, 190
　moral epistemology of 4, 61–4, 199, 209 nn.9–10
　notion of self-evidence 118
prima facie duties. *See also pro tanto* duties
　Rossian 71–4
Prinz, J. 160
production of justification 175, 185–6, 197–8
proposition 50–1, 54
　analytic 125–6
　differences between belief and 176–7
　independently credible 82, 176
　self-evident (*see* self-evidence)
　true 208 n.10
pro tanto duties 73–4. *See also prima facie* duties
　competency 101–2
　conflicts of 96–103, 178–81
　generalist view of 91–4
　hierarchy of 76, 78–9, 94–6
　moral pluralism in 74–7
　self-evident 118–19, 125–6, 195–6, 214 n.110
prototype theory 225 n.38
Pryor, J. 34–5
psychology
　impact of evolution on 147–8
　of intuition 11–24, 37, 201 nn.6, 10
　of moral intuition 43–7, 133–4, 157–64
　of moral judgement 139–44
　of self-evidence 119–20
Pust, J. 21, 51, 52, 55, 203 n.29
Putnam, H. 14, 53

quality of choice 155–6
quasi-perceptualism 3–4, 13, 32–9, 46–7
　of emotion 133, 160–4

rational intuition 19–21, 203 n.32
　episodic character of 22
　modal character of 21–2
rationalist deontology 142–4
rationality, and emotions 162–3
rational judgement 96
Rawls, J. 53, 55, 64, 66, 89
realism 69–70, 77, 210 n.29

reason 215 nn.121, 126
　distinction between emotion and 138
　and duties 97–101
　and moral intuition 144–7, 205 n.14
reason-tracking 163, 223 n.56
recalcitrant emotions 161, 223 n.53
reductionism 13–19, 202 n.14, 204 n.46
　argument against 24–31
reflection 2–3, 21, 65, 85–6, 199
　Audi's method of 113–14, 217 n.32
　conclusion of reflection 41–2, 120–3
　further reflection 77–8, 86–7, 106–7, 110–12
　on *pro tanto* duties 95–7, 99–101, 121
　substantial reflection 39
reflective equilibrium 53, 64, 89–91, 106–8, 113, 115, 132
regress 101, 187–8
Reid, T. 212 n.62
reliability/reliabilism 222 n.41
　of deontological moral intuitions 149–51
　of moral intuitions 1, 41, 46, 106–7, 115, 166, 168–86
reparation 76, 78–9, 95
representationality, of perceptual experience 34–6
rightness 211 n.39
　and goodness 62–4, 70, 72, 211 n.50
　pluralism about 69, 74–6
　and practice 101–2
Roberts, R. C. 160
Roeser, S. 210 n.29
Rosch, E. 183
Ross, W. D. 59–60, 209 n.7
　ethical framework of 94–103, 178–81, 199, 211 n.39
　influence on Audi 105
　on intuitive induction 212 n.63
　on moral epistemology 4, 64, 77–80, 203 n.28, 208 n.1, 209 n.18
　on moral pluralism 67, 74–7, 211 n.55
　on *prima facie* duties 71–4, 118–19 (*see also pro tanto* duties)
　on self-evident propositions 80–6, 119, 130, 214 n.110

theory of justification 87–91
Russell, B. 87

Sauer, H. 222 n.46
Scanlon, T. 67, 129, 162–3, 215 n.126
scepticism 138–9, 221 n.31
  about epistemological intuition 3
  against intuition as evidence 49–54
  types of 219 n.2
Searle, J. 15
seeing other similarities 99–101
seeming intuitionism 67–8
self-evidence 2–3, 70, 212 n.76, 213 n.82, 214 n.110, 219 n.64
  Audi's account of 4, 42–3, 105, 108–11, 116–21, 216 n.25, 218 n.50
  Audi's account of, alternative to 123–7
  inferential justification for 81–2, 105–6, 108
  and intuition 55
  justification for 77–8, 87–91
  Prichard's account of 64
  of *pro tanto* duties 95–7, 99
  Ross's account of 80–7, 119
  seeming account of 127–31, 133
  Sidgwick's notion of 116
  Stratton-Lake's account of 219 n.63
self-evidence intuitionism 67–8
self-evident truth 111–12, 117, 192, 195
sensible theory 215 n.1
sentimentalism 59, 160–1, 220 n.19
Shafer-Landau, R. 114, 124, 169
Shaftesbury, Lord 59
Shaver, R. 211 n.55
Sidgwick, H. 43, 59, 64–7, 116, 203 n.28, 207 n.41
Singer, P. 219 n.2, 221 n.30–1
  evolutionary debunking argument of 5, 138–9, 147–51, 156, 164
Sinnott-Armstrong, W. 114, 224 n.11, 225 nn.37, 44
  critique of 175–81
  epistemological intuitionism account of 157, 186–91, 195–8, 219 n.2, 225 n.49

on irrationality of emotions 161–2
rejection of epistemological intuitionism 5, 166–75, 182, 226 n.60
Skorupski, J. 69–70
social intuitions 138–9, 144–7
  similarities between moral intuitions and 156
soft self-evidence 109–11
Sosa, E. 18, 204 n.50, 222 n.44
Spinoza, B. 10
Stratton-Lake, P. 14, 67, 98, 205 n.14, 211 n.50, 215 n.126, 219 n.63, 222 n.43
strong classic intuitionism 60–4
substantial reflection 39
Swain, S. 137–8

tentative belief 51
Thomson, J. 85–6, 220 n.9
thought experiments 14–15, 37, 53, 85–6, 90, 203 n.32, 204 n.47
Timmons, M. 114, 220 n.19
Tolhurst, W. 35, 114, 169
translucency 37–9, 47, 158
transparency 37–8
trolley dilemma 140–1, 143–4, 149–50, 220 n.9
Tropman, E. 117–18, 225 n.38
truth 108–9, 222 n.43
Tucker, C. 205 n.1

unconscious thought 144–5, 155–6
Urmson, J. O. 98
utilitarianism 75

Van Inwagen, P. 18
Väyrynen, P. 168

Weinberg, J. 137–8
Williams, B. 66–7
Williamson, T. 13, 49, 54–5, 202 n.16, 203 n.34, 207 n.5
Wittgenstein, L. 4, 11, 60, 65, 68, 71, 86, 210 n.28
Woodward, J. 155–6
Wright, J. 159

www.ingramcontent.com/pod-product-compliance
Lightning Source LLC
Chambersburg PA
CBHW062132300426
44115CB00012BA/1895